THE ART OF THE POPES

THE ART OF THE POPES

FROM THE VATICAN COLLECTION

*How pontiffs, architects,
painters and sculptors
created the Vatican*

Edited by Maurizio Fagiolo dell'Arco

Texts by Angela Cipriani, Marcello Fagiolo dell'Arco,
Maurizio Fagiolo dell'Arco,
Maurizio Marini, Vitaliano Tiberia, Enrico Valeriani

Greenwich House
Distributed by Crown Publishers, Inc.
New York

On page 2: a detail of Raphael's fresco *The Liberation of St. Peter*, in the Room of Heliodorus. St. Peter in chains is woken by the angel who has come to free him.

Translated by James Ramsay

This 1983 edition is published by Greenwich House, a division of Arlington House, Inc., distributed by Crown Publishers, Inc.

Library of Congress Cataloging in Publication Data
Main entry under title:

The Art of the Popes from the Vatican Collection

Bibliography: p.
Includes Index.
1. Art, Italian – Vatican City – Addresses, essays, lectures. 2. Art – Vatican City – Addresses, essays, lectures. 3. Christian art and symbolism – Vatican City – Addresses, essays, lectures. I. Fagiolo dell'Arco, Maurizio, 1939–   .II. Cipriani, Angela.
N6920.A72   1983   708.5′634   82–25135
ISBN 0–517–40883X

The quotations from the Bible are taken from the Revised Standard Version.
The quotations from *The Divine Comedy* by Dante are taken from Charles S. Singleton's translation (Routledge & Kegan Paul, London, 1971).
The quotations from *Ten Books on Architecture* by Leon Battista Alberti are taken from James Leoni's translation, 1755 (reprinted by Alec Tiranti Ltd, London, 1955).

Printed and bound in Italy by Arnoldo Mondadori Editore, Verona

CONTENTS

'Beatus es Simon Bar Iona: quia caro et sanguis non revelavit tibi, sed Pater meus, qui in caelis est. Et ego dico tibi, quia tu es Petrus, et super hanc petram aedificabo Ecclesiam meam, et portae inferi non praevalebunt adversus eam. Et tibi dabo claves regni caelorum. Et quodcumque ligaveris super terram, erit ligatum et in caelis: et quodcumque solveris super terram, erit solutum et in caelis.'

'Blessed are you, Simon Bar-Jona! For flesh and blood has not revealed this to you, but my Father who is in heaven. And I tell you, you are Peter, and on this rock I will build my church, and the powers of death shall not prevail against it. I will give you the keys of the kingdom of heaven, and whatever you bind on earth shall be bound in heaven, and whatever you loose on earth shall be loosed in heaven.'

(Matthew 16: 17–19)

Detail of the view of Rome, showing the Vatican, painted by Antonio Danti between 1580 and 1583, in the Gallery of Maps.

FROM ROME, CITY, TO THE UNIVERSE

Books will continue to be written on the art of the Vatican. Not only because the treasures contained within these few square miles appear to be inexhaustible, that the boundaries of historico-critical reappraisal are for ever being widened, but because each generation needs to rewrite the history of the art of the popes; which is another way of saying, the history of Italian art, or rather, of the arts in Italy.

Perhaps nowhere is history's unbroken chain more in evidence than within the confines of the minuscule papal state: from the beginnings of the late-Roman era to the reverberant affirmation of Constantine; from the 'autumn of the Middle Ages' to the triumph of the Renaissance; from Baroque through Neoclassicism to the eclecticism of the 19th century. The aim of this book is to take stock of all these historical developments, but adopting a new approach by, first of all, explaining the history of an idea as it acquires the dogmatic force of an ideology; and then the history of a particular place, which started out with such inauspicious beginnings, and became in time a focal point for a whole city.

Originally, this vast holy place was an unhealthy marsh; Caligula, and Nero after him, had a private circus here; and it was here that the first Apostle was martyred. There was perhaps a foreshadowing of this in its use as a necropolis (it will be remembered that Hadrian built his mausoleum only a stone's throw away from the Vatican Hill). The Edict of Constantine (313), proclaiming equal rights for all religions, ushered in a new age; only ten years later, work started on the huge basilica. Less than a century later occurred the first sack of Rome (Alaric and the Visigoths in 410): the myth of temporal Rome was destroyed. It was not until the middle of the 9th century, after numerous reverses of fortune, that Leo IV decided to enclose the citadel within walls and the basilica became a fortress. The link with

the city itself is first in evidence around the end of the 13th century, with the construction of the *passetto* (or *corridore*) joining church and castle. This was as far as it got, for at the beginning of the following century the Roman pontifex moved to Avignon. Under Nicholas V (1447–55), scholar, humanist and founder of the Vatican Library, Rome became temporarily a center of Humanism; plans for a new St. Peter's were set in motion.

The jubilee years of 1450 and 1500 were the occasions for new work on the church and other edifices. With Julius II, in the early 16th century, the basilica and citadel appeared to be about to be transformed into a mausoleum (witness Michelangelo's grandiose plan for a tomb as nucleus of the basilica); later came the concept of *umbilicus mundi*. A complete architectural and artistic restructuring program was embarked upon, but the sack of Rome in 1527 brought the dreams of Bramante, Raphael, Michelangelo, and Julius II to a halt. Again, it seemed like the end of civilization: instead a miraculous flowering of the arts was about to take place. These artists, employed for the most part in the Vatican fled from Rome, to carry the impress of their genius (the so-called Raphaelesque style) throughout the entire peninsula, from the Veneto to Sicily, from Lombardy to Naples, thus creating a universal Italian idiom.

Soon, however, the Roman skyline was to be dominated by the most magnificent dome ever built by man – a veritable symbol of the cosmos, of power: *urbi et orbi*. More and more, attempts were made to give tangible meaning to spiritual power, even though that power became increasingly temporal, for example, Pius IV's *civitas pia* and *Roma resurgens*, Sixtus IV's *ecclesia palatina*, and so on. With the passing of every decade a new star was to appear in the constellation of sacred palazzi and places of worship: a museum here, an obelisk there, a library next to the new courtyard, a chapel which either followed or preceded the colonnade. Within this confined space, life took on a momentum of its own transforming out of all recognition both sacred and residential

quarters alike – destruction invariably giving way to reconstruction.

The advent of Baroque saw the refounding of the basilica. In the remaking of the new basilica commissioned by Pope Urban VIII Barberini, and the new city envisaged by Pope Alexander VII Chigi, artists such as Bernini were accorded considerable freedom of scope. With the full approval of the pope, Bernini's double-focus piazza (laid out according to the 'Copernican' principle), established, with its succession of dramatic, compellingly 'propagandistic' figures, the cult of the image which was to become the dominant European stylistic idiom for the next hundred years and more, that is until it gave way to Neoclassicism.

The contributors to this book, rather than follow the customary method of exploring the great periods of Vatican art in purely aesthetic terms, have taken history as their starting point, examining artistic masterpieces as documents of an age and, occasionally, as springboards for culture. The Fra Angelico cycle, for example, is analyzed within the context of Nicholas V's cultural policies; the tomb portraiture is seen in terms of 'eternal life' which every pontiff wished to see emphasized in art; an understanding is sought of the new value placed on the arts by this Power (for it is against this papal Weltanschauung that patronage must be judged). Historical and political events are thus seen in conjunction with their artistic image.

Some comment about the illustrations, which form such an important part of this book, is also called for. The photographic selection runs parallel with the attempt at historical and artistic analysis. Where, for instance, a cycle of frescoes is analyzed, it is also sought to present them in their totality. Thus Raphael's masterpieces in the genre are also to be seen as brilliant decoration for rooms – study, audience-chamber – in everyday use by the pontiff. The classical and Christian exhibits of these magical museums are subjected to the most detailed examination and systematic categorization. Always the individual object is related to the overall

The hiding place where towards 315 the supposed remains of the Apostle Peter were walled up. The remains came originally from a rough grave a few yards away: this was officially declared by Pope Pius XII in 1950 to be the Apostle's tomb, but was found empty.

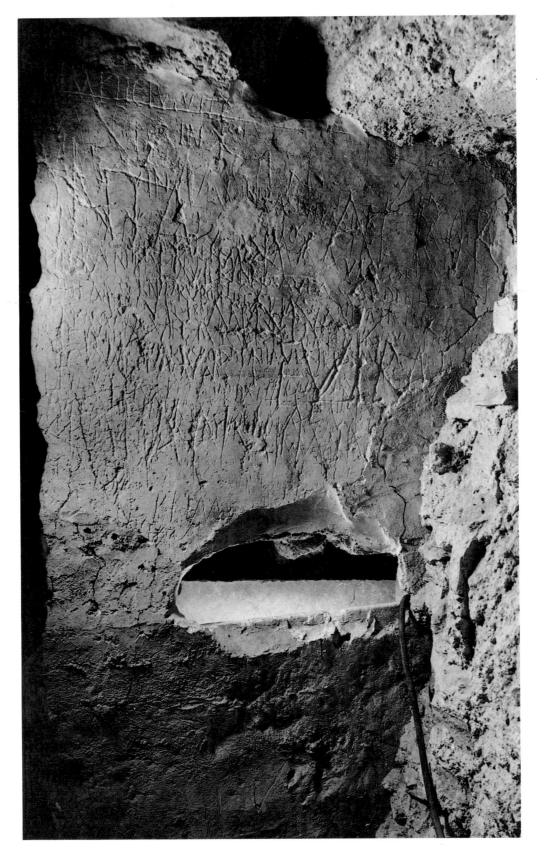

historical and artistic context.

Over the centuries the Vatican grew to become a citadel of the spirit, but above all of culture. The concepts of *propaganda fide* and *urbi et orbi* can be seen as having a common motive – to find an effective voice in society, through the medium of culture and art. It is precisely these initiatives that are set out in this book, an encyclopedia, one might say, of a certain power embodied in sublime images as consummately perfect as the dogma that inspires them.

The book also treats of other, less obvious aspects, such as the way in which a church can become a palace, and then grow to embrace a whole 'city.' Slowly, over the centuries, an institution has come into being, which today appears crystallized, of truly global proportions, embracing at once life and death, church and city, the sacred and profane. In a sense the Vatican resembles a Middle-European type *Residenz*: the royal palace of the spirit which identifies with 'paradise.' Under Pius IV, when the palaces were acquiring beautiful gardens (a *casina* and a loggia, two atriums, and an oval naumachia), the pontiff appeared as a new Apollo, fashioning his own Parnassus, complete with 'academy' and 'museum,' the sacred places of the daughters of memory, and the pavilions of culture. On the city side was to arise the colonnade, presenting, in its turn, a new type of *paradeisos*, architecturally more natural than urban. In sum a theatrical setting that does not seek to emphasize the image of grasping power, as it might appear to do, but rather to promote the idea of a place of delights: 'paradise' or 'theater of the sun' – whichever it may be.

The Vatican's long history as a 'city of the arts' ends, naturally enough, with the termination of the temporal power of the Roman pontifex. Nonetheless the last fading flashes of artistic activity are of interest in the general context of Italian culture, from the period even of the 'second Rome,' already in its decline, with the pope besieged and finally, following the fateful 20 September 1870, exiled in his gilded cage. The last pope-king, Pius

IX, who taught the Romans to call him 'Father,' having added to his 'liberal' image the attribute 'infallible,' decided at the end of his life that he wished to be buried in San Lorenzo fuori le Mura — outside the ancient Vatican City which thereafter declined from a center of culture into a refuge for individual artists, seeking among other things, 'spiritual' recognition.

Perhaps the book's distinctiveness lies in its attempt to integrate the history of art with an artistic vision of history. It is to be seen as a comprehensive guide to this wonder world of altar paintings, classical statues, illuminated books and noble façades, frescoes, mosaics and chapels, secular gardens and solemn tombs . . . . Once inside the basilica, one becomes a participant in this extraordinary synthesis of time and space. Starting with the tomb where the faithful come to venerate Peter, one is caught up, in turn, in the sumptuous exuberance of Baroque, in the extravagance of Rococo, vying with the austerity of Neoclassicism; and so on to the 18th-century mosaics, the frescoes and inlaid floors. One comes to a realization of the true meaning of Time as exemplified in the ancient symbol of the serpent swallowing its own tail — the myth of 'eternal return.' Where now Bernini's triumphant *baldacchino* towers, marking the point of departure of a civilization born, as ever, in blood, there reposed in the 14th century, a majestic polyptych by Giotto, now in the Pinacoteca. This work expresses the perpetual duality of the place, and may almost serve as a symbol of the entire ethos of the Vatican. On the one hand we see God enthroned amid a circle of saints, and there also is the donor, Stefaneschi; on the other side of the polyptych St. Peter sits enthroned amid a similar circle of the blessed. For an instant, the eternal Logos and apostolic power have touched; this alternation will always be present in a place which claims to be a reflection of the world. A 'city' in the form of a palace, and a basilica in the form of a 'city': that unity in diversity is the generative nucleus of an affimation that resounds from *urbe* to *orbe*.

Perhaps in no other place is the inexorable progress of civilization so clearly defined: the alternations of wretchedness and splendor, shrinkage and growth, the affirmations of art and the contradictions of thought, the conservation of the past and prevision of the future.

11

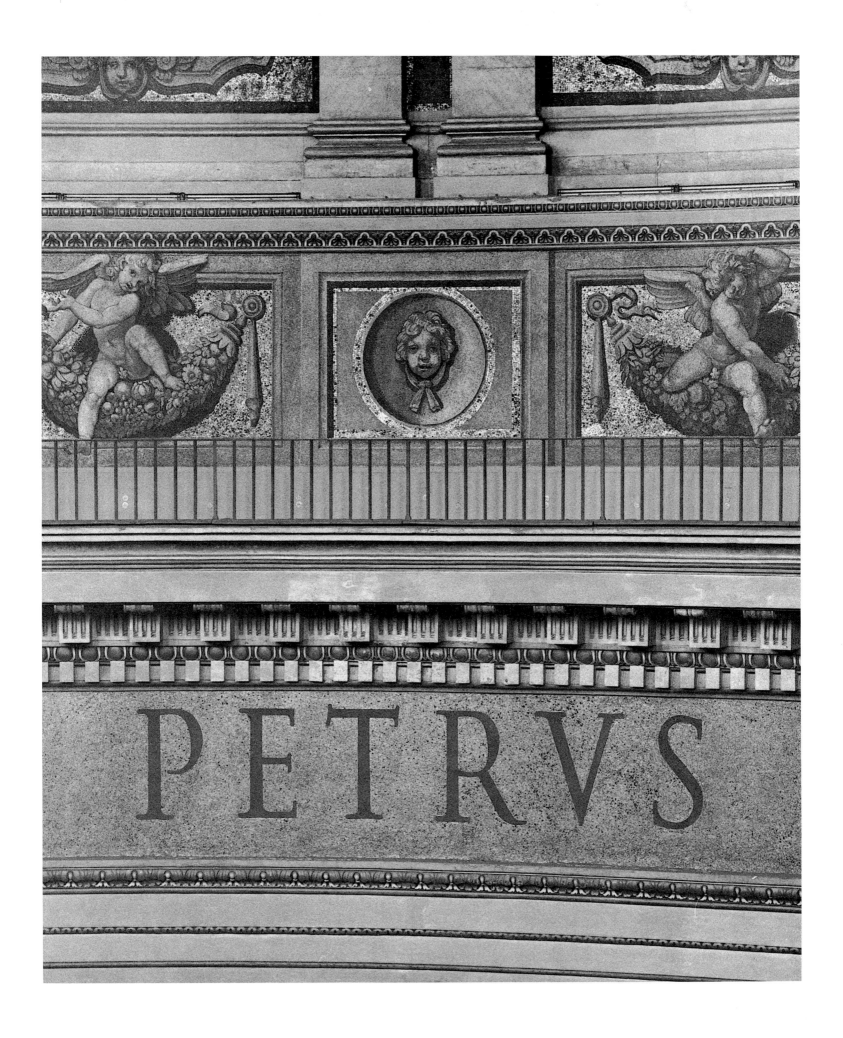

THE ROMAN PONTIFICATE
The ethos of a sacred city

'Thou art Peter, and upon this rock I will build my Church.' These prophetic words of Christ – apart from the intentional ambiguity and untranslatable pun: Greek *petros* = rock – enshrine the destiny of an *ecclesia*, or New Testament 'community of the elect,' which, two thousand years after, is still seeking to find the true meaning of Christ's message to his successor.

Does *ecclesia* mean the new community of this world, or that of the kingdom of Heaven? Is it a real *civitas*, or an aspiration to *Civitas Dei*? An edifice of stone and flesh, or the *Renovatio* at the end of time to which the Apocalypse alludes? Here is the essential dualism – and point of contention – that underlies the whole history of Rome and the papacy, up to the fateful year 1870. The coexistence of the two *civitates* has been resolved in various ways throughout that time.

To begin with, the nickname conferred by Jesus on the fisherman Simon (Cephas or Petros: stone, rock) inevitably points to an assimilation of the disciple with the Master: Christ himself was the 'cornerstone' of the Temple (the image crops up in varying forms in both the Old and the New Testaments). If therefore Peter is the foundation stone (and, in material terms, the Vatican basilica is built over his tomb), then Christ is the true crowning-piece of the Christian *opus*.

Once in Rome, Peter himself took up the metaphor when addressing the faithful of Asia Minor:

Come to him, to that living stone, rejected by men but in God's sight chosen and precious; and like living stones be yourselves built into a spiritual house, to be a holy priesthood, to offer spiritual sacrifices acceptable to God through Jesus Christ. For it stands in scripture: 'Behold, I am laying in Zion a stone, a cornerstone chosen and precious, and he who believes in him will not be put to shame.' To you

therefore who believe, he is precious, but for those who do not believe, 'The very stone which the builders rejected has become the head of the corner,' and 'a stone that will make men stumble, a rock that will make them fall'; for they stumble because they disobey the word, as they were destined to do. (I Peter, 2, 4–8)

Christ is stone, his apostle is stone, his disciples are 'living stones,' in a structure at once material and spiritual:

So then you are no longer strangers and sojourners, but you are fellow citizens with the saints and members of the household of God, built upon the foundation of the apostles and prophets, Christ Jesus himself being the cornerstone, in whom the whole structure is joined together and grows into a holy temple in the Lord; in whom you also are built into it for a dwelling place of God in the Spirit. (Ephesians, 2, 20–22)

Peter-Petros stands at the center of a new world, in a preordained strategy of progressive appropriation of the political power-center of the ancient world – the Rome described by Peter and John as 'Babylon.' The crucifixion of Christ had constituted the last act of ancient history, in the same Jerusalem – 'center of the earth' – that had seen the birth and death of the first man (the summit of Golgotha or Calvary derived its name from the skull of Adam, which was buried there); similarly the Vatican Hill, with its tomb of Peter, became the new Golgotha, just as *Roma caput mundi* was to be called to a new mission of central authority. Constantine's basilica on the 'Petrus' was homologous with the temple built by Solomon on the 'rock' – the altar of holocausts sanctified by David for reconciliation with God.

Three crucial events took place between the years 64 and 70: the burning of Rome, which was said to have been instigated by Nero; the martyrdom of Peter and Paul, cornerstones and columns of the Church; and finally the destruction of Jerusalem and the temple, interpreted

as vengeance for the slaying of Christ (and perhaps as a prefiguration of the burning of Rome-Babylon foretold by John).

The triumphal entry of Titus into Rome (AD 71), immortalized in the bas-reliefs on the Arch on the Via Sacra, can be seen as not just the return of a conqueror replete with the spoils of Jerusalem (subsequently the Vatican basilica received from Constantine the columns said to have come from the Temple of Solomon), but as, in a sense, the translation to Rome of the very idea of Jerusalem. If therefore Jerusalem had initially been 'Romanized' under Herod the Great, and then, so to speak, 'Babylonized' through the carrying into exile of its most precious trophies, then by a curious twist of history it was again Rome, the new Babylon, that replaced Jerusalem in the providential plan that brought about the progressive consolidation of the City of God.

John saw Rome-Babylon lit up by lurid lightning flashes:

I saw a woman sitting on a scarlet beast which was full of blasphemous names, and it had seven heads and ten horns . . . and on her forehead was written a name of mystery: 'Babylon the great, mother of harlots and of earth's abominations.' And I saw the woman, drunk with the blood of the saints and the blood of the martyrs of Jesus . . . the seven heads are seven mountains on which the woman is seated; they are also seven kings, five of whom have fallen, one is, the other has not yet come, and when he comes he must remain only a little while. As for the beast that was and is not, it is an eighth but it belongs to the seven, and it goes to perdition. (Revelation 17, 3; 5–6; 9–11)

The blood of the martyrs and the death of the fifth king (Nero) presage the downfall of the 'Whore' and the final victory of the Lamb. Indeed the fire of AD 64 seemed to fit in with a specific design if, as seemed to be the case, Nero himself was the arsonist. This crazed incendiary gesture, on the anniversary of the Fire of the Gauls (333 BC), and hymned by Nero as a metaphorical burning of Troy, marked the end of an era for the unfortunate capital: an end of the squalor of a chaotic, labyrinthine city, and the beginning of a construction program for a *ville radieuse*, with broad streets and squares open to the sunlight. Marrying, in a sense, the cult of the sun with that of fire (the fiery chariot of the sun purifying the city of its ancient disorderliness?), Rome was reborn, renewed like a phoenix, from the flames.

This image (used by Martial in homage to Domitian) accompanied a belief – taught also by the Stoics – that at the end of time the world will be destroyed by fire. From the syncretism of the late imperial period, there then emerged the palingenetic theory of a world renewed after destruction in a ritual fire: with the triumph of the just, and the death of all wrongdoers; at last the kingdom of universal happiness would have arrived.

Over the succeeding centuries Rome became not only *caput mundi*, but – with the Edict of Caracalla extending Roman citizenship to every subject of the Empire – a very synthesis of the world, and a living image of *orbe* became *urbe*. By a kind of reverse process, the patient strategy of the Christians was to respond to the centripetal gravitation to the pagan capital, with the foundation of a catholic *ecclesia* expanding centrifugally into the world; to the universe made city, they opposed in secret a *civitas* aspiring to universality.

In the grand, sweeping synthesis of St. Augustine, history is seen as an ever-alternating conflict between the *civitas terrestris* and *Civitas Dei*: the two often appear inextricably entwined, like the tares in the wheat, yet Rome-Babylon, in all its good and evil, provided a temporary image of a cosmo-political association tending towards the higher unity of the City of God which draws its citizens from all nations, irrespective of different languages, customs, and laws, pursuing and strengthening that which all the various nations put at the service of peace on earth, provided it does not hinder religion in its quest for the supreme, true God.

The myth of pagan Rome did not end with Constantine, but with the apocalyp-tic sack of 410. St. Jerome believed that the entire world perished in the ruins of that one city; St. Augustine retorted that Rome will not die unless the Romans die – the city of stone may well have been destroyed, but the 'living stones' remained to ensure the rebirth and continuance of the city of destiny. *Civitas Dei* was yet to make progress in human history, through successive phases of conquest, and through that strategy of universal conciliation that was to reach a crisis with the schisms and the Reformation.

Nero is also important in the present context for his espousal of the cult of Mithra (the Sun), with which the emperor was identified. His vast statue (vying with the Colossus of Rhodes), stood in the hall of the *Domus Aurea*, Golden House, the earthly recreation of the *Regia Solis*, the Kingdom of the Sun. The largest room in the Domus, a *coenatio* dominated by the imperial throne, the very epicenter of the Neropolis and of the whole universe, rotated continuously, reproducing the movement of the heavenly spheres: the sovereign, the 'New Sun,' playing his lyre, saw himself as Apollo presiding over the harmony of the spheres, and like Apollo he felt he was founding and refounding cities by the power of his cosmic music.

Significantly, the *Regia Solis*, the center of rotation of the cosmos, stood in the center of Rome, not far from the *Regia* of Numa Pompilius and the *pontifices maximi*; by contrast the *Regia christiana* was to occupy an eccentric location, not the Vatican, but the Lateran. And, if the throne room itself symbolized the cosmos (the movement of of rotation around the sun-emperor directly evoking the idea of a heliocentric cosmos, tying in with the beliefs of those Stoics who had greeted Nero's rise to power with enthusiasm), the huge area of the rest of the Golden House afforded an image of worldly dominion.

Before Constantine, the interdependence of politics and religion, temporal power and spiritual power, had reached its height with Aurelian (270–75), who adopted the Sun cult as the official state religion, uniting all the solar divinities of the East into a single god conceived as the moderator-supreme of the universe. The Sun was called *Conservator, Restitutor Orbis*, and *Dominus Imperii Romani*. Alongside and above the traditional *pontifices maximi* a college of *Pontifices Dei Solis* was created. Thereafter the emperors never abandoned sun-worship.

The centralization of religious as well as political power in Rome applied also to the nascent cultus of Christianity: in a dispute concerning the episcopal See of Antioch, Aurelian granted the Italian bishops – and especially the Bishop of Rome – the right to recognize and thus sanction elections of other bishops. However, it is likely that he feared the danger of competition with the Sun cult, which Christianity represented, despite, or perhaps because of, what both religions shared in common. It is probably to this period that we can date the oldest known Christian mosaic, in the mausoleum now under the Vatican grottoes. In this mosaic Christ is shown riding in the chariot of the sun, in the middle of a symbolic vine. The assimilation of Christ with the sun – a device to win over the general populace, brought up on sun cults – was justified by metaphors of *Sol Justitiae* and *Sol Salutis*.

The Church Fathers had to fight long and hard to combat the latent 'heliolatry,' which constantly burst out in heretical movements (the Heliognostics or *Deinvict-iaci* in Gaul) or in superstitious rites. In the 5th century St. Leo denounced the still prevalent adoration of the rising sun, practised even on the steps of St. Peter's itself; it is said that, one of the reasons for the siting of Giotto's mosaic of the *Navicella della Chiesa* (the Barque of the Church) on the inside of the portico, facing the façade of the basilica, was the desire to confront with a suitably pious image those who, even as late as the 14th century, would turn their backs on the basilica (the façade looks east) in a last act in a last act of adoration of the rising sun.

To return to Aurelian, we have tried to demonstrate elsewhere in this book that the plan of the city walls – which meant a new 'layout' of imperial Rome (it was to remain virtually unchanged until 1870) –

can be affiliated with two symbols, both connected with the ideology of Rome and the worship of the sun and the cosmos: the eagle and the seven-pointed star.

As an organic and zoomorphic motif, the eagle was much in evidence in urban design (a town to the northeast of Rome still attests to this fact in its name: L'Aquila), but it was particularly with Rome and the expansionist policies of the Empire that the eagle is indissolubly linked (eagles were of course the insignia of the Roman legions). It had a special significance for Aurelian whose victorious campaigns carried him from Gaul to Palmyra and Egypt. Apart from its significance as a symbol of victory, to which we shall return, the eagle was also a solar symbol, as 'king of the heavens,' the bird of Jupiter, of Apollo, and of the sun, the only living creature able to stare straight into the incandescent orb.

Traditionally, the eagle was the instrument of *consecratio* or *apotheosis*, when the soul of the emperor was assumed up to heaven (this symbol dated from the remarkable apparition of an eagle rising from the flames of Augustus's funeral pyre). It was at the same time the messenger of Jupiter. The eagle design was ultimately a symbol of the consecration (according to Roman religious custom, buildings, places, and towns could all be deemed sacred) of Rome as the city of the sun and seat of the deified emperors (*divi*).

The second, but not the last, design of the Aurelian walls, in the shape of a seven-pointed star, has connotations with the star that appears – at various times, and with varying symbolic purpose – on imperial coins (also relating to Jupiter and *Dea Roma*); Aurelian was also the first emperor to wear a diadem decorated with a star. The walls form the diadem and crown of the city. Conversely, one thinks too of the *corona muralis* or *corona turrita*, the battlemented or tower-adorned crown that was given as an award to soldiers in a successful siege, or presented to towns (e.g. the statue of Tyche at Antioch), and also offered to Cybele, mother of the gods and the sun, whom Rome worshipped as *Magna Mater Deorum*, and who could well have been assimilated with the 'great mother' metropolis of the world through her role as protector of cities as well as of agriculture.

The seven-pointed star is also an obvious cosmological reference to the seven 'ruling' planets and their interrelation (they were commonly rendered in visual terms as a seven-pointed star, or as a hermetic stellar citadel), as well as to specific Roman historical, ritual, and geographical data; the seven kings, the seven hills, and the *Septimontium*, the group of seven hill settlements.

However, the supreme star, the omnipotent heavenly body of salvation, was of course the sun, especially in the iconography of Eastern art, in which it is indeed depicted as a star. The 'crown' of walls thus represents a sort of *corona radiata*, the attribute of the sun and the emperors who were equated with the sun. Viewed in this manner Rome becomes the Heliopolis of the West, the 'City of the Sun' (*Sol Invictus*), in the same way that the emperor was identified with the sun, enthroned amid the planets, in accordance with the monarchic line of thought of the Stoics.

Aurelian's 'solar program' (always a secret, and known to us today only through sparse clues, given the curious absence of information about the walls in historical sources) was taken up in a remarkable fashion by Constantine, through the key importance of the *chrismon*, the monogram of Christ (☧ = *chi* + *rho*, the first two letters in the Greek spelling of Christ, XPIΣTOΣ), which appeared to him on the eve of his victory over Maxentius in October 312. This monogram then took the place of the eagle on the standards of the Roman legions. That this was no traumatic break with the past, nor a revolutionary new departure, is demonstrated by a series of events leading up to the ultimate triumph of Christianity, which one might say was an example of Aurelian's concept of a syncretic reconciliation of all monotheistic religions being taken to an extreme.

In 310, at Trier, Constantine had his first 'vision' (even in this phenomenon of inspired revelations, the example of Aurelian served as a model). During a visit to the temple of the sun, Apollo and Victory appeared to him with a prophetic sign of thirty years of imperial rule ahead of him (*Tricennales*: XXX). The fatidical character 'X,' at once a letter and a number (ten or *decussis*, the divine numeral par excellence), a sign of consecration and a solar symbol (the Gallic tradition testifies to this), thus signified 'Victory' in the mysteries of the cult of the sun, traceable back to 307, which Constantine only renounced at his deathbed baptism.

Again in 310 the fiercest persecutor of the Christians, Galerius, suffering from a severe illness, having supplicated Apollo and Aesculapius in vain, appealed directly to the Christians to pray to their God. This was about the time of the Edict of Nicomedia, drawn up perhaps in 310 and promulgated on 30 April 311 with the signatures of Constantine and Licinius, the future signatories of the Edict of Milan. It was no ordinary act of tolerance, but a politico-religious pact of universal pacification; indeed it had great importance in the early Christian doctrinal disputes, with its identification of orthodoxy on the one hand, which, according to the tradition already approved by Aurelian, was the thinking of the Bishop of Rome, and with the many heresies on the other, all declared to be at variance with 'the very founders of the faith.' Bloody battles were the outcome. The apparent spirit of tolerance was thus – doubtless due to the influence of the higher echelons of the Christian hierarchy – contradicted by a declaration of war against heresies. The Edict of Milan, signed in 313 by Constantine and Licinius, not only declared the state's tolerance of Christianity but also legalized its practice, as well as, nominally at least, annulling the difference between the orthodox communities and the heretical sects. Constantine subsequently attempted the great balancing feat of a reconciliation of the different views and beliefs, in the overall interest of the concord of the state, as proved by his well documented initial support of the Church

of Rome, and his later leanings towards Arianism; it was an Arian bishop who in the end baptized him.

In 312 Constantine experienced his famous vision, of which there are various contradicting documentary records. According to Lactantius (313), Constantine was advised (possibly in a dream) to set a heavenly symbol on his standards before the battle with Maxentius's forces: this symbol was an elaboration of the victory symbol X transformed into the monogram of Christ (*chrismon*). It is possible that the emblem of the six-spoked solar wheel had already been adopted among the insignia of the Roman legions.

The sun and the solar cross were hence taken up as divine symbols, auguring victory. Similarly, the various stages of Aurelian's spectacular career had been marked by solar 'manifestations.' In all crises, the sun god was said to have protected Rome and her emperor. One of the emperor's many visions took place under the walls of Emesa, the city of the Sun-god Elagabalus, when the god appeared to him, promising victory: it would appear that Aurelian had already consecrated his army to the sun. The many solar symbols on the legionary standards (later testified to by the *Notitia dignitatum*) must indeed have been placed there on Aurelian's orders, forming so to speak a springboard for the new worship of the Sun-Christ. The eagle, the other symbolic emblem of Aurelian's Rome, had likewise featured in history and myth as a symbol of victory: for instance, an eagle appeared to Jupiter before his decisive battle against the Titans. It was no mere coincidence that the eagle became connected with the *chrismon* in the paleochristian iconography of the *crux invicta*, the cross victorious over death through the event of Christ's resurrection.

We have attempted elsewhere to show how Constantine, after his victory over Maxentius, also used the *chrismon* as a supreme symbol of exorcism and victory, over and above the urban Roman dual emblem of the eagle and the sun. While the center of Rome remained a conservative stronghold of pagan worship (here Constantine confined himself to renovating the former basilica of Maxentius, and the senate erected the great arch, *compendium imperii*, near the Colosseum in his honor), the great Christian buildings rose along the imagined axes of a *chrismon*, often taking in areas of imperial property as well of course as the graves and tombs of the martyrs.

The six axes of this *chrismon* touched on and indicated points of exceptional interest:

To the north, the Milvian Bridge, the site of the historic defeat of Maxentius;

To the northeast, on the Via Nomentana, the covered cemetery and adjoining mausoleum of St. Costanza;

To the southeast, the Lateran complex on the outskirts of the city, with the church of St. John, begun in the winter of 312–13, and originally dedicated to the Saviour as an offering for victory (just as Aurelian, after the victory of Emesa, built a votive temple to the sun); outside the walls, along the Via Casilina, the cemetery-basilica at Tor Pignattara, with, nearby, the tomb of St. Helen;

To the south, on the Via Appia, the Basilica Apostolorum, with the relics of St. Peter and St. Paul, on the site of the present San Sebastiano;

To the southwest, along the Via Ostiense, the basilica of San Paolo fuori le Mura;

And finally, to the northwest, the basilica of St. Peter, founded after 319.

The western arms of this enormous *chrismon* are, in a manner of speaking, 'synthesized' by the churches of St. Peter and St. Paul, while the southern arm leads down towards the basilica dedicated to both Apostles, and the eastern arms extend to the tombs of the imperial family, in that section of Rome orientated roughly in the direction of Constantinople (where Constantine was to erect his own tomb, close to the basilica of the Apostles). It is noteworthy that the two greatest churches, the cathedral of St. John Lateran and the Vatican basilica, lie on the same axis, which became the symbolic axis of Christian Rome; and at the center of this same axis cluster the greatest monuments of pagan Rome: the Via Sacra, the Campidoglio, the Basilica of Maxentius and the Arch of Constantine, as well as the Colosseum.

This *chrismon* of urban planning therefore forms an eloquent image of the outspreading of Christianity. In the same way that the Aurelian walls were the radiating crown of the sun, the constellation of Christian basilicas was both the martyrs' crown and the aureole of faith. If as *caput mundi*, all roads led to Rome, so it was from Christian Rome, the new Jerusalem, that all roads left, carrying the Christian message following the apostolate of Peter and Paul.

Up until 326 Rome remained the point of equipoise (perhaps compromise) between paganism – solidly maintained by the senate at the city's center, and still adhered to by two thirds of Romans – and Christianity, with its monuments scattered around the periphery. In 326 Constantine triumphantly celebrated the twentieth anniversary of his rule (*vicennales*). He was at the height of his power. Yet at the same time it had become clear that his hopes of making Rome a Christian capital, or at least a united capital, could never be realized.

Leaving Rome, never to return (not even on occasions of family tragedies), he now turned all his attention to Constantinople, the New Rome, then arising alongside Byzantium and which was *consecrata* in 328 and solemnly inaugurated in 330. Only in Constantinople, the hinge between East and West, would the ideal organic fusion of solar religion and Christianity be achieved, as well as the healing of the internal divisions within Christianity, evidenced by the wide extent of the Arian heresy.

Constantine was proclaimed the 'new Moses,' the 'thirteenth Apostle,' being identified with both Christ and the Sun. His *palatium* was at once *Regia Solis* and *palatium Salomonis*. The circular forum of Constantine, around which the New Rome gravitated, had at its center a porphyry column containing, inside the base, the palladium of Rome together with relics of the saints; on top was a statue with an

On the following pages: a detail of the *Creation of Adam*: the hand of God gives life to the first man, on the ceiling of the Sistine Chapel, frescoed by Michelangelo between 1508 and 1512.

effigy of the emperor. This was an ancient statue of Apollo (attributed to Phidias, possibly originating from Rome's mother-city, Troy-Ilium), reworked to resemble Constantine. Holding a spear in one hand, and in the other a globe surmounted by a cross, and with seven sun rays (containing relics of the wood and nails of the Cross) around its head, it was venerated as an allegory of Christ.

To return to Rome, however, the process of Christianization, initiated by Constantine, proved irreversible; and Constantine it was who, albeit exonerated by history of having any connection with the infamous 'Donation' (see page 22), assured the future temporal power of the popes (though the Bishops of Rome only assumed this title later, with their assertion of primacy, in the Western world at least).

Throughout Rome's history there had been examples of combined temporal and spiritual power: the kings had also been priests, and similarly Augustus was pontifex, and several emperors were high priests of privileged cults (e.g. Elagabalus, who took his adoptive name from the sun god worshipped at Emesa). At the same time these two forms of power had frequently been independently administered: thus, under the Republic, the *rex sacrorum*, the king of sacrifices, and the *pontifex maximus*, who ruled separately from his *regia* on the Via Sacra.

With Diocletian the process of self-glorification reached its logical apogee in self-identification with the divinity, after the example of the great Eastern monarchs. Constantine renounced this prerogative, in line with Christian beliefs (although after his death the senate declared him *divus*), but in recompense made himself the protector and, in a sense, the head of the Church, appointing himself supreme judge and conciliator, as an 'external' or lay bishop (this was how he styled himself at the Council of Nicaea). Clearly, under the rule of Constantine the popes played a subordinate role, with the result that Christianity consolidated its roots in Rome under a dual authority: a benign form of caesarism-papism.

It was Constantine personally, together with his family, who undertook the building of all the places of worship and administration of Church affairs. Thus emerged the cathedral with its adjoining baptistry, and the residence and offices of the bishop; a Palatine church for the emperor's mother and her court; and five or six covered cemeteries situated on various roads leading from the city, and linked with places of worship.

As a result, the Lateran became the religious, political, and administrative center of the Christian community. The new basilica — described as an 'audience chamber of Christ the King' — was purposely built away from already inhabited land (the area continued uninhabited until 1870), among fields and possibly vineyards, serving as an allegory of the seed of Christianity planted in the mystic vine. In subsequent centuries the popes created important new buildings, and sought to increase building activity in the vicinity of the Lateran — the city within a city, the *caput mundi* of Christendom.

To begin with there was absolute centralism: baptisms could only be performed by the pope in the Lateran, and the entire city congregated in St. John for the most important ceremonies; later, other churches acquired baptistries, and liturgical stations were established, so that the pope could officiate in these satellite churches. The new religion, as it grew in independence and power, remained centered on the Lateran. No longer was this just a place of worship and administration, it was also a place of justice, with spectacular executions carried out before the statues of ancient justice: the bronze wolf and the bronze tablet of the *Lex Vespasiani* (the decree of the senate conferring on Vespasian that *potestas*, later to be transfered to the pope by Constantine).

In time the Lateran became a fortified citadel and a papal court in the fullest sense: a *palatium* which comprised the residences of the pope and various functionaries, reception and banqueting rooms, service areas, storerooms, chapels, and ambulatories. After the year 1000 it

became the center of a considerable agricultural complex: vegetable gardens, vineyards, orchards, mills. It was also the site of an open museum of 'marvels' from antiquity; besides the bronze wolf and the Vespasian tablet, there was the equestrian statue of Marcus Aurelius (identified as that of Constantine rather than the philosopher-emperor who had persecuted the Christians), and three 'honorary' columns, surmounted respectively by a Priapus, and the head and hand (the latter bearing an orb: symbol of world dominion), from a colossal statue of Constantine.

While many of these symbols of ancient power were later transferred to the Campidoglio, no longer a seat of power, almost all the functions of the Lateran were to be taken over in modern times by St. Peter's.

If the Lateran was the *caput mundi* recognized by papal authority, St. Peter's was the heart and soul and in effect the true center of the faith, consecrated as such by the devotional longing of the whole of Christendom. The Trophy of Peter, the humble tabernacle built over the Apostle's tomb in the second century, was a symbol of his victory over death, analogous with Christ's *crux invicta*. The most sublime moment following Constantine's victory at the Milvian Bridge was not his triumphal procession to the Capitol, but his halt before the Trophy in the Vatican, now consecrated as a 'new Capitol.' The Constantinian basilica of St. Peter was to see an uninterrupted flood of pilgrims, especially once Rome — with the fall of Jerusalem to the Arabs in 640 — remained the only true holy city in the West, the *altera Jerusalem*.

After the construction of the Leonine walls (847–53), the Vatican complex took on a distinctly cosmopolitan aspect, with the founding of the *scholae*: civil-military organizations and quasi-legations from many countries such as those of the Saxons (whence the name Santo Spirito in Sassia), the Lombards, the Frisians, and the Franks.

Now seems an appropriate moment to introduce the subject of the relationship

21

between Church and Empire, as it was in the Carolingian period that this became explicitly defined, through the forged 'Donation of Constantine,' on which the temporal power of the popes was based. The two chief Apostles had followed Christ in drawing a rigorous distinction between what is God's and what is Caesar's.

When Constantine 'emigrated' (to Constantinople), the Church acquired *de facto* hegemony in Rome. Indeed, according to Leo I (440–61), it was the See of Peter alone that ensured that Rome retained its position as *caput orbis*. Gregory the Great (590–604) was the first to set up a temporal government in the full sense of the word, controlling substantial territories in central and southern Italy. In the following century the ecclesiastical state gained legal authority with the donation of Pepin, King of the Franks, to Stephen II (754) of those parts of central Italy occupied by the Lombards and previously Byzantine possessions. Rome thereby cut its last links with the East, to ally itself permanently with the Western world.

The coronation of Charlemagne in St. Peter's (800) ratified this alliance between the two foremost powers of the West, the papacy and the Empire. It was about this time that the 'Donation of Constantine' was first heard of. This fictitious document purported to prove that the emperor, on the point of withdrawing to Constantinople, gave to Sylvester I (314–35) complete autonomy over the lands around Rome, and a presumed sovereignty over Italy and indeed the whole of the West. Thus the 'barbarian' Charlemagne was received in Rome as a faithful vassal rather than as emperor and heir to Constantine. The emperor was greatly disturbed by a ceremony that placed him in an inferior position to the pope. Around the year 1000, Otto III tried to reassert the authority and autonomy of the Empire in its dealings with the papacy, elaborating the theory of a double theocracy, in which nevertheless the emperor had the upper hand.

To counter this move, Gregory VII

(1073 or 1074), with his *Dictatus Papae*, accorded the pope the role of absolute monarch, conferring on himself both the right to chose the emperor and a right to the imperial insignia, a right claimed to have been conceded by Constantine. It is with Gregory VII that the papal tiara – interpreted as a crown – first became the *triregno*: the first diadem symbolizing regal dignity; the second, added by Boniface VIII, imperial dignity; and the third, appearing for the first time at Avignon, on the tomb of Benedict XII (1334–42), being of unclear symbolism. Innocent II (1130–43) was described in panegyrics as 'Caesar and sovereign of the whole world' and 'true emperor.' The ideology of the emperor-pope reached its acme with Innocent III (1198–1216), and experienced a last revival with the proud Boniface VIII (1294–1303), who is said to have replied to the imperial ambassadors: '*Ego sum Caesar, ego sum imperator,*' (I am Caesar, I am emperor.)

The concept of caesarism-papism, born with Constantine, was therefore inverted into a kind of 'papal caesarism,' founded in turn on the putative 'Donation.'

Ahi, Costantin, di quanto mal fu matre,
 non la tua conversion, ma quella dote
 che da te prese il primo ricco patre!
(Ah, Constantine, of how much ill was mother, not your conversion, but that dowry which the first rich Father took from you!) (*Inferno* XIX, 115–117)

From his invective against the simoniac popes, Dante proceeds to express nostalgia for the balance of these two major powers, in that imperial Rome elected by providence as *lo loco santo/u'siede il successor del maggior Piero* (the holy place where the successor of great Peter has his seat) (*Inferno* II, 23–24).

From the prehistory of the 'City of the Sun' we finally arrive at the metaphor of the 'two Suns': papal power illuminating the path to eternal beatitude, and imperial power revealing the way to eternal happiness.

Soleva Roma, che 'l buon mondo feo,
 due soli aver, che l'una e l'altra strada

facean vedere, e del mondo e di Deo.
 L'un l'altro ha spento; ed è giunta la spada
 col pasturale, e l'un con l'altro insieme
 per viva forza mal convien che vada
(Rome, which made the world good, was wont to have two Suns, which made visible both the one road and the other, that of the world and that of God. The one has quenched the other, and the sword is joined to the crook: and the one together with the other must perforce go ill) (*Purgatory* XVI, 106–111)

Nor is the other metaphor of the eagle neglected in the *Divine Comedy*. The anti-Christian emperors of Rome-Babylon strike at the chariot of the Church like an eagle. Constantine too is an eagle who descends on the chariot-barque, leaving behind the plumage of the 'Donation': *O navicella mia, com mal se' carca* (O little bark of mine, how ill you are laden) (*Purgatory* XXXII, 129); and the *Cinquecento diece e cinque* (Five Hundred, Ten, and Five) (*Purgatory,* XXXIII, 43), the DXV of vengeance – Dante's cryptic phrase would seem to refer to a temporal ruler, probably Henry VII, who would resolve the dialectic of the 'two suns' – is also an eagle. The enigma Beatrice offers Dante allowed three possible solutions: a great emperor (the universal monarch, sole helmsman of the ship of the world, of whom Dante speaks in the *Convivio*), a great pope (*Dominus Xristi Vicarius*), and the Sun-Christ himself (*Dominus Xristus Victor – or Vltor*).

PAPAL POLICIES IN MODERN ROME. 'THE ADMINISTRATIVE CENTERS' AND THE DECLINE OF TEMPORAL POWER

A later section of this book deals with the fundamental stages in the formation and evolution of the Vatican City as the focal center of the pontiff's dual authority. Here let us consider the cultural policies of the popes with regard to the city under two complementary aspects, which make the modern history of the 'second Rome' occasionally somewhat contradictory. On the one hand the expansion and increase of the centers of power, with the creation of satellite nuclei or administrative centers beyond the Tiber; and on the other the siege and 'reduction of the Vatican,' leading to eventual exile, until the denouement of 1870.

One might begin this account with the fateful urban-planning ambitions of Nicholas V (1447–55), who envisaged building a new papal palace at Santa Maria Maggiore as a summer retreat. Yet in some ways it would be preferable to start with the initiative of Paul II (1464–71) who, in enlarging his cardinal's mansion in the very heart of the city, was in a certain sense creating another Vatican (many later popes used it as a second residence): the Palazzo di San Marco (later renamed the Palazzo Venezia), which included the old church, reducing it to the status of a court chapel. The façade of the church, with its double loggia, seems to echo the Loggia della Benedizione built by Pius II in front of St. Peter's. Adjoining the palazzo, which stood alone and had the appearance of a castle, was the Palazzetto Venezia, with its raised garden, a miniature reproduction of the Vatican's *paradiso* or *pomerium*.

Though Paul II may have felt 'persecuted' (to take up one of Nicholas V's fixed notions), Alexander VI (1492–1503) was in a much worse plight. In 1494 the victorious forces of Charles VIII of France were encamped across the Tiber. Hence the pope's retirement to the Vatican, and the undertaking of the great fortifications and urban reconstruction works, of which more will be said later.

Julius II (1503–13), Alexander's bitter enemy, then adopted a policy of attack as opposed to defense. One of the results of this aggressive attitude towards the city was the construction of the long, straight thoroughfare of the Via Giulia, at the center of which, in a large piazza, Bramante was to build the Palazzo dei Tribunali. In the same piazza, Bramante is thought to have designed the Palazzo Sforza Cesarini – then the Apostolic Chancellery (the post of chancellor being held by a nephew of the pope).

The Palazzo dei Tribunali, conceived as a castle or 'citadel of Justice,' brought under one roof the ecclesiastical and civil tribunals (the former had hitherto occupied the *palatium Innocentianum* in the courtyard of St. Peter's), as well as providing lodgings for the judges, thus expressing in tangible form the ethical and metaphysical concept of *justitia* of the pope-emperor.

Under the two Medici popes, Leo X and Clement VII, the city spread itself in the area of the ancient Campus Martius (Campo Marzio), where a modern quarter developed, constructed around two new arterial streets, the Via di Ripetta (or Leonina) and the Via del Babuino (or Via Paolina, after Paul III who finished it). Particularly important was the Leonina, planned by Raphael and Antonio da Sangallo the Younger, which formed both a more suitable approach to the Vatican from the Porta del Popolo, and a privileged route to Leo X's new Medici palazzo, designed as part of a grand project by Giuliano da Sangallo (later it became the Palazzo Madama; originally it was to embrace the Piazza Navona, making it the Medicis' 'courtyard').

This intense flourish of expansion was offset, however, by an equal process of 'reduction' with the sack of 1527, when Clement VII and his entire court were besieged in Castel Sant'Angelo. The city suffered major destruction, from which it recovered only in the next decade. With the momentous triumphal entry of Charles V into Rome, in 1536, the Romans and Paul III Farnese (1534–49) were able to show the emperor not a city still suffering from the sack of nine years before, but one in which the vestiges of ancient Rome stood out along a *via triumphalis*, a processional route following the 'stations' of the *Septimontium*, the Palatine, the Colosseum, the Forum Romanum, and the ancient arches (of Constantine, Titus, and Septimus Severus), alternating with which were temporary triumphal arches. For the occasion old tumbledown houses had been demolished, and new streets laid out; the whole city was in a forment of reconstruction.

The visual symbol of Paul III's power in the city was the Palazzo Farnese, which became the hub of a new quarter, with the opening up of a large piazza and a street converging on the main entrance to the palazzo. At the same time the Palazzo Venezia was integrated into an ambitious plan connecting it, by means of a *passetto*, to the tower built by Paul III on the Ara Coeli as the fulcrum of a Capitoline citadel wholly dominated by the pope. A contemporary indeed noted that the pope had 'constructed a heavenly stronghold, but not to fend off suspected enemies, of which he has none – he needs no stronghold who rules on earth in the name of the Lord of Heaven – but in order to equal the immortal gods, and so that God who, leaving heaven, might be able to boast another Olympus on earth with a lord of the earth.'

In 1557 Rome came close to being sacked again, when the irresponsible policies of Paul IV (1555–59) dragged the state into a new war with Spain, and the Duke of Alba's army only narrowly failed in a night attack below the very walls of the city.

The next pope, Pius IV (1559–65), at once consolidated and developed the city's fortifications, as well as setting in motion an energetic program of new building and urban reconstruction. Contemporary records show him in constant movement from one part of the city to the other, even at the expense of his already frail health. 'His Holiness suffers from a slight gout in one knee, yet never stays in any one place; he may lunch at San Marco, then in the evening sup and sleep at Ara Coeli; or he is to be found in his apartments at the Vigna Giulia, or in St. Peter's, or in his garden at Montecavallo, ever restless.' This apparent restlessness (inherited partly from Paul III) reflected more a deliberate attempt on the part of the Milanese Gian Angelo Medici (nicknamed 'il Medichino' to distinguish him from the Florentine Medicis) to enhance his image of 'omnipresent,' thereby reaffirming the pope's position as 'guardian angel' (*angelo custode*) and 'doctor' (*medico*) of the city.

The new residential and administrative

A detail of the Throne of St. Peter in the tribune of the basilica, a triumph of sculpture in bronze created by Bernini between 1656 and 1665. Four Doctors of the Church hold up the symbol of St.

Peter's power. In this detail one can see on the left St. Ambrose from the Latin Church and St. Athanasius from the Greek Church on the right.

centers were not planned in single unrelated units, but as part of a fast mutually interrelated urban-planning scheme. The new, long straight thoroughfare of the Via Pia (possibly conceived by Michelangelo, who designed the Porta Pia itself), in particular became the power-axis of the pope and his eminent nephew and secretary of state Carlo Borromeo.

From the notional starting point of the Palazzo Venezia, the epicenter of all the new construction work, this axis meets, in succession, the Palazzo Colonna (given to Borromeo), the Quirinal (where Paul III had once thought of creating a papal summer residence), and then the complex of the *horti bellaiani* (also given to Carlo Borromeo). Thus from the twin-centers of the Vatican-Lateran urban plan (or its reduction to a single center) the planning was now definitively polycentric. Both the administrative centers and the basilicas came to be linked by a modern system of straight streets designed to accommodate the latest means of locomotion: the carriage.

Pius IV's plans for the urbanization of the semideserted areas on the Pincio, Quirinal, Viminal, Esquiline and Caelian continued to be implemented under Gregory XIII (1573–85) and Sixtus V (1585–90) – Rome in its modern lineaments was beginning to take steps. Under Gregory the ideology of *Roma resurgens* reached its height. By Pius IV's time the population was double (80,000) what it had been at the beginning of the century; under Gregory XIII it increased to 140,000 (however, a census at the end of the century registered 110,000, and the population remained stationary throughout the next century). In view of the jubilee year of 1575 the basilicas were restored, and churches built or rebuilt that were to have an important effect on the architectural style of the Counter Reformation, not to speak of the formative influence of some façades dating from this period on the baroque style later.

The restoration of the Acqua Vergine and the Trevi led to the construction of an elaborate system of fountains. Numerous public and private edifices were erected, partly due to building regulations that favored works of urban improvement, like the new tower of the Campidoglio, the granaries at the Baths of Diocletian, the Collegio Romano, the University (Sapienza), and many other educational, charitable and medical institutions.

The main new thoroughfares to be opened under Gregory XIII: the Via Merulana or Gregoriana, the Via Appia Nuova, and the Porta San Giovanni were only the completion of Pius IV's projects. A number of projects, initiated under Gregory XIII, were to be finalized by Sixtus V: among these were the erection of the Vatican obelisk in St. Peter's Square, and the completion of the restoration work on the Alexandrine aqueduct (renamed 'Felice' by Sixtus V). There was also the grandiose urbanization scheme drawn up in 1573, but never actually realized: 'On Wednesday morning,' one document tells us, 'the Pope rode over to St. John Lateran, where he ordered that the street leading from that church to Santa Maria Maggiore, and those from the other seven basilicas, be made straight, like the Strada Pia, for the Holy Year.'

The first street completed under Sixtus V was the Strada Felice, which intersected the Strada Pia, running presumably from the Piazza del Popolo (Santa Maria del Popolo now took the place of San Sebastiano as one of the seven basilicas), past Trinità dei Monti and then Santa Maria Maggiore, to Santa Croce in Gerusalemme. This cruciform network of streets, straddling the deserted hills or *monti*, was both a cross of exorcism and consecration. Santa Maria Maggiore, the basilica adjacent to the papal Villa Montalto (which the pope, Felice Peretti da Montalto, had started to build some time before), now took on a role of unique authority, situated as it was at the center of a 'star' layout of streets.

We have elsewhere sought to show that the town planning of Sixtus V was a sort of self-portrait, to be seen in terms of the crest he chose in ascending the Chair of Peter: the hills surmounted by the cross and star, to be duplicated almost exactly in the design of a great cross and star of streets on the hills of Rome; the allusion to Mary *maris stella* also must not be forgotten. Felice Peretti was born in Grottammare (literally 'cave by the sea'), as the pope himself liked to put it, 'in a cave,' an obvious analogy with the birth of Christ. His parents, exiles twice over (from Dalmatia, then from Montalto), were fervent devotees of the Madonna (who more than once had miraculously saved the young Felice). Santa Maria Maggiore, the greatest Marian church in Rome, was also specially dedicated to Christ's nativity as in it were contained the relics of Bethlehem: swaddling clothes, hay, and manger.

Under the pope's plan, the basilica was to become both a court church (adjoining the Villa Montalto, which had become the largest in Rome) and, with the addition of a new chapel, a papal tomb (his own); its dome would be a reminder of the dome-tomb of St. Peter's now brought to completion, according to Michelangelo's plans, by the prodigious efforts of Sixtus himself. Furthermore, the pope had the old medieval crib transported to the new chapel. Thus in his funeral chapel, Sixtus V, 'born in a cave,' surrounded himself with the most revered relics of the Bethlehem cave-stall, paradoxically equating his last resting place with the nativity of Christ. And Sixtus V had yet another extraordinary idea: to steal the Holy Sepulcher from the Turks and transport it to tiny Montalto delle Marche. The Holy Sepulcher would therefore find a new home in Sixtus's native land, while the relics of Christ's birth lay forever preserved beneath the pope's tomb. And if Montalto was to take the place of Jerusalem, another town in the Marches, dear to the pope, had for long been a surrogate Nazareth: Loreto, where the house of the Madonna, the place of Christ's conception, was preserved.

Sixtus V's choice of the hills and the cross as his crest relate to the idea of the Church (the Hill of God) and Christ; but above all, the inclusion of the star indicates a symbolic identification between the pope, the Church, the Madonna, and Christ. Elsewhere we have

tried to illustrate how Sistine Rome was to be not only a city in the shape of a star (*in syderis formam*, the panegyrist Bordino wrote), but a constellation of such: six of the seven basilicas, according to the new Sistine canon, would be disposed like the stars of Ursa Major, while the greatest temple of all, St. Peter's, would occupy the place of the Polestar in Ursa Minor. Viewed in this way, St. Peter's would flank the temple of *Maris stella*, and each would contain the elements of birth and death: with the crib in the 'womb' of Santa Maria Maggiore, in the equivalent position to the tomb of Peter as cradle of the Church. The Madonna is the Polestar, as is the greatest of all churches, as is, Peter; Sixtus's faith in God is also the Polestar (according to one panegyrist, the pope had 'always put his confidence in God,' that God who, like the Polestar, remained ever constant).

Finally, the concept of the Polestar applies to the pope himself as the ultimate point of reference and security for his city and the world. 'One star stood for security,' we read in a funeral oration, 'and this was clearly the Pole, which sailors call the North Star and Sixtus it was, that brightest of stars, who opened up to the faithful the sure way by which they might reach the heaven of yearned-for peace.'

The Quirinal palace, begun by Gregory XIII, continued by Sixtus V, and completed by Paul V, was now firmly established as the second papal *palatium*. Atop the hill that was said visually to dominate the city (as one epigram put it: *Colle Quirinali praestat qua mitior aura,/vertice et summo subdita Roma patet* – Rome starts with the Quirinal hill whence [comes] milder airs, and spreads itself at the feet of its lofty heights), the Tower of the Winds became a new focal point of the urban panorama, alongside the Campidoglio tower, and echoing the other Tower of the Winds in the Vatican (both built by Gregory XIII).

The desire for maximum visual domination of the area is attested by one writer, who attributes to the pope the aim of 'dominating not only the seven hills but

also as far as the sea.' Embellished with gardens and fountains, and fortified like a citadel by Urban VIII (who also built nearby, as an out-of-town residence, the Villa Barberini), the Quirinal looked like becoming the sole *caput* of the city when Alexander VII pondered (and consulted his advisors on the subject) whether to transfer his court lock, stock, and barrel onto the hill – where already there were important papal offices such as the *Dataria*. It is significant that at the time of the last pope-king, Pius IX, the Quirinal passed from being the favorite papal residence, to become the palace of the Savoyard kings, three quarters of a century before it became the favored 'palace' of the Republic.

For reasons of space, various other developments of parallel administrative power-centers and/or projected shifts of the center cannot be gone into here. Nevertheless, it is worth mentioning the plan of Innocent X (1644–55) to move all or at least part of the papal court to his family seat, the Palazzo Pamphili in the Piazza Navona: the Piazza was altered so as to become a 'Pamphili courtyard,' with the construction of the Fontana dei Fiumi and the court chapel of Sant'Agnese in Agone.

Undeniably, the main axis of Rome was gradually shifting from the Vatican to the Piazza Veneto and the Quirinal. The commercial, financial, and social center, of which until the mid 16th century the Campo dei Fiori had been the hub, moved first to the area of the Piazza Navona, then towards the Corso (the main axis projected by Alexander VII, who contemplated creating a 'Chigi courtyard' with a large piazza in front of his family palazzo, where Bernini dreamt of siting Trajan's column alongside the Antonine column), and finally to the area around the Piazza di Spagna, so-called to commemorate the clash between the two greatest Catholic powers, Spain and France. Another project carried out under Alexander VII was the construction of steps leading up to Trinità dei Monti, as a monument to the glory of the Sun King.

Let us also skim over the dramatic events of 1800 onwards – a thousand years

after Charlemagne, and five hundred after the exile to Avignon – which saw a return of the 'persecutions': the French supremacy, the 'republic,' the exile of Pope Pius VI, and a new imperial coronation, in France this time rather than in Rome, by a pope (Pius VII) clearly subordinate to the 'new Charlemagne,' Napoleon. Rather, let us end by considering briefly the rule of the last pope-king, Pius IX.

During the longest ever pontificate (1846–78), Pius IX was once again, like Julius II and Sixtus V before him, a pope who aimed at modeling both city and state in the image of his own vision of the world. The long epitaph on his tomb tells us that: 'He dedicated himself to promoting the public good, in the sciences and in the arts, in both town and country; with the railways and telegraph he improved communications; everywhere he was concerned for beauty and progress especially in Rome. To him is due the creation of great numbers of episcopal sees and constitutional hierarchies; he encouraged the founding of seminaries and the decoration of new churches, marvelous in numbers, and was a wonderful inspiration to piety.'

Here then are the main strands of his policies: active involvement in the city and environs, encouragement of science and the economy under the banners of 'communications' and 'progress,' consolidation of the hierarchy and Church structures, and the fostering of social services as an exercise of piety and religion. His use of the arts – as *instrumentum religionis* and hence *instrumentum regni* – was in the hope of an eventual cultural and spiritual consensus among his subjects. According to apologists, the pope wished, 'with the minister for fine arts, to enhance the Romans' love of religion and worship, to promote in them the culture of their spirit.'

An impressive amount of this was achieved between 1850 and 1870. Despite the recurrent economic crises and cutbacks in public spending, it could nevertheless be said that 'no pope has done more to embellish this eternal city with new buildings.' Building sites multiplied, financed by the state, and occasionally out of the pope's own pocket: 'It is marvelous,' we read, 'to see every day new works and important monuments rising up, which would be described as great even in times of prosperity, but which must be regarded as colossal in these difficult and calamitous times.'

As well as the traditional renovation work in the old quarters, new buildings were also erected in the uninhabited parts of the city inside and outside the walls. An overall plan of redevelopment of public services was set in operation, concentrating mainly on the least well served areas; the city also acquired stations and bridges, factories and barracks, museums and observatories, public washhouses and post offices, new prisons, and the monumental Verano cemetery.

Together with the civic refurbishing of Rome went the restoration of both pagan and the Christian monuments. The church-building projects were on an unprecedented scale (a report of 1865 mentions 'the restoration, renovation, and decoration of no fewer than forty-eight churches in Rome alone, some built up from the very foundations,' with the dual aim of 'collective edification' and 'the greater glory of God.' We shall confine ourselves here to the most important of these ecclesiastical projects, some of which were possibly undertaken with the 1875 jubilee year in mind. The pillars of St. Peter's were refaced with white marble, the Canonica was enlarged, and a temporary council chamber built.

At Santa Maria Maggiore, the pope's initial choice for his own tomb (in honor of the Virgin, and perhaps also in homage to the memory of Sixtus V), Pius IX renovated the chapel where the earlier pope was buried and commissioned the new *Confessione* below the high altar (where, in 1800, a statue of Sixtus V was placed). St. John Lateran gained a new *Confessione* (reliquary) and plans were made to move the old apse (using a system of rollers powered by steam), an operation carried out by Andrea Busiri Vici in 1868. A new cruciform piazza was completed in front of the basilica in 1870. San Lorenzo fuori le

Mura, which the pope eventually chose as his last resting place, is perhaps the most outstanding example of 19th-century 'period restoration' combined with modernization, as seen in the substitution of new frescoes over the ancient decoration. However, the most notable worksite of 19th-century papal Rome was San Paolo fuori le Mura which, following the fire of 1823, was almost fully restored to its former glory under Pius IX.

Magnificence and reliance on Providence are mentioned in contemporary hagiography as the two guiding principles of Pius IX's policies. The syndrome of the 'pope-father' continued to grow, almost to the point of absurdity as evidenced by this contemporary quotation: 'The first names Romans teach their children to say is not that of their own father, but that of Pius IX. The first cry from the cradle now is no longer one of pain, but of gladness: the name Pius IX.' Ever since the general pardon (*Editto del perdono*, 1846), Pius had popularized the image of himself as a father at once stern and merciful, concerned for the physical and spiritual well-being of his great family, wishing to strengthen the ties within that family both through progress in faith and faith in progress,

This notion of enlightened paternalism derived sustenance from deep in the pope's own personal experience and psychology. In his early days the young Mastai was a much loved superintendant of a hospice for poor children; later he took over the direction of the Ospizio di San Michele, the 'great house of mercy,' where he was in charge of some 1200 young people, all there for very different reasons: it was at once a school for abandoned children, a school of arts and crafts, and a house of correction for 'fallen' young men and women.

Mastai saw through highly effective reforms, making better use of resources and potential, and introducing new activities and regulations. It is quite likely that even after becoming pope, Pius IX retained to some extent the attitude of the director of a hospice-factory-prison. Through his paternalistic eyes — whether

enlightened or despotic — the city must have seemed a broader version of the 'citadel of mercy' in Trastevere, and indeed the entire state could be seen as one huge hospice or, even worse, a vast panopticon, with the prisoners at all times under the eyes of the warders.

Without going so far as to describe this Roman administration as a 'complicated machine' or a 'prison for life' (Pianciani), nevertheless the view of the city as a total institution accounts well for the intensive four-facetted program of production, assistance, education, and correction.

As a counterweight to the *leggenda nera* — the black legend — of the Risorgimento writers, there arose the concept of the 'good father.' Following on from the 'liberal' image came that of the 'infallible' pope — until 20 September 1870 saw the pontiff consecrated once and for all in the guise of 'martyr.'

Yet, 20 September 1870 was a watershed. The fall of the pope-king at last brought to an end the interminable autumn of the Middle Ages. Previously, as Paolo Brezzi has observed, the situation was indeed still almost medieval, with the Inquisition and the stake, the exclusion of heretics from the community (both the religious and the civil communities), and obligatory presentation of documents testifying to fulfilment of ecclesiastical precepts in obtaining employment or a post in a school, and so on.

'My body, once a corpse,' wrote Pius IX in his will, 'shall be buried in the church of San Lorenzo fuori le Mura. On the modest tomb shall be carved a *triregno* with the keys; the coat of arms shall be a skull.' The papacy had thus come full circle: the last martyr-pope asked to be buried beside the first Christian martyr. Besides the proud, stubborn reassertion of the legitimacy of his own temporal as well as spiritual power, symbolically expressed by the *triregno*, was a disturbing and tragic hint: in place of the heraldic crest there was now an image of death. *Vanitas vanitatum* was the metaphorical seal on the tomb not only of the man, but also of the enmeshing symbol of dominion which had threatened to engulf him.

THE BASILICA AND THE BORGHI
From church to city

Long before becoming a part of Rome, Borgo was a town in its own right, founded on a precise occasion, at a precise moment, with its own individual history and evolution. For these very reasons it may be considered as a showpiece of urban history, an exemplar of the processes of a town's formation and development, which in other circumstances might not be so easily identifiable.

The history of Borgo is linked with that of the Roman papacy, is indeed a direct reflection of it, as step by step its development followed the fortunes of the Church of Rome.

How did it come about that a place so small and insignificant came to play so important a role in the history of the city of Rome? From its very beginnings Borgo was an autonomous town, outside the Aurelian walls which marked the limits of Rome. And it always maintained this 'outside' position, which was first and foremost strategic and political, other than topographical or urbanistic.

A 'SEPARATE CITY'

Even a rapid glance at its history will show the 'separateness' of the Leonine City with respect to Rome. Its complete indifference to the developments taking place within the city, is a verification of the self-assertiveness and eventual consolidation of the temporal power of the Church of Rome following the return from Avignon. The Borgo Vaticano was itself a determining factor in this process, at least during the 15th and 16th centuries; it was under Sixtus V, at the end of the 16th century, that Borgo was officially integrated into the Roman administrative system, as the fourteenth sector or *rione*.

Some of the main town-planning developments carried out in Rome (recent times included) took place in this area; these include the later realized plans of Nicholas V, the opening up of Borgo Nuovo by Alexander VI via the Giulia-Lungara project, not to mention the immensely difficult task of systemizing the piazza before St. Peter's All these works testify to a continued interest in the quarter, resulting in a coherent, monumental, not to say triumphalist, reality brought to a conclusion with the construction of the Via della Conciliazione.

THE MAKEUP AND ORIGINS OF THE BORGO

The Borgo Vaticano is a miniature city in itself. Between the basilica, the castle, and the Santo Spirito complex – each with its differing, well-defined features and functions – there evolved a compact urban zone, uniform as regards architectural style and construction. Of exits from the area, there were few. Around the fringes (these areas have now changed almost beyond recognition, not for the better) there were sectors whose individuality stemmed directly from the way they had evolved over the years: the area below the Janiculum, between the ending of the Borgo Santo Spirito and the Porta Fabrica, was made up of irregular, relatively low blocks of buildings grouped around certain very ancient complexes. At various times other larger buildings replaced these fragmented constructions: the cavalry barracks (near the Porta Cavalleggeri), the Palazzo del Sant'Uffizio, and the recent Aula Nova.

Very different was the area opened up in the mid 16th century by Pius IV, between the *passetto* and the new defensive line established between Belvedere and Castello. Laid out along the old thoroughfare leading to the restored Porta Angelica, this new development consisted of uniform, well-defined rectangular groupings of tall buildings. Despite considerable alterations, this remains the only part of the old *rione* to have preserved any of its original character.

As can be imagined, the successive developments which took place, in time affected the architectural 'texture' of the area, bringing about a complete change of urban character. The original unity and coherence of basically residential buildings so organized as to make maximum use of ever more fragmented lots, gradually became lost. This is all the more understandable when one considers the monumental and prestigious purposes for which these developments were designed.

It is not easy to document the origins of the Borgo since records relating to the Vatican area before the Christian era, when it acquired its symbolic aura, are both few and incomplete. From the beginnings of the history of Rome, the *Ager Vaticanus*, as it was known (the name is probably of Etruscan derivation), was considered sacred. Varro mentions that this vast marshy plain was conquered from the neighboring city of Veii by Romulus himself, under divine providence. Perhaps due to its strategic importance, the area was entrusted to the protection of the goddess Dia, to whom a shrine was dedicated.

NERO – STREET BUILDER

For all the sacred associations of the place, however, the Vatican plain was considered unhealthy, and for a long time remained deserted. Only in the first century AD were attempts made to drain the land; at the same time most of the area became imperial property, and between 37 and 41 Caligula began building a private circus there. It was completed by Nero and named after him. Nero it was in fact who first took an interest in the area and built the Ponte Trionfale, connecting the street of the same name – running from Monte Mario down to the Vatican plain – with the city center. As to the provision of roads in this area in both Roman and medieval times, research has so far been unable to shed much light.

Where all sources agree about the existence of certain roads, the Via Trionfale, and the Via Cornelia, for instance, there is still no definite indication of where they ran exactly. In the case of the Via Trionfale, the most probable theory is that it went northwest from the bridge, joining the Via Cassia at the level of the Giustiniana, having surmounted Monte Mario. The Via Cornelia on the other hand

A detail of Michelangelo's drum of the dome of St. Peter's, the smaller domes can be seen in the foreground.

Below: This 16th-century drawing is a copy of a fresco which used to be in the Vatican Grottoes, and shows a cross section, looking east, of the interior of the old basilica built by Constantine. Bottom: a cross section of Constantine's basilica, showing the portico and part of the pontifical residences, in the model made in 1694 by Carlo Fontana, the pupil and assistant of Bernini. Opposite above left: Letarouilly's model of Constantine's old basilica, looking west. Above right: a model of the Circus of Nero in the *Ager Vaticanus*, made by Fontana in 1694. Below left: the ground plan of Constantine's basilica, showing the respective positions of the basilica of St. Peter and of the Circus of Nero. Below right: the ground plan of the old Vatican as reconstructed by Carlo Fontana.

SETTIONE DELLA BASILICA COSTANTINIANA DEMOLITA NEL VATICANO CON PORTICI E PARTE DELLE ABITATIONI PONTIFICIE

is thought to have followed an east–west axis, roughly corresponding to the present Via della Conciliazione, and taking the Vatican Hill to connect up with the Via Aurelia. These two roads would most likely have intersected at the point of the future Piazza Scossacavalli.

The Vatican plain, known by then as the *horti Neronis*, became inhabited immediately after the fire of 64, when temporary accommodation had to be found for those who had lost their homes. At this time many Christians were put to death in Nero's circus and gardens (both the emperor and public opinion put the blame for the fire on the Christians).

Tradition has it that it was during these persecutions that St. Peter was crucified, and that the place of his crucifixion was the Vatican Hill. This was the first important event determining the future of the area, and it was to have decisive consequences for the city of Rome itself. It is not in the present context of great importance to establish the exact spot where Peter was martyred; what concerns us here is to note the origins of a tradition that was never to be denied, and which was to make this hill the polarizing center of a new social structure.

TOMB AND BRIDGE

Gradually the zone grew as a center of habitation. As well as the short-term housing, a number of funerary erections and monuments appeared, resulting in the creation of a veritable necropolis. The importance of the site was enhanced when the Emperor Hadrian built his own mausoleum there, together with a bridge giving easier access to the city. Built between 113 and 134, the bridge's original name of *Aelius* was later changed to *Sancti Petri*. It consisted of three large central spans, two smaller ones on the right bank, and three on the left.

As well as Hadrian's tomb, situated close to the Via Cornelia, numerous other noteworthy monuments were erected here: among them, the pyramidal *Meta Romuli*, described by medieval guides as the tomb of Romulus or the Scipios; and

VEDVTA DEL CERCHIO NERONIANO CHE MOSTRA IL DI DENTRO ELDI FVORI.

A. Piano, ò Arena per le corse.
B. Spina che divide il medemo in due parti.
C. Obelisco sopra detta Spina oggi la Sagrestia di S. Pietro.
D. Tempietti situati a Conca et altre Deità false.
E. Mete in fine della Spina p. la Terminatione delli giri.
F. Euripo longo circa piedi 10. per il Corso dell'Acqua.
G. Gradini per sedere con sfori p il sito del Popolo.
H. Loggie attorno il Cerchio con ambulatorij.
I. Orificeli.
K. Ingresso contiguo alle Carceri.

L. Coridori e Botteghe publiche.
M. Tempio di Apollo oggi Santa Petronilla.
N. Tempio di Marte oggi Porta fabrica.
O. Elisio (ò Terebinto) oggi habitatione Aviccara.
P. Memoria eretta a Romolo oggi la Vaschetta.
Q. Campi Trionfali e Vaticani oggi Porta Angelica ò Castello con Prati e Vigne.
R. Monte Vaticano oggi il Palazzo Pontificio con giardini.
S. Monte Aureo oggi Villa Barberini habitatione Suentsia e altro che tendono verso S Honofrio.

PIANTA DELLA BASILICA COSTANTINIANA E SITVATIONE DEL NOVO TEMPIO CON IL CONTORNO E LOCO DOVE FV IL CIRCO DI NERONE.

PIANTA DEL VATICANO ANTICO

1. Villa Rustia.
2. Monte Vaticano
2. Campi Neroniani
4. Campi Vaticani
7. T. di Marte
8. Terebinto
9. Strada Trionfale
11. Monte Aureo
12. Memoria di Romulo
13. Campi Neroniani
Campi Vaticani
Strada Trionfale
Campi Vaticani
Prati Quintij
TEVERE
16. Porta Trionfale
15. Sepolcro di Scipioni
17. Equo Trionfale
FIUME
19. Sepolcro di Elio Adriano
20. Ipodromo di Elio Adriano
25. A. D. Adrissi e Onorio
18. Ponte Eliano
LATIO
FIUME
22. Horti de Domitij
Horti de Domitij
FIUME

Scala di Canne 200: cioè palmi. 2000:

the so-called Monument of Nero, circular in shape with two orders, of which by the 12th century little trace remained. In general, however, the area was probably not that different from the rest of the Roman *campagna*, at least where other consular roads were sited.

With the edict of Milan in 313, Constantine recognized Christianity as the official religion. A few years later, in 324, the same emperor started work on a large basilica on the site where, according to tradition, the Apostle Peter was martyred. The building work continued until 349, and was finished under the Emperor Constantius.

This was the second vital stage in the history of St. Peter's: for what had hitherto been but a pious tradition, on the basis of which pilgrims came to venerate the tomb of the Apostle at a more or less exact spot in the Vatican necropolis, now received the chrism of offical recognition by the imperial authorities. The basilica in all its splendor was henceforth the physical representation of the Christian presence in Rome; and it also indicated the

On this page above: three plans for the basilica of St. Peter (left), by Antonio da Sangallo, center and right, by Giuliano da Sangallo. Below; between the spread: the plan by Peruzzi. Left: Michelangelo's plan, which reworks Bramante's Greek cross plan. Below: the wooden model of the dome (1/15th of actual size), which Michelangelo began to work on in 1546.

Opposite above: Bramante's plans for the basilica and the complex including the basilica and the Belvedere. Below left and right: Giuliano da Sangallo's plans for the basilica of St. Peter. Center: Raphael's project.

primacy accorded to Rome over all other places in the Empire, including Jerusalem.

Constantine's basilica, with its five naves, was no different from the other Roman basilicas except by virtue of its size and the plethora of buildings, both sacred and secular, that began to spring up around it. As well as the various memorials and tombs, there also appeared the first service buildings for the pilgrims who were now arriving in daily greater numbers. This, however, did not make the basilica any less isolated from the rest of the city. But situated, as it was, outside the ring of the Aurelian walls, the zone became eventually cut off when, for strategic reasons, the Ponte Trionfale was demolished, probably between 404 and 423.

In 410 Rome was sacked for the first time by Alaric's Visigoths, but it would appear that on this occasion the basilica went undamaged. It was less fortunate, however, when, in 455, Genseric and his Vandals plundered the city for fourteen days. Only three years before, Pope Leo the Great had managed to save the city from attack by the Huns. By now the sway of the Western Empire was virtually at an end: the last of the twenty emperors to rule between 455 and and 475, Romulus Augustulus, was deposed by Odoacre in 476. And therewith began the succession of Romano-barbarian rulers.

The crisis of the Empire inevitably also involved the Roman Church, which was constantly threatened by schisms of one sort or another. Yet it was in this confused and troubled period that Borgo first shows up with an autonomous identity.

GOTHIC WARS

The Gothic wars present an extremely confused picture. In 537, during the year-long siege of Rome by Witigis, the Goths set up a camp in the Vatican area from where they could control the Porta Aurelia and the Porta Transtiberina. Then in 546 Totila occupied the city. After only a short time, however, he had to withdraw with most of his troops. Fearing that the Byzantine army under Narses might return, he tore down a long stretch of the Aurelian walls, to prevent the Romans from defending their city. At the same time he enclosed part of the Vatican plain with temporary fortifications as a winter camp for the, perforce very small, garrison he left behind. These fortifications were centered on the mausoleum of Hadrian, an important strategic point, and it is reasonable to assume that they followed broadly the same course as the first section of the present Borgo *corridore*, and then closed in towards the Tiber.

Although the only documentary evidence concerning this period is provided by Procopius, it is clear that the Vatican area was developing into a zone of enormous strategic importance. This is particularly interesting when one considers the value of Hadrian's mausoleum for the defense of Rome. The future Castel Sant' Angelo, as it was to become, is a fundamental part of Borgo's history – one need only observe how the whole area is orientated around the Ponte Elio-Castello-Basilica grouping. Furthermore the Ponte Elio, one of the few places where the Tiber could be crossed, was strategically controlled by the castle.

At all events Totila's camp did not survive long, nor do any traces of its presence remain. A certain anonymity attaches to Borgo over the next three centuries.

During this time various important centers had grown up around the Vatican basilica: these were the *scholae*, which had started as hostelries, colleges, and churches to receive the pilgrims from every country. The first *schola* was founded by the Saxon King Ine of Wessex, in 728, and gradually others followed: those of the *Longbardorum*, *Bohemorum*, *Frisonum*. The Saxon *schola* remained the most important, however, to become the nucleus of the Santo Spirito complex.

The process of the urbanization of Borgo only really began under Leo IV, as already mentioned. Between 847 and 855 this pope built a ring of walls stretching from the castle to the basilica, up the Vatican Hill, and doubling back towards the river, to end at the Saxon *schola* complex. Historians have always taken this as the true beginning of the Vatican citadel – and indeed the whole Vatican complex is to this day known as the *Città Leonina*, the Leonine City. The reasons why Leo built this wall remain obscure. The most acceptable theory is that he was prompted to do so after the fearful events of 846, when the Saracens succeeded in sacking the basilica. It is also known that both Charlemagne, and Lothair after him, insisted on the basilica being rendered immune to external attack.

THE BORGO AS AN ALTERNATIVE ROME

What is important is that a new town had been created, completely separate from Rome, an alternative Rome in fact. There were various factions in the city, not a few of which were openly hostile to the imperial power, and hence also to the still somewhat shaky power of a pope inclined to ally himself with the emperor. It was

PERILLVSTRI DNO MEO COLEND. DNO IACOBO BOSIO, SACRI.
INVICTI ATQ ILL ORDINIS S. IOANNIS HYER IN ROMANA CVRIA
NEGOTIORVM PROMOTORI DIGNISSIMO

during this period that the Leonine City acquired its unique role in the dialectic between secular and religious power, the repercussions of which are still to be felt.

By the end of the 11th century, the quarter had developed a complex urbanized structure of its own. One of the most striking features was the large number of churches and oratories clustering around the basilica. Among these, three main groups can be identified: the first group, the oldest, consisting of the four monasteries immediately beside the basilica, whose purpose was to supply singers for the choirs: S. Martino, SS. Giovanni e Paolo, S. Stefano Maggiore, and S. Stefano Minore; the second comprising the churches of the four *scholae*: *Saxonum*, *Frisonum*, *Francorum*, and *Longobardorum*.

This conglomeration of buildings extended from the slopes of the Janiculum and the Vatican Hill down to the Tiber. The third group of churches was situated

From the basilica to the castle. Opposite above: a detail of the Borgo from Antonio Tempesta's 1593 plan of Rome. Below: a plan by Antonio da Sangallo the Younger for a wall to enclose the Borgo.
On this page below left: fireworks at the castle.

to celebrate the feast of St. Peter and St. Paul, drawn by Nicolaus van der Aelst at the beginning of the 17th century.
Below right: a view of Castel Sant'Angelo, in a drawing by G. B. Faletti, dating from the second half of the 16th century.

on the pilgrim routes, along the so-called 'portica,' from Castello to the basilica, and included the screen of houses dividing the piazza from the portico of the basilica.

In fact at this period there was no piazza as such. From the various accounts and chronicles (there remains no pictorial record), it would appear that the houses of the Borgo came right up to the steps of the basilica. From the same written sources can be deduced the street layout of the area.

PILGRIMS' ROUTE

The main pilgrim route stretched from the Ponte Sant'Angelo, along the 'portica' to the basilica. An alternative route was that of Borgo Santo Spirito, which could also be reached from Lungara, via the Porta Santo Spirito, and which ran parallel to the Borgo Vecchio, striking the basilica at a tangent. The rest of the area, between the portica and Leo IV's walls, consisted of a maze of narrow streets.

Another way of approaching the basilica from the north was by the so-called *ruga francigena*, which (though it is impossible to say exactly how it ran), probably corresponded to the later Via di Porta Angelica, flanking the papal palace, to arrive at the Porta Viridaria – now filled in, but still visible in the surviving remains of the Leonine walls incorporating the *corridore*. However, the *ruga* disappeared for ever when Boniface IX had a piazza built between 1389 and 1404.

In the years 1277–80 Nicholas III constructed the *passetto* (which then became known as the *corridore*), a corridor built into the top of the Leonine walls in order to connect Castel Sant'Angelo and the papal palace. In 1305 Clement V transferred the papal see to Avignon. As a result the Borgo, as well as the basilica, entered a period of decline, which lasted about a century. Not until 1377, after lengthy negotiations, did the popes leave France and return to Italy.

One of the chief subjects of these negotiations was the ownership of Castello. In 1363 Pope Urban V approached Orso Orsini (whose family occupied Castello at the time) on the matter. Having once gained strategic control of the Vatican zone, when on the death of Orsini in 1367 the Church acquired possession of the castle, one of the major stumbling blocks in the way of a return to Rome was removed.

In this way the question of autonomy or perhaps one should say antinomy – as affecting Borgo in its relationship with Rome, was heightened. The condition laid down by the papacy as the guarantee of its return to Rome was simply the right to immune itself within its own fortified *città*. In this the papal thinking was not merely defensive, it could even be construed as aggressive, in that control of Castello, from Borgo, and hence of the Ponte Sant'Angelo, meant that the pope could strike at the very heart of the city of Rome, notably the part enclosed within the curve of the river, which was the most populous quarter at the close of the 14th century. The return of the papacy from Avignon marked an upturn of major proportions in the fortunes of the Church of Rome, and in its rise to temporal power. A new dawn had begun for the basilica of the first

Apostle and the city around it.

The metamorphosis of Borgo took some time however. In 1415 the Pisan antipope John XXIII made an attempt to restore the walls of the Leonine City and the *passetto*, but with no great success. The woeful condition into which the Vatican complex had been allowed to fall, led, in 1437, to an appeal to the pope by the canons of St. Peter's, worried at the state of disrepair of the streets and houses, and even the basilica itself.

RING OF WALLS

The first extensive works program was carried out by Nicholas V, whose pontificate lasted from 1447–55. His program actually covered the entire city. The plans for Borgo, though, were especially thorough, inasmuch as they embraced the quarter as a whole, without treating the basilica as a separate entity. Defense was a prime consideration, and a major feature of the pope's plans was an impregnable ring of new walls.

Thus from the *Città Leonina* to the *Civitas Dei*, the earthly Jerusalem. Nicholas V's political program was exemplary

in its lucidity. Corresponding to his somewhat peremptory view of the temporal power of the Church of Rome, his town planning ideals included a radical restructuring of the Vatican citadel and a series of major operations in the city itself, to be seen as evidence of the pervasive, ever tangible presence of the Church.

Of his grand projects very few in fact came to be realized. Rossellino started on the restoration of the basilica, laying the foundations for the new apse, and work also began on the defensive system, though only the gate tower – which still bears the pontiff's name – was actually completed.

Work was halted by Nicholas's death, and almost twenty years went by before any new projects got under way. On the occasion of the 1475 Jubilee, Sixtus IV restored both the Santo Spirito complex and the eponymous *borgo*, most notably the part at the bottom of the steps leading up to the church of SS. Michele e Magno, the former *Schola Frisonum*. At the same time a street was opened near the *corridore*, joining the area in front of Castello with the palazzi and the basilica. Originally called the Via Sistina, this new street

later became the Borgo Sant'Angelo.

New building work was also put in hand for the next jubilee. In 1496, in preparation for the jubilee year 1500, Alexander VI commissioned Cardinal Raffaello Riario to provide for a new street to run parallel with the Borgo Vecchio, linking the basilica more conveniently with the Ponte Sant'Angelo. This completely straight street was begun in April 1499 and opened on Christmas Eve of the same year. During its construction much of the *Meta Romuli*, the presumptive tomb of Romulus or the Scipios, was demolished. To encourage building development along this new street, a truly grand thoroughfare which became the main approach to the basilica, attractive concessions were offered to those who built along it, one condition being that any building had to be at least seven Roman *canne* tall – approximately fifty feet. Named after the pope who had planned it, it was still called the Via Alessandrina until quite recently, although more popularly known as the Borgo Nuovo.

It was now that the quarter really 'took off.' All that had been done between the return from Avignon and the end of the

Opposite: the massive buttress of the walls with the large coat of arms of Pope Paul III at the junction of Via Leone IV and Viale del Vaticano. Right: a frontal view of the basilica with the façade by Carlo Maderno and above it Michelangelo's dome.

15th century had been with the aim of remodeling the Vatican citadel to meet the exigencies of papal policies. Nicholas V's concern for defense was amply borne out by the unreliability of alliances and shifts in the political balance of power, both internal and external; yet he had also been activated by a certain sense of 'showmanship,' an aspect that was to be further developed under his successors. The opening of Via Alessandrina, with the specific injunction imposed on those who owned the adjacent land to build in accordance with certain standards, is symptomatic of the papacy's desire to bring home the fact of the reality of its power in the temporal sphere.

PLANS FOR A NEW BASILICA

In 1503 Pope Julius II was elected to the See of Peter; besides commissioning Michelangelo to design his tomb, he took up where his predecessors had left off in the matter of building projects. The basilica now entered the crucial phase of its history. Interminable wrangling and heated debate surrounded the plans for the new building. The architect called in to supervise the work was Bramante, chosen in preference to Sangallo, and he proposed a central plan within a square, with a huge semispherical dome resting on four piers. Sangallo's design had been a Latin cross. And the great arguments in the years that followed were over the differing symbolism of the Greek and Latin crosses.

Construction began immediately, and on 18 April 1506 the pope laid the first stone of the great pillar that was to be known as La Veronica. The other great main piers were started between 1506 and 1514. Meanwhile Bramante acquired as assistants Fra Giocondo and Giuliano da Sangallo. On his death in 1514, direction of the work passed to Raphael, who retained his predecessor's assistants. It was perhaps under Sangallo's influence that Raphael reverted to the design of a Latin cross, which naturally enough Sangallo himself kept to when he took charge of the work in 1520, when Raphael

died. The sack of Rome in 1527 by the Protestant troops of the most catholic king of Spain brought about a dramatic interruption of all building activity. Sangallo nevertheless retained his post until his death in 1546. During these years numerous designs, which were to be repeatedly altered, were drawn up, one of which was a Greek cross design proposed by Baldassarre Peruzzi.

In obvious homage to Bramante, and intended in equal measure as a criticism of Sangallo, Michelangelo, summoned to take over in his old age, reverted to the centralized Greek cross. By the time of his death in 1564 the drum of the dome had been completed.

THE DEFENSES AND THE NEW QUARTER

The rivalry between Michelangelo and Sangallo was not just confined to the rebuilding of St. Peter's. On other occasions the two had clashed: one such encounter having taken place a few years previously over the new defensive walls of Borgo. The traumatic experience of the sack of the city had brought home to the authorities the Vatican citadel's need for

effective defense against attack from outside. Paul III cast his net wide in seeking the advice of experts, military leaders and military architects, including, among others, Galasso Alghisi, Alessandro Vitelli, Montemellino, and Antonio da Sangallo.

Sangallo it was who received the first commission to build the bastion of Santo Spirito and the Porta Santo Spirito, between 1542–45. The plans for the new defenses inspired much bitter controversy. When Sangallo died, Meleghino, Paul III's preferred architect, took over; at the time of the pope's death, in 1549, the walled defenses of Borgo had been completed, although not entirely in masonry: certain stretches of the Gallinaro and Sant'Antonino ramparts were still just earth and wooden stakes. The old Leonine walls were now obsolete, being situated inside the new fortifications and therefore no longer of any functional use.

Reverting to the old theme, as elaborated by Nicholas V, of the New Jerusalem, Julius II determined to give it still greater credence by a massive reconstruction program for the basilica. The very vastness of the plan can be seen as a

further symptom of the desire of the
papacy to provide tangible proof of its
increasing political power. Bramante's
design of a vast dome, echoing that of the
Pantheon, as a crown for the Apostle's
tomb, symbolized the synthesis of temporal and spiritual power, an assertion of
the papacy's ultimate aim. Throughout
the 16th century the popes continued to
pursue the same course of action; and
while the sack of Rome placed a temporary

question mark over the efficacy of this
policy, Michelangelo's dome rose up
nevertheless to attest to its rightness.

Linked indirectly with the restructuring of the defenses of Borgo was the
problem of its administration. In this
context it is worth mentioning that Pope
Julius III, on 22 February 1550, in the
short *Ad fidei constantiam*, appointed his
nephew Ascanio della Cornia as *militum
custodiae corporis nostri, tam peditum*

quam equitum capitaneum generalem
(Captain-General of our bodyguard, both
mounted and foot); and at the same time
conferring on him the title of governor of
Borgo. Through this appointment the
pope once again emphasized the special
status of Borgo, giving it its own independent administration. The post of
governor in fact entailed the exercise of
jurisdiction in civil and penal matters over
the inhabitants of the quarter. To be able
to fulfil his mandate, the governor had his
own court with prisons attached, while to
maintain law and order he had under his
orders a head of police and fifteen guards.
The governor himself came under the
direct authority of the pontiff, by whom
he was received in weekly audience. In
the dispensing of justice the governor
appointed a judge who resided in the
courthouse, and although not on a fixed
salary, received fees and a quarter of all
confiscated goods.

A NEW IMPORTANCE

In view of the increased importance of the
area, and as part of an overall improvement project, on 5 December 1565 Pius IV
ordered the construction of a new quarter
beyond the Borgo *corridore*, in the plain
between the fields of Castello and the
Belvedere hill. Special concessions were
provided for those who went to live there,
ranging from tax exemptions to aid with
house building. One rather curious inclusion in the papal bull *Romanum decet
Pontificem*, where these provisions were
announced, was that they also applied to
prostitutes who had invested at least five
hundred *scudi* in the area, *etiam ex turpi
quaestu acquisitis et acquirendis* (even
acquired or to be acquired by an indecent
profession).

The rectangular layout of the new
quarter, designed by Francesco Laparelli,
was centered on the Borgo Pio, as the main
connecting axis between Castello and
Belvedere. Parallel with it ran the two
other *borghi*: Vittorio and Angelico, their
lesser importance reflected in their more
restricted street area. These three new
borghi were intersected longitudinally by

THE DOME AND THE OBELISK

The short pontificate of Sixtus V (1585–90) brought two further achievements of interest here: the completion of the dome of St. Peter's and the transfer of the obelisk to the middle of the piazza. The work on the dome was directed by Giacomo della Porta, at the time architect of the basilica, in 1588–89. The lantern was added in the following year.

Della Porta, assisted by Domenico Fontana, considerably modified Michelangelo's original plan, raising the curve of the dome – whether for technical reasons, or for better visibility from the piazza, is not clear. Moving the Vatican obelisk on the other hand was part of a much more comprehensive project upon which Sixtus V had embarked within months of becoming pope. A significant feature of the 'Sistine plan,' as it was commonly called, was the erecting of obelisks near the main basilicas, which in turn were all interconnected by major thoroughfares. The Vatican obelisk was of particular interest: it was the only ancient obelisk erected by the Romans to have been preserved *in situ*, in the ruins of Nero's circus, situated only a few yards from the left side of the basilica. On 24

the Via di Porta Angelica, the main transverse axis, and by five less important streets running parallel with it, access to which was provided by arches cut in the now useless, defensively, that is, *corridore*. Laparelli had in fact designed and constructed new fortifications at about the same time, Castello acquiring new ramparts and a rectilinear stretch of wall with outworks in the middle, connecting it with the Belvedere, and enclosing the new quarter of Borgo Pio, as it was called.

Where the road came down from the north an opening was cut in the wall and named after the highway, Porta Angelica.

Borgo had now expanded to its ultimate limits. Pius IV's rebuilding program once again represented an attempt to impose order on an ancient city at the same time offering it new outlets for development. But pride of place went always to the Vatican citadel as the fortified *caput* of a Rome built in the form of a five-pointed star.

they were able to start lifting the obelisk, and it was solemnly consecrated on the 26th, which was slightly later than the date set by the pope: he had wished it to be the 14th, the day of the Exaltation of the Cross. Honors were showered on the papal architect, who had also designed a complete new plan for the Borgo Vaticano.

Yet again a pope imposed his own aims: the city-planning developments in Rome under Sixtus V, so obviously intended as an assertion of his own authority and quasi-omnipresence, are only too well known. The new streets, linking various clearly defined poles such as the basilicas and the numerous obelisks raised near them, in fact had no relevance to everyday urban reality, and were indeed totally extraneous to it. However, this merely served to increase their significance as symbols of power.

THE FINAL LIMITS OF THE BORGO

With the creation of Borgo Pio, the Vatican quarter had reached its maximum size, extending beyond the *passetto* which for centuries had bounded it to the north. Within the old walls the process of urbanization was now complete, virtually no building land being left vacant. The

August 1585 the pope convened a special committee of cardinals to decide where to resite the *guglia* (literally, spire), as it was popularly known.

THE OBELISK RESITED

This committee then organized a competition, which numerous architects and engineers entered (including, among others, Domenico Fontana, della Porta, and Bartolomeo Ammannati). Less than

one month later, on 18 September, the committee met to judge the entries. And although Ammannati's plan was chosen, the job of transporting the obelisk was given to Fontana, in whom Sixtus V had great confidence, having employed him when still a cardinal. Fontana decided that the obelisk should be laid flat, carried to where it was to be resited, and then lifted up again.

The operation began on 30 April 1586, and proceeded apace. By 10 September main elements of the street network and its various poles were by now established. More detailed inspection of the quarter overall will afford a better understanding of the relationships between the bulk of this built-up area and its focal points, notably the basilica.

At the same time we will get an idea of the different phases of urban renewal and decline by which, over the years, the Vatican quarter was totally altered and almost destroyed. This is not simply a lament for all that had been destroyed; but if it is the case that any city or town has its own dynamic of change, then it is equally the case that that dynamic in turn has different processes and trends.

There were basically three entrances into the quarter, even though there were more than three gates in the walls (certain of these, such as the Porta Fabrica and the Porta Pertusa, were of limited usefulness, or were alternatives to others; thus the Porta Cavalleggeri was a duplicate link with Trastevere, via the Janiculum, the more direct route being by the Porta Santo Spirito, along the line Lungara-Porta Settimiana; while as an alternative route to the north, the Porta Castello was less important than the Porta Angelica.

Connecting the quarter to the center of Rome was the Ponte Sant'Angelo, which in practice was the only means of crossing the Tiber at this point. Indeed along the whole length of the city stretch of the river, it was only possible to cross in three places: Ponte Sant'Angelo, Ponte Sisto, and at the Island, the Isola Tiberina, with its two bridges, Ponte Cestio and Ponte Fabricio.

A VITAL BRIDGE

The vital importance of control of the Ponte Sant'Angelo has already been mentioned. In consequence this bridge was well maintained. It had been restored under Nicholas V, who also had the piazza giving onto it enlarged, after a tragic accident in the Holy Year of 1450, when a large number of pilgrims, crowding onto the bridge to cross over to the basilica, fell into the river. The same pope had ordered the building of two votive chapels on the spot, which were subsequently demolished by Clement VII in 1534 and replaced by the statues of the Apostles Peter and Paul. The statues presently on the bridge are by Bernini, and date from 1667–70. At the end of the 19th century (1892–93), as part of general work on the river banks (the *Lungotevere*), the smaller arches of the bridge were replaced by a single wider span on either side.

Immediately beyond the bastions of Castello began the most ancient *borghi*. Leading off from the Piazza Pia were the Borgo Vecchio and the Borghi Nuovo (the everyday name for the Via Alessandrina). The area between these two streets was occupied by the Spina – a long line of irregular blocks of buildings extending up to the basilica. The two *borghi* differed not only in that the Nuovo was straight, while the Vecchio was not; they were also differentiated by the 'tone' of their respective buildings.

As already mentioned, the Borgo Nuovo was planned by Alexander VI as the main thoroughfare of the quarter; accordingly the buildings flanking it had to be 'up to scratch.' The first building of importance, going towards the basilica, was the church of Santa Maria in Traspontina, with monastery attached. The present church, which has survived the modern demolition of the quarter, was built to replace another, of very ancient origins, mentioned in old records as *ecclesia Sanctae Mariae in Traspontina* or *in Turrispadina*: it stood on the old *platea Castelli*, and was torn down in 1566 to make way for the new fortifications. Work began on the new church (designed by Sallustio Peruzzi) in the same year; Battista Ghioldo subsequently took charge, until his death in 1581. The building was completed by Ottaviano Mascarino in 1587. The church was consecrated (while it still lacked a choir) on 8 February 1587.

BRAMANTE'S PALAZZO

After a block of buildings belonging to the Cappella Giulia came the Palazzo Giraud-Torlonia, which still stands today on the right-hand side of the Via della Conciliazione. Attributed by Vasari to Bramante, this palazzo dates from the beginning of the 16th century; however, it was still not habitable in 1504. In the following year its owner, Cardinal Castellesi di Corneto, presented it to Henry VII of England. In 1519 Cardinal Castellesi fled to Venice, having been implicated in a plot against the pope, and the palazzo became the English embassy, until it eventually passed to Cardinal Campeggi. Towards the end of the 16th century Campeggi let it to Tolomeo Gallio, cardinal of Como, who commissioned Ottaviano Mascarino to carry out a number of internal alterations. Then in 1609 the palazzo passed to the Borghese family, thence again to the Campeggi, then to the Colonna, who let it to Queen Christina of Sweden.

The Spina's blocks of buildings were interrupted at this point by the broad Piazza Scossacavalli, connecting Borgo Nuovo with Borgo Vecchio. Giving onto this piazza, in the middle of which was a fountain, were the church of San Giacomo a Scossacavalli, the Palazzo dei Penitenzieri, and the Palazzo dei Convertendi.

San Giacomo a Scossacavalli had ancient origins, its name deriving from a legend dating back to Constantine's mother, St. Helena. According to the legend, the horses transporting the stone on which Isaac was said to have been laid for sacrifice, which Helena wished to be kept in St. Peter's, refused to go beyond this point, regardless of their drivers' imprecations and whippings (*Scossacavalli* literally means 'horses' shock'). A more mundane explanation of the name traces the root to *coxa caballi*, referring to fragments of an equestrian statue which still remained on the site in the Middle Ages. The old church, also known as San Salvatore in Bordonia and San Salvatore in Portico, was rebuilt in the 17th century and then demolished to make way for the Via della Conciliazione.

The Palazzo dei Penitenzieri, on the Via della Conciliazione, is now a hotel. Built in the 15th century by Cardinal della Rovere, it is attributed to Baccio Pontelli. After della Rovere's death, it passed to

Left top and center: two drawings by Maarten van Heemskerk which show the square of St. Peter's circa 1533 and (bottom) a drawing by Giovannantonio Dosio, dated circa 1570, which shows the Borgo Nuovo at the junction with St. Peter's square. Above: a drawing by Carlo Fontana of Bernini's campanile with plans for its restoration.

Cardinal Alidosi, then to Cardinals d'Aragona, Salviati, Madruzzo, and Visconti. Cardinal Pallotta owned it up till 1620, when it was given to the Penitenzieri di San Pietro, who had been left homeless by the broadening of the piazza in front of the basilica.

The other palazzo on the Piazza Scossacavalli, the Palazzo dei Convertendi, was a fusion of several houses in the early 16th century: those of Cardinal Accolti, Raphael, and the Zen. It had various owners: the Alicorni, the Peretti, and the Spinola families. In 1665, under the ownership of Cardinal Gastaldi, part of the palazzo was made over to indigent bishops and part to the Istituto dei Convertendi. Restored by Gregory XVI, it was demolished during the construction of the Via della Conciliazione. Partly rebuilt on the right-hand side of the Via, it is now the seat of the Congregazione Orientale.

Continuing up Borgo Nuovo, the next building was the Palazzo da Brescia, at the top of Borgo Sant'Angelo where it led off from Borgo Nuovo. The palazzo was built in 1515–16 on a triangular site for Leo X's doctor, Giacomo di Bartolomeo da Brescia. There are, however, no clues as to who designed it. Vasari puts forward Raphael, while Titi, in 1763, suggested that it might in fact have been Peruzzi; other writers simply describe it as being in the style of

The Egyptian obelisk originally stood to the south of the basilica, up against the chapel of St. Andrew. Sixtus V took the decision to change its place, and various plans were submitted for the work, which are recorded in the inscription (top left). This tricky task was finally given to Domenico Fontana. Between April and September 1586, the obelisk was removed from its base and placed in its present position.

Raphael, without going any further into the matter. Even the pictorial records which have come down to us fail to throw any light on the matter. At all events, certain stylistic characteristics indicate that it was indeed the work of the Raphael school. It survived virtually intact until 1937, when it was finally demolished as part of the restructuring of the *borghi*, to be somewhat maladroitly rebuilt in a small street leading off the Via della Conciliazione.

A little farther on, Borgo Nuovo broad- ened to form the small Piazza dei Rusti- cucci (named after the Palazzo Rusticucci that gave onto it). On the left, rose the block of the Priorato di Malta, and the Palazzo Branconio dell'Aquila.

The Palazzo Rusticucci, on the right- hand side of the piazza, stood between Vicolo del Mascarino and Borgo Sant'Angelo. Built towards the end of the 16th century by Cardinal G. Rusticucci, to a design by Fontana and Maderno, it then passed to the Accoramboni. In 1630 St. Joseph of Calasanza took it over as the new home of the Collegio Nazareno. It was de- molished during work on the Piazza Pio XI.

RAPHAEL'S 'TRIAL' BUILDING

Torn down under Alexander VII to make room for Bernini's colonnade, the Palazzo Branconio was the building most certainly attributable to Raphael. It was started some time between 1515 and 1520, pos- sibly not until after 1517, by Giovanni Battista dell'Aquila, a goldsmith and courtier, the custodian of Leo X's jewels. It had great symbolic significance, as the physical embodiment of its owner's success in life, and as the building on which Raphael tried out the basic principles of his architectural aesthetic. Here he explored the relationship between 'modern' architecture and classical antiquity, as interpreted through adaptation and the echoing of the great monuments of earlier times. The model for the palazzo was the markets of Trajan, in the use of the ground floor for workshops, and in the actual definition of sections, by means of precise grading and balancing of space, reinterpreting the spatial values of the curved façade of the earlier building on the level of pure size, yet at the same time asserting a more abstract harmony and logical rigor.

Known also as the Palazzo di San Martinello, after a church which had been incorporated into it, the Palazzo del Priorato was built in the 15th century and demolished in 1667 to make way for Bernini's colonnade. In an anonymous list of palazzi, made in 1601, the building was described as the 'house of the Priorato of Rome in St. Peter's Piazza, where the cardinal of Ascoli (Girolamo Bernieri) lives. The front elevation measures forty-five paces and the sides twenty-six paces. It has only one row of four windows and a loggia; on one side are workshops. The entrance is not in the middle. This house is tiny, and the upper part is barely adequate for a reverend gentlemen's needs, but the cardinal has certain rented accommodation over towards Borgo where he houses his family, and he has expanded the property towards Borgo Vecchio.'

The Palazzo del Priorato formed the head of the Spina, giving onto the piazza, once the wall of houses stretching up to the basilica had been demolished. On the other corner of Borgo Nuovo, leading into the piazzo, was the little church of Santa Caterina delle Cavallerotte. Founded at the start of the 14th century, it adjoined the Palazzo Rusticucci, the ground, including the kitchen garden of Santa Maria delle Vergini, having been given by Boniface IX. It disappeared in the 17th century, to make way for the colonnade.

OBELISK AND FOUNTAIN

The piazza itself was of an irregular shape. On the left it followed a straight line to align with Borgo Vecchio; on the right, at the entrance to Borgo Nuovo, it spread out towards the *passetto*, where was the Porta San Pietro. The axial position of the obelisk only served to emphasize this irregularity, which the fountain, erected in the widest part of the piazza, did nothing to rectify.

The oldest buildings were in the Borgo Vecchio. Besides the Palazzo dei Penitenzieri, already mentioned, there were the Palazzi Cesi and Serristori, the church of San Lorenzo in Piscibus, and the Palazzo Alicorni, at the corner of the Piazza Rusticucci and St. Peter's square.

Built around 1575 by Martino Longhi the Elder, the Palazzo Cesi belonged to the Cardinal of San Callisto, Francesco Armellini. It suffered severely during the renovation of St. Peter's square, and only the left-hand side of the original building remains.

This palazzo should not be confused with the other of the same name, which is still extant, albeit much altered, behind the colonnade near the Sant'Uffizio. Built in the early 16th century by Antonio Trivulzio di San Giorgio, known as Cardinal Alessandrino, this palazzo was acquired by Cardinal Paolo Emilio Cesi in 1517, and remained in his family for over two centuries. At the beginning of the 17th century the members of the Accademia dei Lincei took to meeting there. When the colonnade was being built, the front was rebuilt to echo the curved line of the colonnade. It is now the Collegio Internazionale di Santa Monica.

The Palazzo Serristori likewise has been greatly altered. Built by Averardo Serristori in 1555, it became the Tuscan embassy. It belonged to the Serristori family up until 1830, when it was sold to the Camera Apostolica, to be used as a papal barracks. The Monti-Tognetti outrage of 1867 resulted in the destruction of part of the building, and the deaths of some of the papal zouaves quartered there. After 1870 it became a barracks for Italian troops, taking the name Caserma Manara in 1902. Used as lodgings for evacuees after the First World War, it was handed over to the Holy See in 1929 to become a children's educational center.

Below: a study for the colonnade of St. Peter's square by Gian Lorenzo Bernini. Bottom: a variant of Bernini's plan for the colonnade in the model made by Carlo Fontana in 1694. Right: a perspective plan of the square by an anonymous artist of the 17th century.

SAN LORENZO IN PISCIBUS

On the same side of Borgo Vecchio, almost on St. Peter's square, was the church of San Lorenzo in Piscibus, popularly called San Lorenzolo. This church too was of ancient origin, being mentioned in chronicles of the 12th century. At one time the church of the Poor Clares, for whom Leo X found other accommodation at the beginning of the 16th century, it then passed into the hands of Cardinal Armellini who owned the little palazzetto next door. In 1659 the Cesi d'Acquasparta family restored the church.

The Palazzo Alicorni was built for a family who orginated in Albania and moved to Rome in the second half of the 15th century. Recalling the traditional design of the Renaissance Roman house, it had a central courtyard, two sides of which were arcaded. The main entrance and the corners of the building consisted of square hewn stone in an otherwise smooth façade. Giovanni Mangone, known as 'Giovannoni' (Big John), who designed it, was one of the lesser architects working in Rome in the first half of the 16th century. Considerably altered in later centuries, it was restored in 1928, only to be knocked down the following year under a new street-planning scheme

following the approval of the Lateran Treaties; it was rebuilt in Borgo Santo Spirito.

The Borgo Santo Spirito formed one of the most important areas between Castello and the basilica; its dominant landmark was the hospital and church, and the Palazzo del Commendatore. As mentioned earlier, its origins lie in the first national *schola*, founded by the Saxons in 728.

On 25 March 1446 Eugenius IV's bull *Salvatoris Nostri* decreed a number of hospital reforms, including restoration of the medieval buildings and the revival of the confraternity of Santo Spirito. In 1471, possibly from designs by Baccio Pontelli, and on the orders of Sixtus IV, the hospital and church were rebuilt. The major element of the new construction was a great hall with arcades along the sides, surmounted by an octagonal dome which matched the altar. New works were carried out between 1538 and 1544 when Antonio da Sangallo rebuilt the church. About the same time, in 1543, Sangallo built the new bastion facing the Tiber, and started work on the gate which, however, remained uncompleted. The years 1555–75 saw the construction of the palazzo on the Via dei Penitenzieri, the conservatory, and the Palazzo del Commendatore.

SISTINE PASSAGE

Under Sixtus V the church façade was reconstructed by Ottaviano Mascarino. In the 17th century Alexander VII ordered certain modifications to the hospital façade, as well as having a mezzanine floor built above the arcades, and two new doorways put in, one at the front, and one at the side. Later, Benedict XIV commis-

Bernini's plan for an elliptical colonnade gave rise to a series of polemics. His enemies submitted a 'counter plan' with twenty-five drawings, of which two are reproduced here (top and center). They were characterized by an exaggerated symbolism, ranging from a circular area suggesting a snake eating its own tail, a symbol of eternity, to the inclusion of a human figure making a gesture of embracing or touching the colonnade with its own extremities, thus referring to the four continents known at the period, and thus implying the unity of the Church. Bernini's plan was not completely carried out, as the third 'arm' to close off the colonnade towards the Spina was never built: this can be seen in the illustration at the foot of the page.

sioned Fuga to extend the Sistine passage in the direction of Castello; Pius IX subsequently had Azzurri alter the entry to the passage. At the end of the 19th century, when work was being carried out on the Lungotevere, this section was demolished, exposing the former elevation of Sixtus IV's structure, the restoration of which was completed in the late Twenties of the present century.

While the road forked towards the Porta Santo Spirito at the church, Borgo Santo Spirito itself continued on beyond the piazza, skirting the basilica, the region of the Porta Cavalleggeri and the Porta Fabrica, to finish in the Piazza Santa Marta, and at the vineyard on the Vatican Hill, owned by the hospital.

Among the many commemorative buildings in the quarter, Santa Maria della Febbre (Holy Mary of Fevers), next to the basilica, recalled, by its very name, the Roman temples to the goddess Febris. Octagonal in shape, it was first transformed into the sacristy of the basilica, and then demolished to make way for the chapel of St. Gregory the Great.

Of more recent date is the Santa Marta complex, constructed in 1538 by the servants of the Palazzi Apostolici, who had formed themselves into a confraternity, to which Paul III granted permission to build a church, a hospital, and a cemetery. Several times restored, the church was then given to the Spanish Trinitari Scalzi by Benedict XIII; it stayed in their hands, with various changes of fortune, from 1726 to 1874, when it passed to the Palazzi Apostolici. In 1882 Leo XIII restored it again and gave it to the Vatican seminary.

This then was the urban 'scene' in the quarter at the beginning of the 17th century, when Paul V, for liturgical reasons, once again reviewed the possibility of altering the basilica by lengthening the nave. To this end a competition was announced, and numerous architects submitted plans, among others, Flaminio Ponzio, Giovanni Fontana, Carlo Maderno, Girolamo Rainaldi, Ottavio Turiani, Niccolò Branconi, Domenico Fontana, and Ludovico Cigoli.

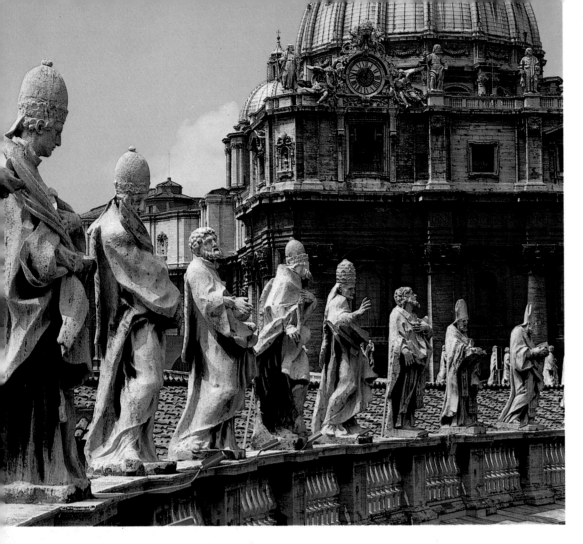

The design chosen was Maderno's, which added three chapels to each side of the nave, so giving the basilica its present form. It should be mentioned that Sixtus V had already intended extending the basilica: in fact, as D'Onofrio points out, there could be no other explanation why the obelisk should have been resited so far away. The new façade was begun in 1607 and finished in 1614. And on 18 November 1626, on the 1300th anniversary of the first consecration, Urban VIII solemnly reconsecrated the transformed basilica. To complete the new front elevation, the same pope ordered two towers to be built in 1637. A few years before, around 1620, Martino Ferrabosco had produced a design for the basilica with two bell towers.

The architect put in charge of the work was Bernini who, in collaboration with Giovanni Battista Soria, started on the symmetrically in each of the two hemicycles. This imposing erection is made up of eighty-eight pilasters and two hundred and eighty-four columns and at the widest part of the ellipse measures seven hundred and eighty-seven feet.

building of the left-hand tower, after carrying out experiments with a wooden model.

Finished in 1641, within a year the tower was showing signs of instability due to excessive weight and poor foundations, and in 1646 the decision was taken to pull it down.

THE CREATION OF THE MODERN SQUARE

These multifarious schemes were to lead finally to the one which was to affect the layout of the entire quarter irrevocably, and which has provided a subject for argument ever since: the definitive design of St. Peter's square. In 1651 an important decision was taken. It stemmed from a proposal by Monsignor Virgilio Spada to the Congregazione della Fabbrica concerning the redevelopment of the whole area between the basilica and the Ponte

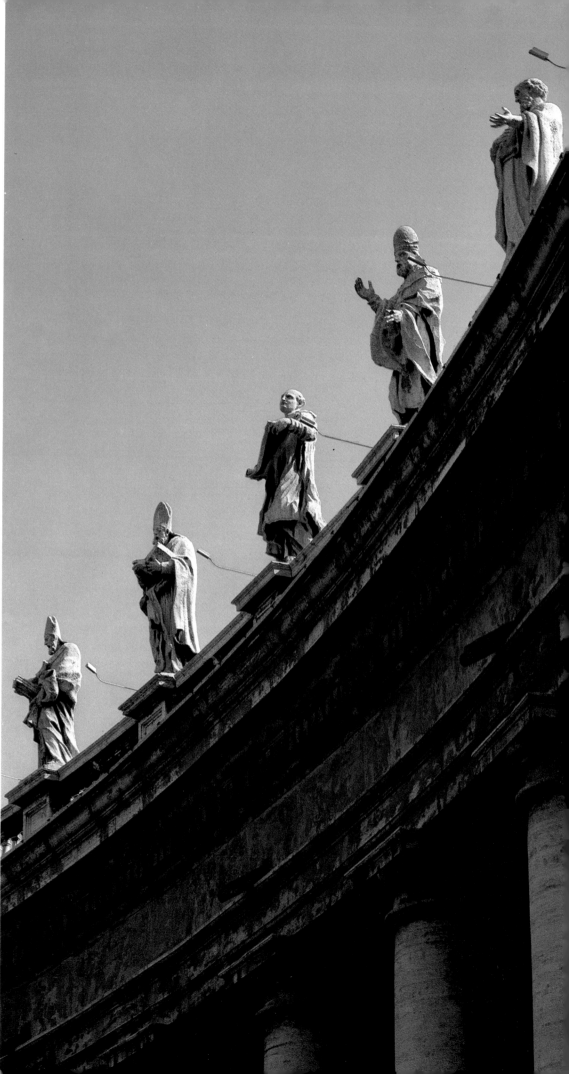

The problem of access to St. Peter's square was raised as early as 1690 in a plan attributed to Carlo Fontana. Later on, many plans were submitted. In 1776, Cosimo Morelli made plans for a hurried demolition of the Spina and for the tidying up of the edges around the gap that would have resulted (opposite page left). At the beginning of the 19th century, Giuseppe Valadier submitted a plan for two gigantic spiral columns modelled on Trajan's column (bottom). In 1916, Armando Brasini conceived a neobaroque macrostructure (below).

Sant'Angelo: it would necessitate the complete demolition of the Spina. A highly complex plan of expropriation was worked out. However, the project was not acted on immediately. Only after some years was Bernini commissioned to make a design for the square. The first official announcement came on 31 July 1656, when Alexander VII declared at an assembly of cardinals that he intended redesigning the square.

Shortly afterwards Bernini presented a design incorporating a rectangle with sides converging towards the Piazza Rusticucci. An experimental beginning was made on the site, but the pope pointed to certain defects in the plans. The next suggestion was for a circular piazza, but this also came to nothing.

On 17 March 1657 Bernini showed the pope and the cardinals a design for an oval colonnade. This was approved and work began. Demolition started in 1658 with the Priorato; then in 1661 part of the Palazzo Cesi d'Acquasparta in Borgo Santo Spirito went, together with the building known as the Arcipretato (the Arch-Presbytery). Finally in 1667 the Penitenzieria and Torre dei Cybo came down, to make way for the left arm of the colonnade. Starting in 1667, Mattia De Rossi, under Bernini's direction, eventually completed the Sant'Uffizio arm of the colonnade in 1669.

THE BERNINI CONTROVERSY

Such an important and involved operation could not of course be undertaken without much controversy. Bernini's rivals and enemies showed their hostility in various ways, the most effective being the production of a 'counter design.' This counter plan was based on a design made by Papirio Bartoli around 1630. A blatantly 'anti-Bernini' document, it consisted of twenty-five drawings on fifteen sheets, listing a number of alleged defects in Bernini's proposals, and suggesting solutions. The dominant feature of the counter plan was its excessive use of symbolism, from the circular-shaped piazza (recalling the serpent biting its own tail, symbolizing eternity), to the inclusuccessive drawings all show different ideas, none of them very clear-cut. Above all it is impossible to say for certain (i.e. scholars cannot agree) what the fate of the Spina was to be. Was the *interrompimento* to act as a sort of filter between the solid bulk of the Spina and the empty expanse of the square, or was it to have been itself a block along the axis created by the demolition of the Spina?

With the completion of Bernini's work, such as it was, a long cycle of construction in the quarter was brought to a close. Indeed this immensely complex restructuring of the square had the most profound consequences for the whole area, a considerable section of which had been sacrificed to make way for it. The process of destruction of the preexisting urban makeup, which had started several hundred years before, so to speak, and which had brought the quarter 'up in the world,' now reached its climax. The basilica and piazza no longer needed to be protected by a whole quarter and defensive walls. The idea of clearing away the Spina, first advanced by Virgilio Spada, was by no means put out of court by Bernini; and as we shall see, it was to become a veritable leitmotiv of Roman architectural planning, with architects competing – sometimes with rather ludicrous results – to resolve this knotty problem.

Perhaps nowhere is there to be found a better example of the interplay between urban renewal and ideology than here. Cities undergo constant change. In other words it is wrong, or historically unacceptable, to see a city as ever being 'finished,' or to lament its state, seen as once perfect in a supposedly 'golden age.' And the processes of change are intimately linked with the dynamic structures of urban organization, i.e. are never merely an automatic, mechanical embodiment of some particular form of sociopolitical reality, but are themselves an integral part of the reality.

After the 'Berninian' phase, a whole plethora of projects for the definitive shape of the square was forthcoming. In 1690 Carlo Fontana presented a weighty

sion of a human figure touching the colonnade with all four limbs, symbolic of the then four known continents, and therefore of the Church's universality.

In the event Bernini's design was never fully realized. The 'noble interruption' planned for the Spina end of the square was never built. Although it is almost certain that a third arm of the colonnade was envisaged, the way in which Bernini intended to incorporate it is far from clear:

study in which, after giving an account of the history of the basilica and the piazza, he put forward a new design with numerous illustrations. Basically this entailed demolishing the Spina, tidying up what remained of the two Borghi, and building a third complex, complete with bell tower, which would be some distance from the square but connected to Bernini's colonnade by means of two corridors similar to those which were already in place.

Interior of the basilica.
Partial views of Maderno's nave, with polychrome marbles, half columns, pilaster strips and medallions of the popes, as conceived by Gian Lorenzo Bernini.

THE DEMOLITION OF THE SPINA

In 1776 Cosimo Morelli (who had already produced a design for the sacristy of basilica – though it had not been taken up) advanced another plan which proposed a somewhat insensitive tearing down of the Spina, but with little indication of what was to be done with the huge space which would result. The plan also provided for the insertion into Piazza Pia, at the start of the new street, of two rather stunted colonnades with statues on top.

A NEW VISTA

At the beginning of the 19th century two further plans were put forward, one by De Tournon (the prefect of Rome during the French occupation), the other by Joseph Valadier. Both these plans necessitated the destruction of the Spina. Valadier also suggested placing two huge columns – modeled on that of Trajan – at the head of the street, described by Paolo Marconi as 'a gratuitous, grandiose design [in which Valadier] carries to the extreme the fashion for long perspectives which only lessen the effectiveness of the object they are supposed to embellish.' It was therefore self-contradictory, since the whole purpose of pulling down the Spina was to improve the view of the basilica and square – especially the former, with its dome, which was conceived as forming the central point of a magnificent approach vista.

Once again, in 1881, the demolition of the Spina was proposed as part of a general 'tidying-up' plan, but the proposal was vetoed by the Giunta Comunale. Plan followed plan; in 1883 Andrea Busiri suggested replacing the dilapidated houses of the Spina with a double colonnade, which would reach as far as the Piazza Scossacavalli.

In 1913–15 Erich Gugler of Columbia University put up yet another plan for the restructuring of the sector, showing Piazza Pia as circular and colonnaded, with the addition of another obelisk, counterbalancing that of Sixtus V, at the top of the great street opened up by the

demolition of the Spina. In 1916 Armando Brasini designed a vast baroque-style 'macrocomplex,' rather incongruously fitting in between the tiny houses of the Borghi, and extending almost to within sight of Ponte Vittorio.

Action was finally taken in the Thirties. In fact in the years following the Concordat of 1929, new designs came shooting off the drawing boards like sparks from a catherine wheel. Few were mentionable, let alone memorable.

We shall not here go into the pros and cons that have been bitterly argued for the past thirty years and more over the design which was finally accepted and put into execution, that of Marcello Piacentini and Attilio Spaccarelli. The earliest mention of the plan was in 1934 in a series of articles in which Piacentini and Spaccarelli presented their solution to the thorny problem of the entrance to Bernini's square. They were not, however, in complete agreement as to how this should be done; Spaccarelli, for instance, was not convinced that it was necessary to demolish the Spina. Their differences were soon resolved, however, and in February 1936 they were jointly commissioned to draw up a definitive design, which was then presented to Mussolini in the Sala Paolina in Castel Sant'Angelo on 20 June. The following week the designs were ex-

hibited in Raphael's Loggia for approval by Pius XI,' On 28 April 1937 the job of demolishing the Spina began. That part of the project was soon completed. The program, interrupted by war, was not resumed until the end of the Forties; it was completed, however, in time for Holy Year 1950.

END OF THE BORGHI

The construction of the Via della Conciliazione finally marked the end of the Borghi. For Holy Year 1500 Alexander VI had ordered the construction of Borgo Nuovo; Holy Year 1950 saw the final disappearance of that 'elegant' thoroughfare. For reasons of prestige, of power and grandeur a street had been destroyed which itself had been brought into existence for precisely those same ends, even though with Alexander VI these pretensions had not yet been formulated. In over 450 years of assiduous practice they were to be nourished and perfected, academic taste allowed to prevail over concepts more sensitive to the demands of urban development. Under the banner of *ad propagandam fidem*, an area with the tradition of more than four centuries behind it, had been sacrificed to a thirst for aggrandizement, with results that give cause for dismay.

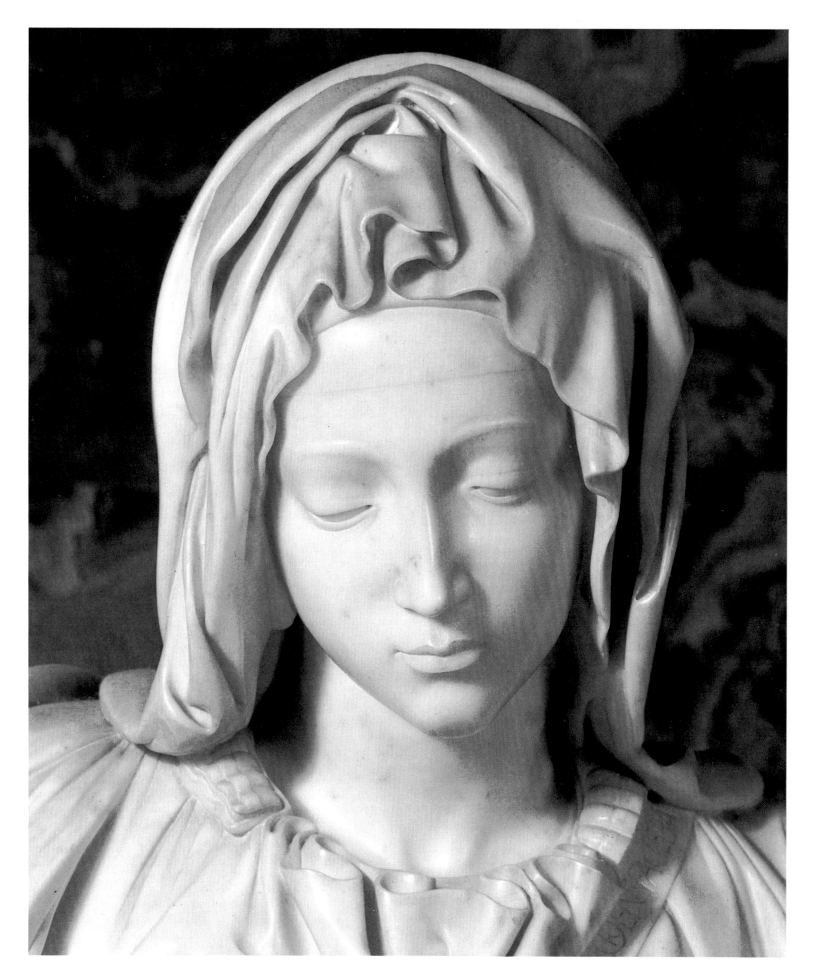

Below: a detail of the gilt coffering of the vault of the central nave. Opposite: the interior of the dome decorated according to the designs of Giuseppe Cesari by Cavalier d'Arpino in 1590 during the pontificate of Sixtus V.
In the spaces between the gilded ribs are the figures of Christ, the Virgin, St. John the Baptist, St. Paul, the Apostles and angels.
On the lantern ceiling, the figure of God appears from the clouds to give benediction. The drum is pierced by sixteen windows which illuminate this grand architectural creation. The dome is the largest in the world and measures one hundred and thirty-eight feet in diameter.

Below: a detail of the drum of the dome. In the frieze below the drum, there is an inscription in mosaic on a gold ground bearing the words of Christ which are held to justify papal authority: '*Tu es Petrus et super hanc petram aedificabo ecclesiam meam et tibi dabo claves regni caelorum.*'

Opposite: a view of the dome, looking towards the apse. In the background arises the dramatic ensemble of the Chair of St. Peter.

On the following pages: views of the minor cupolas.

BASES · PILARVM
EX · LAPIDE · TIBVRTINO · MARMOREAE
$\overline{LIX}$ · PONTIFICATVS · AN · $\overline{XIII}$

Opposite: a holy water stoop in the basilica. Below: an angel making music on the arch over the entrance to the Scala Regia.

On the following pages, left: a detail of the throne, and (right), the bronze baldachin, a masterly work by Bernini, erected between the years 1624 and 1633 over the tomb of St. Peter. The tall spiral columns are designed to evoke the memory of the columns which for over a thousand years formed a screen in front of the sacellum of the medieval basilica; they support a cornice from which hangs a cloth imitating those that hung from portable baldachins; four volutes join at the top to support a golden globe and the cross. The huge columns frame the throne, which appears dramatically and triumphantly against the background.

The lantern which crowns the Michelangelesque dome. Michelangelo was able to direct the work on the dome up to the completion of the drum. He died in 1564, and after his death, Giacomo della Porta took up the task of directing building operations and brought the work to completion between 1588 and 1589. Below right: the large coat of arms of Alexander VII Chigi on the trabeation of Bernini's colonnade. Opposite: the clock on the façade of the basilica.

THE VATICAN FRESCOES
A microcosm of the history of art

Works of art are a way of communicating with the transcendent. Nowhere is this illuminating, liberating thought more sublimely expressed or more variously explored than in the Vatican. Constantinian architects and mosaicists vied with each other in their different mediums to trump beauty with yet higher beauty; and in this they blazed the trail for Arnolfo di Cambio and Bramante as the latter in his turn did for Antonio da Sangallo the Younger, Michelangelo, Raphael, Bernini, and so on and so on.

A history of the Vatican frescoes must necessarily take into account (it cannot be otherwise) the intense spiritual desire of the popes and their artists (the papacy's visual right hand) to be part of the 'civilization of the image.' The tomb of Peter was the magnetic center, recognized as a *Depositum Fidei*. The popes, the heirs, both spiritual and temporal, of the Roman emperors, themselves *duci* and *pontifici* (though the seat of temporal power, despite appearances to the contrary, remains the Quirinal palace), have over the centuries, within an area of some one hundred odd acres, concentrated an incomparable collection of art treasures.

FRA ANGELICO AND EARLY HUMANISM

The decoration of the chapel of Nicholas V (1447–55) was entrusted to the Dominican Fra Giovanni da Fiesole, better known as Fra Angelico, whose period of artistic maturity (1451–77) coincided with the early flowering of Humanism. The artist chose for his subject the martyrdom of SS. Stephen and Lawrence, and the whole work is highly evocative of the physical and spiritual sufferings of mankind. The setting, one of realism, with buildings amid natural scenery, a clear light picking out, along with other details, the poor and destitute receiving alms at the hands of St.

The Stanza della Segnatura, a detail of the *School of Athens* by Raphael. The figure bending down with a pair of compasses in his hand represents Archimedes and resembles the great architect Donato Bramante, who was commissioned by Julius II to rebuild Constantine's basilica in the Renaissance style.

Lawrence. What the artist has depicted here is a slice of 'real life': mothers with children, beggars, cripples, the blind, the air of mystic hope which pervades the work in no way lessening its psychological impact as a counterbalance to the splendors of the Renaissance.

The fact that human wretchedness combined with temporal exaltation were treated in so realistic a manner could account for the ultimate fate of Fra Angelico's works for Nicholas. His other commissions from the pope included the decoration of the pontiff's tomb, study, and a chapel dedicated to the Holy Sacrament. The frescoes which adorned the study and the chapel of the Sacred Heart were said to have been destroyed to make way for a staircase. In reality they were victims of the manner in which works of art not yet old enough to be classed as antiques, become 'outdated' by changes in fashion and cultural tastes. It was because Constantine's basilica was falling down that it was rebuilt on the principles of Bramantesque classicism. It was different with Fra Angelico's figures which were regarded as archaic and *démodés*. In the same way, when Pope Julius II della Rovere transferred his private appartments to the second floor of the papal palace, he commissioned Raphael to cover over the frescoes by Piero della Francesca, Luca Signorelli, and Bartolomeo della Gatta, while partly preserving those of Perugino, Baldassarre Peruzzi, Sodoma, and Lorenzo Lotto. Greater respect was shown to the frescoes of Melozzo da Forli, who in 1477 depicted the foundation of the Vatican Library (1475) on the ground floor of the Nicholas wing, showing Sixtus IV appointing Platina as first librarian, responsible for systemizing the vast store of material that was to form Rome's first public library.

PINTURICCHIO AND THE BORGIAS

Similar treatment was meted out to Bernardino di Betto or Pinturicchio, as he is commonly called, who worked from the end of 1492 to 1494 on the frescoes in the private appartments of Pope Alexander VI.

The perennial Vatican conflict between the temporal and spiritual sphere (an easy target for anticlericals and schismatics alike) was crystallized by Rodrigo Borgia's ambitious political, economic, and artistic activities. Having, despite himself, come to the See of Peter, he was patron to various artists including Bramante – and indirectly the young Raphael – and Leonardo da Vinci, whom he engaged as a military engineer. He strove to unify Italy under the banner of papal-Borgian Rome, his sword arm being his son Cesare, a former cardinal and hero of Machiavelli's *Prince*. He sought to improve Vatican finances by every possible means, to help in financing his rebuilding of the Petrine edifices in the idiom of the Renaissance.

However, the other side of the coin comes up in Pasquino's damning epitaphs: *Furie, perché del sangue e dell'eccidio l'orgia/cessò d'un tratto, e pace, e gioia ora ne arride?/È morto Borgia* (Furies, why has all the blood and the orgy of killing suddenly stopped, and peace and joy now shine through? Borgia is dead). And again: *Sextus Alexander iacet hic: conduntur et unalquae coluit: luxus, lis, dolus, arma, neces* (Here lies Alexander VI. With him is buried all he worshipped: luxury, discord, deceit, violence, and crime).

THE AGE OF RAPHAEL

The Raphael Rooms, as they are known, the official part of the residence of the pontiffs from Julius II to Gregory XIII include the Cappella Niccolina (Chapel of Nicholas V), and the library or Stanza della Segnatura.

Betweeen 1508 and 1511 Raffaello Sanzio (to give him his Italian name) worked on a sequence of frescoes for the library, depicting the three highest spiritual absolutes of Humanist Neoplatonism: the True, the Good, and the Beautiful. Truth (both supernatural and rational), goodness, and beauty are portrayed respectively in: the *Disputation on the Holy Sacrament* (or *Triumph of Religion*), the *School of Athens*, the *Virtues* and *Laws*, and finally *Parnassus*. On the other hand the subject chosen for the decoration of the dining room next to the papal kitchens, a room of quite imperial dimensions where the pope liked to listen to music, was of a more mundane character – the fire of Borgo.

The Raphaelesque theme throughout is one of allegorical didactism, from the depiction, in the Room of Heliodorus (1512–14) of God's intervention on behalf of the Church, to the political undertones in the fresco of *Leo I Repulsing Attila*. This latter fresco includes a foreshortened vista of Rome, with the Colosseum, the Amphitheatrum Castrense, and ruins of aqueducts and basilicas. The scene is rendered particularly dramatic by a stormy sky, in which miraculously appear St. Peter and St. Paul, threatening the barbarian hordes; other features, such as the fires and the treatment of the hills, contribute to make this one of the key models for the landscapes of Annibale Carracci and Domenichino.

Innumerable developments in both technique and critical sensitivity received a stimulus from individual details of paintings such as the *Expulsion of Heliodorus from the Temple*, notably, in this case, the deep perspective, imbued with golden light and impalpable shadow, in which is framed the figure of the priest at prayer, caught in the reflected light (brilliantly conveyed) of the candles and torchlights. In the foreground there is an explosion of action, while on the right, calm and majestic, being borne aloft in his *sedia gestatoria*, appears Julius II. The painting is both a reaffirmation of Julius's policy – the expulsion of the barbarians from the Church's domains, and a signal to his enemies as to his spiritual and temporal intentions.

Likewise the *Liberation of St. Peter* is to be seen as an assertion of the Church's freedom on earth. Light is here portrayed in three different forms: natural-nocturnal (the moon), artificial (torch-light), and miraculous (the radiance of the angel). Among those influenced by Raphael's treatment of light were Lanfranco and Domenichino, together with Caravaggio, Elsheimer, and Gerard van Honthorst.

From the point of view of form and concept, the *Mass of Bolsena* is outstanding: the portraits and still lifes, vibrant with color (one notes particularly the chair carriers, cardinals, and the

pope), already prefigure the immediacy of such outstanding masterpieces by Raphael as the *Portrait of a Cardinal* (unidentified), in the Prado in Madrid, and the *Portrait of Julius II*, in the National Gallery in London. In the velvety pinks and shimmering damasks, the virtuoso contrasts of tone and texture, Raphael shows himself the equal of Titian in his mastery of handling color.

The years 1517–24 saw the decoration of the last room, the Room of Constantine, which was used for official ceremonies (*caenaculum amplior*). In 1520, before the room was finished, Raphael had died. The Sala of Constantine concluded the Raphaelesque cycle of frescoes. The manner of execution of these latter frescoes types them as forerunners of both Mannerisim and Baroque. The main scenes are painted onto a background of faked tapestries, which lends an air of temporariness to the frescoes as if they were being used for some special occasion.

Raphael probably left some drawings for the *Victory of Constantine over Maxentius*, but the end product is a fusion of various styles and ideas – a 'cooperative' effort, to be echoed, almost to the point of plagiarism, in the workshop of Peter Paul Rubens in Antwerp. Giulio Romano, Francesco Penni, and the other assistants combined the Raphaelesque idiom with ideas which derived from Trajan's column (as previously in the *Victory at Ostia*): antiquity was in the process of being rediscovered. The dynamic of the folds and swirling edges of the 'tapestry' is clearly inspired by the spiraling narrative bands on columns such as that of Trajan. The *Vision of the Cross*, the *Baptism of Constantine*, and the *Donation of Rome* reiterate the theme of the earthy apotheosis of the Church.

Raphael was now to experiment with painting onto real tapestry, which led to his cartoons for the tapestries, made by Pieter van Aelst of Brussels, for the Sistine Chapel during the papacy of Leo X. These are usually referred to as the Old School, to distinguish them from those of the New School, made for Clement VII. A subsequent device of the Mannerists was to

Above left: the Room of Constantine, which was frescoed after Raphael's death by Giulio Romano with the assistance of Francesco Penni and Raffaelino del Colle. Below: the Room of Heliodorus, frescoed by Raphael. Opposite: the ceiling of the Stanza della Segnatura.

copy not only the subject (an example is Baldassarre Croce's decoration of Santa Susanna in the Via Pia, now the Via XX Settembre), but also the distinctive color tones and thready texture of tapestry, as seen in such painters as Taddeo and Federico Zuccari, Cesare Nebbia, Baldassarre Croce, and Paris Nogari.

Raphael had already experimented with freer, not to say startling shapes and compositions, as in the *Healing of the Lame*, the *Conversion of Saul*, and again, *St. Paul in Prison*, with the perplexing figures of the beggars, the gigantic horses, and the strange personification of the earthquake. Everything stands out with the almost reversal effects of photographic solarization which, with the filaments of gold infiltrating the areas of matt and luminous color, and the undulation of the surfaces, impregnate the vast expanses of fabric with the vibrant vitality of light, while at the same time emphasizing the reality of the vision.

Grotesque allegorical motifs (a Roman style of ornamentation, rediscovered by Raphael in the Domus Aurea, Nero's Golden House on the Oppian Hill) were used for costumes and minor milieu such as private baths (e.g. those of Cardinal Bibbiena, Julius II's secretary), smaller loggias as in Leo X's apartments, and the second-floor loggia of the Bramante wing of the Cortile di San Damaso (which contains a group of frescoes by Raphael dating from about 1517). Commissioned by Julius II to capture the view of Rome from the papal palace, the loggias occupy three floors, of which the first and third floors were decorated by Giovanni da Udine, one of the fathers of Italian still life, much used by Raphael for this type of decoration: floral groupings, grotesques, combinations of musical instruments, etc.

The frescoes of the second-floor loggia, reached via the Room of Constantine, are known as 'Raphael's Bible' from their subject matter. His own contribution was limited to preliminary directions. Nevertheless, besides the usual harmonious fusion of his ideas with those of Giovanni da Udine, Giulio Romano, Francesco Penni, and Perin del Vaga (with the

additional assistance of Raffaellino del Colle, Polidoro Caldara da Caravaggio, and others), a new element is detectable here, reflecting the anthropocentric tendencies of Humanism: the incidence of man with his surroundings. For perhaps the first time, the world as a whole is seen as Creation, the mirror and image of God — indeed, given that these rooms look out over Rome, *caput mundi*, it could hardly be otherwise.

Nature is no longer represented as mere background or as a microcosm (the Flemish pictorial convention), but assumes philosophical and cultural values (second only to man) in the unfolding of History; Nature in all its moods: the cycle of light and dark, sun and rain, the whiteness of winter snows and the flaming hues of autumn, imprisoning all motion and thought. The moon and stars attend the primal activities of man, they also preside

over his birth, so that they acquire the role of anthropomorphic deities or symbols linked with a supreme power. In this immeasurable world of forms and images, man alone is projected in time, that is to say, in History, passing from primordial pantheism to Humanistic man-centeredness, finally to annex to himself the role of Creator. Creation and Creator represent the two poles of human consciousness.

The acceptance of the world as a reflection of the deity was more or less an omnipresent element of culture, even though the certainties of Humanism were eventually to lead to a doubting that dramatically exteriorized man's spiritual questing. The perspective box which Humanist thought had built around itself, had begun to crack, and Raphael was among the first, if not the first, to realize this.

MICHELANGELO – THE AGE OF TRANSITION

Following the sack of Rome in 1527, traditional values and social relationships came under severe strain. Individual imagination and empiricism were given free rein as men became more aware of their own dimension in relation to Nature.

But it was the Baroque era that was to expand men's notions of place and space. Meanwhile the transition from the cosmic scene-setting representation of creation to an archaeological one, which Rome laid before the eyes of Raphael and his followers, was accomplished wholly within the terms of 'history painting.' Towards the end of the century, however, attempts were being made to measure the world and the stars (e.g. the Gallery of Maps and the astrological cosmogony of the *Zodiac* decorating the Room of Gregory XIII which the pope dedicated to his native city of Bologna). The ethical farewell was summed up by the Humanist motto of Marten van Heemskerck: *Roma, quanta fuit/ipsa ruina docet* (the very ruins teach the greatness of Rome). But the universe had taken on a twofold image, seen in the dual search of the Absolute, as evinced in the tragic yet lyrical apocalyptic creativity of Michelangelo, and the consequent discovery of an earthly and cosmic reality, the definable limits of which were for ever receding, ever more uncertain.

Both the Sistine ceiling and the *Last Judgement* (1508–12 and 1533/5–41 respectively), express the existential pessimism of this great genius in his portrayal of the prehistory and the posthistory of mankind. In *Genesis* and the *Dies Irae*, Michelangelo develops the themes of the 15th-century frescoes (1481–83) on the lives of Moses and Christ, frescoed on the Sistine walls by the major artists of the time: Perugino, Botticelli, Domenico Ghirlandaio, Cosimo Rosselli, and their *équipes* which included such artists as Pinturicchio, Piero di Cosimo, Bartolomeo della Gatta, and Luca Signorelli. Most probably Perugino was in overall charge of the work, and he himself painted the altarpiece for the *Assumption* as well as the first two panels of the *Story of Moses* and the *Story of Christ*. These three compositions, together with two lunettes above depicting Christ's forerunners (by Michelangelo), were expunged, not without some hesitation it must be said, by Michelangelo to make way for the *Last Judgement*.

The history of the decoration of the Sistine Chapel is therefore in some ways a sad one, highlighting, as it does, the extinction of works which are forever lost to posterity. While the 15th-century frieze and the ceiling retain their architectonic partitions, presenting a chain of individual episodes, for example *Christ Giving the Keys to St Peter*, the *Meeting of the Daughters of Jethro*, the *Delphic Sibyl*, and the *Creation of Adam*, with linking entablatures and niches containing the figures of popes, and throughout the acorn motif of the della Rovere family crest, the

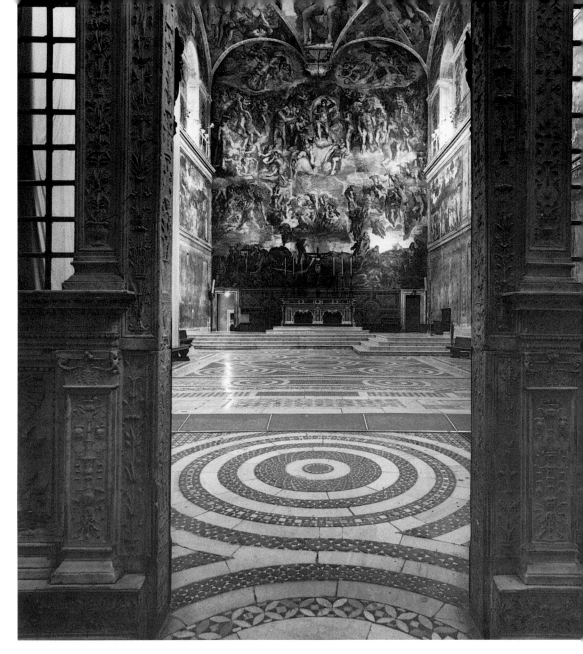

Last Judgement by contrast is a turbulent whirlpool of bodies in empty space revolving around the fixed absolute of Christ the Judge. Against a cerulean background, body-souls float almost weightlessly, some wafted up to the empyrean, others thrust down to hell. One marvels at the magnitude of the work and its conception.

From a compositional point of view, there are three main blocks with distinct centers of gravity: at the bottom the group of angels waking the dead with their trumpet blasts; at the top the instruments of the Passion; and in the center, the numinous mediator, Christ the Judge. The terrible thunder of the trumpets, the chorus of the redeemed, Charon's oar strokes, and the anguished cries and cursings of the damned are proof not only of Michelangelo's final shattering of the architectonic spatial values (illusory) of

Humanism, but of his own striving for an all-embracing artistic idiom. The Sistine apocalypse is the prototype of total art as subsequently developed in the Baroque.

It seems inevitable that current restoration work on both the ceiling and the *Last Judgement* will give the lie to one of the most mistifying misrepresentations in art criticism, namely that Michelangelo did not know how to handle color. It is now clear from an examination of some of the Vatican masterpieces that his colors had succumbed to the dusty overlay of centuries, to the glues used, and to oxidization due to humidity. The first inkling of this came to light during the cleaning of one of the lunettes of Christ's forerunners, that of Eleazar and Mathan.

It is commonly held that Michelangelo was under an obligation to Pope Sixtus V della Rovere to decorate the Sistine Chapel (named after a previous della Rovere

The Borgia Rooms. The coat of arms and emblems of the Borgia family, from the ceiling of the Sala delle Arti Liberali.

pope, Sixtus IV). However, his unwillingness to undertake the job has perhaps been exaggerated. At the beginning (c. 1508), he took on two assistants, Jacopo d'Indaco and Francesco Granacci, both well versed in the art of fresco; yet they were soon dismissed and replaced by raw apprentices whose job it was to prepare the mortar and apply the second layer of plaster. Michelangelo did the rest of the work himself – a remakable testimony to his professional integrity.

The art of fresco, of which this outstanding genius revealed himself a consummate master, demands great creative sureness of hand, since the paint is applied to the plaster while it is still wet (hence the term fresco, 'fresh'), so that it actually penetrates directly into the plaster. Michelangelo was able to work at tremendous speed (without the normal preparatory cartoon, which was generally used for reference in transferring the drawing to the plaster), yet for all that was an expert and refined colorist.

The lunette mentioned earlier bears no trace of any preparatory composition, merely the basic architectonic outlines on which the figures are sketched in black brush strokes, then painted over with red, pink, white, green, shades of azure, and ochre lacquer. The sheer vigor of the painting is in some ways reminiscent of the sculptor's chisel, but there is no doubting the authentically pictorial deftness and dynamic compositional inspiration. Thus we find broad, restless brush strokes, swift and taut, tending ever upward, and an equal concern both for completeness of vision and elaboration of detail (for instance, individual locks of hair, ribbons, anatomical details, and the purse, band, and key at the woman's waist). Possessed eyes haunt us, and faces devoid of grace are contrasted with faces of such beauty as could only come from the artist's own neoplatonic idea. Legs dangle down from the 'nest' below the ceiling, while other figures loom up and away into the shadows.

In his other lunettes the Tuscan-Roman master reveals the same command of color. When restoration work is complete (some

Above left: a detail of Cardinal Bibbiena's little stove decorated under Raphael's supervision in the loggetta which overlooks the Marshal's courtyard. Below: the Stanza della Segnatura, a fresco by Raphael of Alexander the Great placing the poems of Homer in the tomb of Achilles.

(c. 1542–c. 1550). One can almost find a pretext for the unleashing of primordial forces in the supreme exaltation of faith through conversion and martyrdom; the dualistic portrayal of good and evil, light and darkness of Caravaggio's decoration for the Cappella Cerasi in Santa Maria del Popolo owes much to these works.

The frescoes of the *History of the Church* in the Sala Regia – the work of Giorgio Vasari (1572–73), Lorenzo Sabatini, Francesco Salviati, Taddeo and Federico Zuccari (the minor scenes by Orazio Samacchini, Marco Pino, and Livio Agresti, and the wall stuccoes by Daniele da Volterra) – are elegant, extenuated, and ultrarefined. The rich coffering of the barrel-vault ceiling, designed by Perin del Vaga (active with Raphael: notably the work executed in Castel Sant'Angelo for the Pope Paul III Farnese, whose pontificate lasted from 1534 to 1549), provides a ready answer to many questions concerning secular decorative ideas after the time of Raphael, ideas which in fact originated with Raphael himself, contrasting diametrically with the unrelenting dramatic tension of the mature Michelangelo.

Paul III was as active a patron as could be wished for. He employed Michelangelo for his major public and civic works, Titian for the formal portraits of his family, Antonio da Sangallo the Younger as court architect, because of his general availability, and Perin del Vaga for his incomparable ability to create the most spectacular 'set-pieces.'

It was the fantastic world of Perin and the other exponents of Pauline Mannerism that identified with the needs of a society which, while witnessing the advance of the Counter Reformation and the reforms of the Council of Trent (convoked by Paul III to stem the flood tide of Protestantism in Europe), at the same time refused to have anything to do with the neofeudalistic ideas of Farnesian politics. Perin then may be described as the spiritual heir of the early Humanist decorative artists, a Gentile da Fabriano working in the idiom of 16th-century Mannerism.

Two further exponents of this 'neo-courtly' manner of painting are to be

twelve years hence), this will quite likely be seen as the most astounding cultural event of the century – a century with little otherwise to redeem it.

Michelangelo also painted the frescoes in the adjacent Cappella Paolina (Pauline Chapel) which gives onto the Sala Regia – the *aula magna* of the popes, used for the reception of ambassadors.

THE MANNERIST REACTION

The advent of Mannerism coincided with the general spiritual and intellectual upheaval resulting from the sack of Rome, and evolved from the dark, tortured muscularity of late Michelangelesque art – typified in sculpture in the various tragic Pietàs, in architecture in the rugged timeless walls of Santa Maria degli Angeli in Rome, and in painting in the nihilistic shadows (suffused, though, with the rich splendor of gold) of the Pauline Chapel frescoes, where the theme of Divine Grace is dramatically explored in the *Conversion of Saul* and the *Crucifixion of St. Peter*

encountered in the Sala Ducale: Marco Pino and the Fleming Paul Bril, who had a decisive influence in the emergence of landscape as a major theme of art. The brothers Bril, Paul and Mathys, who painted the *Martyrdom of St. Clement* in the Sala Clementina, had little sympathy with the figurative tradition of Raphael and Michelangelo, while the artists working in the Library of Sixtus V had their minds firmly fixed on recovering the forcefulness of late Renaissance art. The Library played an important part in the development of late Mannerist painting.

THE BEGINNINGS OF BAROQUE

Among these fresco painters were some who later came to be recognized on their individual merits. Apart from Bril, there were Ventura Salimbeni, Giovanni Baglione, Giovanni Battista Ricci, Andrea Lilio, Orazio Gentileschi, Avanzino Nuzzi, and others, whom it is difficult to distinguish on the brilliantly colored walls, or in the less eye-catching stuccoes and grotesques executed in the Raphael-Giovanni da Udine tradition. The Library was extended in 1611 by the Borghese pope Paul V, the new rooms being decorated in 1620 by Giovanni Battista Ricci with *Scenes from the Life of the Pope*: of later date are the *Plans of Rome* (Duperac and Lafréry, 1577) and the *Canonizations of Carlo Borromeo and Frances of Rome.*

A champion of Mannerist orthodoxy was the eminent Roman artist Giuseppe Cesari, known as the Cavalier d'Arpino, who was head of a most successful workshop, *Alla Torretta*, in the Campo Marzio. Here a certain Michelangelo Merisi came to work for about eight months sometime in 1593. It was probably Arpino who first instructed the young Merisi – better known as Caravaggio – in symbolism and allegory, introducing him to a more sophisticated style of painting at the start of his Roman career. He put the young apprentice to paint 'from the natural': flowers and fruit compositions, as subsidiary details in grander works, and it was from this that he soon devel-

oped the pictorial parity between flowers and fruit and 'figures' which was the hallmark of his revolutionary naturalism.

With Arpino – who worked on the decoration of the third-floor loggia in the Sala Vecchia degli Svizzeri and the Sala dei Palafrenieri – we return to St. Peter's (he drew the cartoons for the mosaics in Michelangelo's dome, 1603–12) and finally enter the new century, which was to see the complete and irresistible advance of 17th-century artificiality.

The four pendentives of the dome feature the Prophets (1599), the work of Giovanni de' Vecchi, Cesare Nebbia, and Pomarancio, while on the lantern's internal calotte is depicted God the Father descending from the heavens, and blessing the world. It is revealing to note the professional 'gloss' of these works, which do not escape a certain conventional standardization (in fact the same cartoon of God the Father was used for the lantern of the Cappella Santori in St. John Lateran, 1606–07). The mosaics depicting the *Chorus of Angels in Adoration* in the upper section of the dome date from 1606–07, while the putti and cherubs in the tondi are from 1608–09.

The decoration of the dome was finished on 25 March 1612, under Arpino's supervision, several artists having collaborated in the work including the future disciple of Caravaggio, Orazio Gentileschi. Mosaics, rather than the customary frescoes, cover the inside of the basilica. Many of the altarpieces were in fact replaced by mosaics, and over the years, with repetition, this medium became more detailed and fussy, losing in its preciousness, the original freshness of the dome mosaics.

FROM CARAVAGGIO TO POUSSIN

As has been suggested, the 17th century saw the first real artistic revolution: that of Caravaggesque naturalism. In 1605 the Palafrenieri di Sant'Anna commissioned the artist to paint the *Madonna and Child with St. Anne*, intended for the new altar of the confraternity in the restored basilica. The painting provoked bitter controversy

(for reasons which remain obscure), and it was rejected by the Signori Cardinali della Fabbrica (literally, the Lord Cardinals of the Building). The only writing in the artist's own hand to come down to us is in the form of a guarantee for the work: 'I, Michelangelo da Caravaggio, am content and satisfied with the picture I have painted for the Compagnia di Sant'Anna, I have written and signed this in faith, on the 8th day of April 1606.'

The painting was removed after only two days on show (14–15 April). We know that the painter was unable to defend his work, or even to offer a substitute, as he did in other instances, since on 28–29 May he was involved in a murder. On 16 June the painting was bought by Cardinal Scipione Borghese.

Though Caravaggio had now left Rome, naturalism continued to flourish in the work of notable artists such as Giovanni Antonio Galli, called Spadarino, whose work has always remained curiously ambiguous and elusive, even though at times it has echoes of Gentileschi, Cecco del Caravaggio, and Carlo Saraceni. He was fond of silvery color tones and his figures are often rather delicate, recalling those of the early Caravaggio. In 1629–30 he produced for St. Peter's a painting of *SS. Valeria and Martial* (now in the Museo Petriano), in which the decapitated saint is shown holding her own head – an eminently Caravaggesque piece of shock-naturalism.

In 1629 another naturalist, the French artist Valentin de Boulogne succeeded (through the intervention of Cardinal Francesco Barberini, nephew of the francophile Urban VIII, in having an altarpiece, the *Martyrdom of SS. Processus and Martinian* accepted in preference to one by Francesco Albani. An authentic masterpiece, it is now in the Pinacoteca Vaticana, having been replaced by a mosaic. It exemplified the need to break away from the formalized academic style, popularized by Bartolomeo Manfredi, which besmirched the heritage of Caravaggio. It has a highly personal imaginative concreteness that offers a challenge, from within, to Manfredi's

conventionalized notions (on which Valentin's works had hitherto been based), echoing elements of Caravaggio's own *Martyrdom of St. Matthew* (in the French church of San Luigi dei Francesi in Rome). These 'real' Caravaggesque elements were in turn perhaps influenced by the contemporaneous work, *Martyrdom of St. Erasmus* (c. 1628–29) by Nicolas Poussin.

Valentin's fellow Frenchman Poussin is the true heir of the classicist trend, introduced to Rome by the brothers Carracci (Annibale, Agostino, and Ludovico) of Bologna, and their Accademia degli Incamminati, some of whose members were to number among the leading artists of the 17th century. One of these was

Guido Reni, one of whose mosaics in St. Peter's is derived from *St. Michael the Archangel Conquering the Devil* in Santa Maria della Concezione. Another of his works, the *Crucifixion of St. Peter* (now in the Pinacoteca Vaticana, originally in the church of San Paolo alle Tre Fontane), reveals an 'emended' naturalism, intended as a counter to Caravaggio's version of the same subject in Santa Maria del Popolo. More robust, with suggestions of Dosso Dossi and Caravaggio is the *Entombment of St. Petronilla*, another mosaic copy of the original (now in the Capitoline Gallery), by Giovanni Francesco Barbieri, better known as Guercino.

Another artist of the Carracci school was Domenico Zampieri, called Domenich-

ino, the torchbearer of classicism after the death of Annibale Carracci. Perhaps the most famous of his mosaics are the *Martyrdom of St. Sebastian* (copied from his own painting in Santa Maria degli Angeli), and the copy made from another painting of his, the *Communion of St. Jerome*, said to be the most famous picture in Rome in the first three decades of the 17th century. This painting was executed for the Franciscans of the Ara Coeli in 1614 and later transferred to the church of San Gerolamo della Carità in Rome. Napoleon carried it off in 1797; it later returned to Rome, and is now in the Pinacoteca Vaticana. In this work, despite a whiff of naturalism, the main stylistic emphasis is clearly academic. The composition is built

The Sistine Chapel. Opposite: a detail of the *Punishment of Korah, Dathan and Abiram* by Botticelli. Right: detail of *Christ Giving the Keys to St. Peter* by Perugino.

around elegantly balanced masses (with a landscape opening in the center), and in both this and the rich harmonization of colors is evident a deep concern for what might be described as didactic serenity.

The other master of the Carracci school, Giovanni Lanfranco, was responsible for the magnificent flight of angels around the cross (the *Triumph of the Cross*) painted in fresco in the chapel built by Francesco Borromini to house Michelangelo's *Pietà*: here we are made to realize that Baroque has at last arrived.

Poussin in particular, with his *Martyrdom of St. Erasmus* (commissioned in 1627 with the backing of Cardinal Francesco Barberini and Gian Lorenzo Bernini), represents a point of juncture of several different cultural movements: that of the Counter Reformation, with the resurgence of the cults of the very earliest martyr saints; that of Humanism, with the cult of Raphael, Titian, and Veronese; and that of the Stoic Caravaggesque drama (as also interpreted by Valentin), in which a holy martyrdom is for all that a brutal murder.

The gruesome subject matter is exposed to the full light of day, a genuine reflection of the all-embracing light of the Godhead, rather than the suffusing brightness of classical inspiration, which thereby becomes the revealing inner light of philosophical reflection: and hence the viewer is brought to private contemplation.

In Baroque therefore the cyclical approach to art gave way to more explosive effects of sudden movements of drama. From the racked classicism of Andrea Sacchi (for instance, the cartoons for the mosaics realized by the great Giovanni Battista Calandra for the Cappella della Colonna: *St. Thomas Aquinas with St. Peter and St. Paul* (1632), and *St. John Damascene* (1634–36); and for the Cappella di San Michele Arcangelo: *St. Leo the Great* (1638–39), and *St. Dionysius* (1639–47), we progress to the speckled chiaroscuro of the great marble altarpieces of Alessandro Algardi, and finally to the resplendent bronze and gold 'machines' of the artificial universe of Bernini, and the sophisticated stucco work of Pietro da Cortona.

THE CAPPELLA NICCOLINA

Between 1451 and 1477 Fra Angelico worked on the chapel of Nicholas V – a narrow room with lancet windows. His *Histories of SS. Stephen and Lawrence* express profound sympathy with the physical and spiritual sufferings of humanity. At the same time the town scenes and landscapes are rendered with as much perceptive depth as the gold-embroidered dalmatics of the two deacons and the rags of the poor. A down-to-earth record of poverty showing the underside of Humanist splendor.

Cappella Niccolina.
The *Histories of SS. Stephen and Lawrence*.
Fra Angelico (Giovanni da Fiesole, called Beato Angelico; Vicchio di Mugello 1387 – Rome 1455).
Below: St. Stephen is ordained deacon by St. Peter and distributes alms.
Opposite above: St. Stephen preaching and disputing in the Sanhedrin.
Below: the martyrdom of St. Stephen.

Cappella Niccolina.
The *Histories of SS. Stephen and Lawrence*.
Fra Angelico.
Opposite: St. Lawrence receiving the treasures of
the Church from St. Sixtus.

Below left: St. Sixtus ordains St. Lawrence
deacon.
Below right: St. Lawrence distributing alms.
Bottom: the trial of St. Lawrence in the presence
of the Emperor Decius, and the martyrdom of the
saint.

THE 15th-CENTURY FRESCOES OF THE SISTINE CHAPEL

The greatest artists of the 15th century were engaged to decorate the lower part of the chapel of the della Rovere pope Sixtus IV – thereafter to be known as the Sistine Chapel.

Perugino, Botticelli, Ghirlandaio, Cosimo Rosselli and their assistants (including Pinturicchio, Piero di Cosimo, Bartolomeo della Gatta, and Luca Signorelli) worked closely together to create immensely inventive visual stories of Moses and Christ. Here, the virtuoso graphic techniques of the Umbro-Florentine school (dominated by the flowing lines of Botticelli and Ghirlandaio) is combined with the whimsical inventiveness of Piero di Cosimo and the anatomical exactitude of Signorelli; at the same time the Humanist interest in landscape has become evident – even if only as a setting for Man (whether Christ, or some Biblical character). In these landscapes,

note the importance of classical ruins, stressing the value of history. In the work of Michelangelo, landscape then disappears, to be rediscovered in the 17th century.

The Sistine Chapel.
The *Story of Moses and of Christ*.
Below: Moses with his wife Zipporah and the circumcision of their sons.
Perugino (Pietro Vannucci; Citta della Pieve 1448 – Fontignano 1523) and Pinturicchio (Bernardino di Betto; Perugia 1454 – Siena 1513).
Opposite above: The Passage of the Red Sea.
Below: Moses on Sinai and the Worship of the Golden Calf.
Cosimo Rosselli (Florence 1439–1507).

On the following pages: the Burning Bush, Moses killing the Egyptian and chasing the Midianites from the well, the Daughters of Jethro.
Sandro Botticelli (Florence 1444–1510).

The Sistine Chapel.
The Story of Moses and of Christ.
Opposite above: Moses entrusts the Rod to
Joshua, the Death of Moses.
Luca Signorelli (Cortona 1450–1523).
Below: the Punishment of Korah, Dathan and
Abiram.
Sandro Botticelli.
Below: detail from the Death of Moses.

The Sistine Chapel.
The Story of Moses and of Christ.
Left: detail from the Temptation of Christ.
Opposite above: the Baptism of Christ.
Perugino.
Below: the Cleansing of the Leper.
Sandro Botticelli.

On the following pages, above left:
the calling of St. Peter and St. Andrew.
Domenico Ghirlandaio (Domenico Bigordi;
Florence 1449–1494).
Above right: Christ giving the Keys to St Peter.
Perugino.
Below left: the Sermon on the Mount.
Below right: the Last Supper.
Cosimo Rosselli.

THE BORGIA ROOMS

In a continual interplay between reality and phantasy – a sort of visual 'alchemico-hermetic transmutation': the Philosopher's Stone that turns base metal to gold – Pinturicchio here gives an interpretation of the complex psyche of Pope Alexander VI Borgia. Seeing himself as, in a sense, simultaneously a magician and Alexander the Great, this enigmatic pope yearned to transform paintings into jewels, stucco into gold, and the whole of pagan mythology into Christian faith. His attempts at recreating the classicism of the Empire and its culture (art, music, geometry, epic) on a level of complete universality led to a kind of neopaganism which, while providing a springboard for the great geniuses of the High Renaissance, also paved the way for the Lutheran schism.

The Borgia Rooms.
Sala dei Santi.
Pinturicchio.
Right: the Virgin and Child with cherubs.
Below, from left to right: the Legend of St.
Barbara, the Visitation, Susanna and the
Elders.
Opposite: the Myth of Io, Argus and Mercury.

On the following pages: the Disputation of St.
Catherine.

The Borgia Rooms.
Sala delle scienze e delle arti liberali.
Antonio da Viterbo, called il Pastura (*c.* 1450–1509/16).
Opposite above: decorations of the vault, with the coat of arms of Pope Alexander VI, and in the lunettes, the Arts of the Trivium (Rhetoric and Geometry).
Below and center: Arts of the Quadrivium (Arithmetic and Music).

Sala delle Sibille.
Workshop of Pinturicchio.
Above right: a partial view of the vault with, in the lunettes, Ezekiel and the Cimmerian Sibyl and Jeremiah and the Phrygian Sibyl.

Sala dei Misteri della Fede.
Pinturicchio.
Below right: the Adoration of the Magi.

THE SISTINE CHAPEL CEILING

On the ceiling of the Sistine Chapel Michelangelo depicted the most primal elements of human history as recounted in the Bible, integrating them – both aesthetically and in terms of content – with the earlier 15th-century wall frescoes. What we have therefore is a continuous visual narrative, the individual scenes being linked by a complex system of painted pilasters and capitals, and entablatures and thrones, amid all of which is an endless variety of human figures (differentiated as much in composition as in symbolic significance). The *Separation of Light from Darkness* shows the Eternal Father at once transparent (the face and arms) and almost tangibly physical (emphasized by the folds of drapery); the exceptional rendering of tactile physical reality combined with explosive supernatural energy in the *Creation of the Sun, Moon and Planets* terminates then in the incomparable *Creation of Adam*, in which creature and Creator face each other in a tense overriding equilibrium, caught the split second before the two fingers meet.

The *Creation of Eve*, the *Expulsion from Paradise*, the *Flood*, and the 'ante' Christ figure of Noah all show other aspects of the artist's troubled Humanist spirit.

Going through the various Prophets and Sibyls who had predicted the coming of Christ, Michelangelo then depicts the families of Christ's genealogy. As current restoration work has revealed, these groups (three figures in each) were painted direct on the wet plaster, without the normal aid of a preparatory cartoon.

The Sistine Chapel.
The Ceiling.
General view.
Michelangelo Buonarroti (Caprese 1475 – Rome 1564).
On the following pages:
the Sistine Chapel.
Genesis.
Michelangelo.
Above left: Separation of Light from Darkness.
Below left: Creation of the Sun, Moon and Planets.
Above right: Separation of Land and Sea and Creation of Fishes and Birds.
Below right: the Creation of Adam.

The Sistine Chapel.
Genesis.
Michelangelo.
Left: the Creation of Eve.
Below: Fall of Man and the Expulsion from
Paradise.
Opposite above: Noah's Sacrifice.
Below: the Flood.

On the following pages: the Drunkenness of
Noah.

The Sistine Chapel.
The Miraculous Delivery of Israel.
Michelangelo.
Below: the Punishment of Haman.
Bottom: David and Goliath.

The Sistine Chapel.
The Miraculous Delivery of Israel.
Michelangelo.
Below: the Brazen Serpent.
Bottom: Judith and Holophernes.

On the following pages:
Sibyls and Prophets.
Michelangelo.
Left: the Erythraean sibyl.
Center: the Lybian sibyl.
Right: the Persian sibyl.

118

The Sistine Chapel.
Sibyls and Prophets.
Michelangelo.
Right: the Delphic sibyl.
Below: the Cumaean sibyl.
Opposite above: the Prophet Isaiah.
Below: the Prophet Jeremiah.

On the following pages, above left: the Prophet
Joel.
Below: the Prophet Zechariah.
Right: the Prophet Daniel.

The Sistine Chapel.
Sibyls and Prophets.
Michelangelo.
Opposite above: the Prophet Jonah.
Below: the Prophet Ezekiel.
Christ's Forerunners.
Michelangelo.
Right, from top to bottom: King Solomon with his parents; the family of King Rehoboam; King Asa with his parents.

The Sistine Chapel.
The Ignudi.
Michelangelo.
On this and opposite page: five of the figures of
the Ignudi from the ceiling.

THE RAPHAEL ROOMS

The great achievement of Raphael was his consumate fusion of Renaissance Humanism with the genuine spirit of classical culture. His frescoes painted for Pope Julius II give visual form to the three highest spiritual categories of Neoplatonism – the True, the Good, and the Beautiful. The figures in the *Fire of Borgo* and the other scenes depicted here represent a prodigious field of technical experimentation, in which the seeds of numerous future artistic developments are sown.

There are obvious differences of 'spirit' between the artists who worked on the Sistine Chapel and the Borgia Rooms in the 15th century, between the challenging dramatic polarities of Michelangelo, and the absolute universe, with its allegorical and consciously meaningful compositional approach, of the *School of Athens* and the *Parnassus*. Science, Art, and Faith are brought together in a supreme synthesis by means of color, compositional structure, and the mingling of legendary or mythical and real characters. Julius II wished to 'drive out the barbarians' from the domains of the Church; *Leo I Repulsing Attila* and the *Expulsion of Heliodorus from the Temple* convey clear warnings to those wishing to remain within its fold. The *Liberation of St. Peter* emphasizes unmistakenly the freedom of the Church on earth.

The Raphael Rooms.
The Room of the Fire of Borgo.
Raphael Sanzio (Urbino 1483–Rome 1520).
Below: the Fire of Borgo.
Top right: the Oath of Leo III;
Center: the Victory at Ostia;
Bottom: the Coronation of Charlemagne.

The Raphael Rooms.
Stanza della Segnatura.
Raphael.
Below: the Virtues.
Bottom: the Disputation on the Holy Sacrament.
Opposite above: the School of Athens
Below: Parnassus.

On the following pages, above left: detail from the Disputation on the Holy Sacrament.
Below: detail from the School of Athens.
Right: detail from Parnassus.

The Raphael Rooms.
The Room of Heliodorus.
Raphael.
The Liberation of St. Peter.

On the following pages, above left: the Expulsion of Heliodorus.
Below: Leo I repulsing Attila.
Above right: the Mass of Bolsena.
Below: details from the Mass of Bolsena.

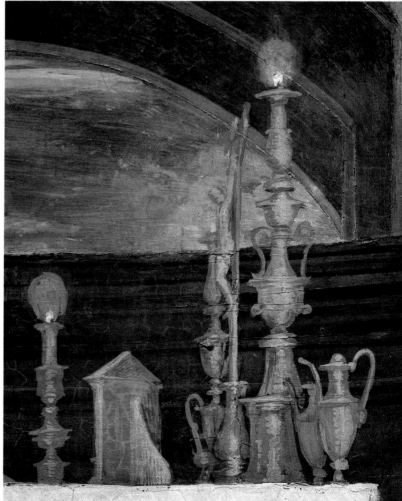

The Raphael Rooms.
The Room of Constantine.
After Raphael (?), carried out by Giulio Romano
(Rome c. 1492–99 – Mantua 1546); Francesco
Penni (Florence c. 1488 – Naples 1528);
Raffaellino del Colle (Sansepolcro c. 1500–66).
Right: detail from the Donation of Constantine.
Below: the Baptism of Constantine.
Opposite above: the Vision of the Cross.
Below: the Donation of Constantine.

THE LOGGIA AND THE LOGGETTA

The Raphael Loggia.
Raphael and his assistants.
Opposite: a general view of the second Loggia.
Below: a detail of Abimelech espying Isaac and
Rebecca (the fifth arcade; Giulio Romano).

The Raphael Loggia in the Bramantesque wing of the Cortile di San Damaso is one of the happiest and most successful works of decorative genius ever created. The Biblical scenes are brought together in a unified whole by the exquisite 'grotesques' of Giovanni da Udine, which had a decisive impact on later exponents of this 'minor' decorative branch of Humanist art, accounting for its all-pervasive classical inspiration. Swags and branches of fruit, clusters of musical instruments, military trophies, imaginary animals, and cupids were all taken (though also in fact, for the most part, reworked) by Raphael himself from the recently discovered decorative schemes of Nero's Domus Aurea on the Oppian Hill. The Biblical frescoes, by the various remarkable artists in Raphael's team, display a new technical mastery of the devices of visual narrative. Both the colors and the actual composition include striking contrasts, and marked *chiaroscuro* (effects of light and shade), flowing lines of drapery, and 'snatches' of landscape, all combining to form a dynamic visual progression which actively harmonizes with the real townscapes of Rome and the real, changing light of day framed by the windows.

The Raphael Loggia.
Assistants of Raphael.
Opposite, above: the Creation of the Animals (first arcade; Giovanni da Udine, Udine 1487–1564).
Below: the Flood (third arcade; Giulio Romano and Francesco Penni).
Below center: Joseph relates his Dreams to his Brothers (seventh arcade; Giulio Romano, Francesco Penni and Giovanni da Udine).
Top right: the Crossing of the Red Sea (eighth arcade; Giulio Romano).
Center: Joshua halts the Sun (tenth arcade; Perin del Vaga, Florence c. 1500 – Rome 1547).
Bottom: David is anointed King (eleventh arcade; Guillaume Marcillat, Verdun 1475 – Arezzo 1537).

The Raphael Loggetta.
Giovanni da Udine, Perin del Vaga.
Opposite: general view
Below: grotesques from the vault.

The Raphael Loggetta.
Giovanni da Udine, Perin del Vaga.
Below: two details of the grotesques.
Bottom left: woman with a skein winder.
Bottom right: Cupids forging arrows.

Opposite: grotesque framed by a mythological scene.

THE RAPHAEL
TAPESTRIES

The cartoons by Raphael and his school which the Brussels weaver Pieter van Aelst transformed into tapestries are a magnificent testimony of creative imagination and adaptability. By the very nature and texture of tapestry, we experience here quite different geometrical effects from those of fresco and painting in general.

The series of scenes depicted are grand compositions, resplendent in color, with gold threads sewn into them, giving vibrant atmospheric brilliance. There was also perhaps a more functional motivation behind this: originally intended to be hung around the bottom of the Sistine Chapel walls, where there are no windows, the gold would have shimmered beautifully in the candlelight on ceremonial occasions. The compositions themselves, the curious decorational elements, and the actual weave of the tapestries combine to create an almost dreamlike impression.

Tapestries.
Pieter van Aelst after the cartoons of Raphael.
Opposite: St. Paul in prison and a personification of the earthquake.
Right: the Miraculous Draught of Fishes.
Below: Christ giving the Keys to St. Peter.

Tapestries.
Pieter van Aelst after cartoons by Raphael.
Below: the Blinding of Elymas.
Bottom: the Sacrifice at Lystra.
Opposite above: the Healing of the Lame.
Below: St. Paul preaches to the Athenians.

On the following pages, above left: the Death of Ananias.
Below: the Conversion of Saul.
Right: the Stoning of St. Stephen.

MICHELANGELO'S LAST JUDGEMENT

When painting his *Last Judgement*, Michelangelo had to sacrifice a fresco of the *Assumption* by Perugino and two lunettes, painted by himself, of Christ's forerunners. Yet no one would now claim the sacrifice was in vain. This *Dies Irae* is a swirling mass of bodies centered on the figure of Christ the Judge. Soul-bodies ascend into heaven or are thrust into hell in a gravity-less clear blue light. The artist deliberately manipulates our feelings, so that we sense a kind of psychic annihilation and at the same time a tangible

physical reality. There are three main 'blocks' of compositional focus: at the bottom, the knot of angels waking the dead with violent trumpet blasts; at the top, the instruments of the Passion – the fideistic and earthly means to all resurrection (note too on the bottom left the 'rosaries' of the angels, fulfilling a similar function); and between the two, the erupting Mediator, Christ in Judgement.

The Sistine Chapel.
The Last Judgement.
Michelangelo.
Opposite: general view.
Below: detail with angels sounding trumpets.

The Sistine Chapel.
The Last Judgement.
Michelangelo.
Opposite: detail of Christ the Universal Judge.
Below: detail with St. Peter and the Apostles.

On the following pages: detail of the Resurrection of the Dead.

The Sistine Chapel.
The Last Judgement.
Michelangelo.
Opposite: detail of St. Sebastian.
Right: detail of the skull.
Below: detail of the ferry boat of Satan-Charon.

THE CAPPELLA PAOLINA

The Mannerist reaction, which coincided with the traumatic experience of the sack of Rome (1527), developed from the dark, tense muscularity of Michelangelo's last period. This tortured sensuous spirituality is typified by the totally abstract quality of the 'unfinished' sculptures (e.g. the Rondanini *Pietà*), the transformation of the Baths of Diocletian into a church (the present Santa Maria degli Angeli), and the Cappella Paolina frescoes. Here nihilistic shadows and bursts of golden radiance evoke primordial feelings in the drama of Grace enacted in the *Crucifixion of St. Peter* and the *Conversion of Saul.*

Good and evil, light and darkness, true faith and heresy stand together in stark opposition, and it was from these intense contrasts that the revolutionary art of Caravaggio evolved.

Cappella Paolina.
Michelangelo.
Opposite: the Crucifixion of St. Peter.
Below: the Conversion of Saul.

RELIGIOUS ART OF THE VATICAN BASILICA

Naturalism, Classicism, and Baroque all jostled for primacy in the 17th century. However, none was in fact totally distinct from the others, and what differentiates the religious art of the 17th century from that of previous ages is the remarkable common denominator of sensuality of color and dramatic handling of well observed subjects.

A favorite theme was the horrific sufferings of the early martyrs of the Faith, from Peter (its very emblem, symbolizing through his crucifixion upside-down the earthly reality of Christ and His Heavenly Church), to the obscure Erasmus, and Processus and Martinian. The tacit implications are clear: the champions of the Church assert the triumph of the papacy against Lutheran accusations of worldliness.

Caravaggio, Poussin, Valentin, and Domenichino (with his evocation of the unshakable faith of St. Jerome – a key name of the Counter Reformation), and Lanfranco (in his *Triumph of the Cross*) were all in the end concerned with this same theme of 'existential justification.'

Of the works illustrated on these and the following two pages, Poussin's *Martyrdom of St. Erasmus*, Domenichino's *Communion of St. Jerome*, Valentin's *Martyrdom of SS. Processus and Martinian*, Raphael's *Transfiguration*, and Guido Reni's *Crucifixion of St. Peter* are all produced in mosaics in St. Peter's. Caravaggio's *Madonna dei Palafrenieri*, though commissioned as one of St. Peter's altarpieces, was not in the end allowed to be put there; the fresco of the *Triumph of the Cross* by Giovanni Lanfranco is on the ceiling of the Capella della Pietà.

Right: Martyrdom of St. Erasmus.
Nicolas Poussin (Les Andelys 1594 – Rome 1665).

Opposite above left: the Communion of St. Jerome.
Domenichino (Domenico Zampieri; Bologna 1581 – Naples 1641).
Right: the Martyrdom of SS. Processus and Martinian.
Valentin de Boulogne (Coulommiers 1594 – Rome 1632).
Below: the Triumph of the Cross.
Giovanni Lanfranco (Terenzano 1582 – Rome 1647).

164

From left to right: Raphael, the Transfiguration
of Christ; Guido Reni (Calvenzano 1575 – Bologna
1642), the Crucifixion of Peter; Caravaggio
(Michelangelo Merisi, Caravaggio 1573–1610),
the Madonna dei Palafrenieri.

HALL OF THE IMMACULATE CONCEPTION

In 1858 Pius IX commissioned a picture cycle of the Immaculate Conception from Francesco Podesti. Having to work in close proximity to Raphael's Room of the *Fire of Borgo* – rather a case of unfair competition! – imposed certain demands of respect, which Podesti fulfilled with admirable tact and skill. However, the 'quotations' from Raphael, tinged with Romanticism, and the essentially static quality of these frescoes affect our appreciation of their undeniably sophisticated visual narrative quality.

The *Definition* and the *Proclamation of the Dogma* on the walls, and the *Sybils*, the *Faith*, the *Theology*, and the Old Testament characters on the ceiling and between the windows, all reveal Podesti's ability to translate the idioms of Humanist art into the polished, precise language of academic form and cold 'purity.'

On an elaborate stand on the exquisite 1st-century Ostian mosaic floor is placed the great manuscript of the dogma of the Immaculate Conception, illuminated in Renaissance style by Annibale Cellini.

Hall of the Immaculate Conception.
Francesco Podesti (Ancona 1800 – Rome 1895).

THE LIFE OF THE PONTIFF
The Papal tombs

The gradual evolution of papal power – and hence the power of the Roman Catholic Church – is vividly recorded in the earthly 'memorials' of the popes, from the simple *aedicula* of the first Apostle to the tomb slabs and funerary paraphernalia later, which take us through the early persecutions to the times of spiritual and temporal triumph, with all their subsequent crises, doubts, and transformations.

With the firm establishment of the Christian religion, the idea of a simple memorial marking the spot where the believer lay in expectation, developed into a sort of rundown of his past life, of the earthly achievements by which he hoped to merit resurrection. The symbols, initially of the future, became allegories of the past, historical records, albeit illuminated by Divine Wisdom.

The excellence of the papal tombs as a means of comprehensively surveying the enormous spiritual and cultural changes that have taken place in the Western world, under the direct or indirect influence of the Roman Catholic Church, has long been recognized. Numerous studies from Gregorovius on have explored the changing styles of these tombs, from different, complementary points of view: documentary/bibliographical, historical/critical, artistic/iconological. Such analysis is especially fruitful when simply confined to the tombs and monuments in St. Peter's itself. In this ideal gallery, the contrasts are all the more evident, and as a result the different cultural values reflected in these memorials, eloquent records of their respective ages, are highlighted.

AUTHENTICITY OF THE TOMB OF ST. PETER

In 1940 Pius XII ordered excavation work around the *Confessione*, or tomb, of St. Peter, in order to fulfil his predecessor

St. Peter bestowing benediction; this much venerated statue comes from the old basilica and is attributed to Arnolfo di Cambio. In the background, the Chair of St. Peter by Bernini, who also designed the spiral columns of the baldachin.

Pius XI's wish to be buried as close as possible to the Apostle's resting place. Under the Constantinian basilica a pagan necropolis and numerous Christian graves were discovered. Most important of all, however, was a small funerary monument consisting of two niches, one on top of the other, in the middle of a wall (the famous Red Wall), dating from about the middle of the 2nd century AD.

This extremely simple monument must have been held in the utmost veneration from the very earliest years to have justified the considerable amount of construction work, support walls, etc. found there. On the side of the Vatican Hill, on the site of the necropolis, still in use at the time, a solid foundation for a basilica-martyry was laid bare; that it was the primary focal point was clear. One of the most important results of the Vatican excavations was this archaeological proof that the first basilica, erected by Constantine, was a construction *ad corpus*, i.e. built as the tomb of a martyr.

Old manuscripts allow us to reconstruct the appearance of this unpretentious *aedicula* in the center of the transept, in front of the apse. Of particular interest is the existence of a hollow space at the bottom of the monument itself: in the floor of this hollow was a small opening through which an object could be passed in order to touch the ground of a modest-sized cavity beneath. A typical feature of the rites of veneration at martyrs' tombs, this would seem to prove conclusively that this small monument is intimately connected with the tomb of Peter.

While discounting the changes brought about by the wider developments in the Church's worship, the unique importance of this memorial to the first pope is rendered all the greater by the architectural history relating to it. Thus, while in the days of Constantine, St. Peter's was the only cruciform basilica-martyry in Rome and the Near East, the Carolingian renaissance took it as a model for numerous churches. Similarly, the alterations undertaken by Gregory the Great created the prototype for churches where the body of a saint was venerated – even when

the grave did not predate the church.

Due to the great crowds of pilgrims, Pope Gregory the Great transformed the Constantinian basilica (built essentially as a memorial building) into a place suitable for the celebration of the liturgy, by raising the level of the transept by roughly a meter and a half, and making the upper part of the monument into an altar, leaving the lower part still visible by means of a semicircular corridor round the apse. And it was this altar-tomb, presbytery-crypt format that was copied in other martyries; in the same way that the *confessione scoperta* created in St. Peter's by Clement VIII and Paul V constituted the model for similar altars in Roman basilicas.

ABSENCE OF ANY PRECISE PAPAL TRADITION BEFORE 1300

Examining the area where the bodies of the popes were originally laid, Montini, in his work on the papal tombs, distinguishes four main categories: a) the earliest Vatican graveyard, from St. Peter to St. Victor, during the first two centuries; b) the graves from then on until the middle of the 6th century; c) the cemetery *ad Beatum Petrum* of St. Leo the Great, up to our own day; d) the Lateran complex dating mainly from between the 10th and 12th centuries, almost completely destroyed in the fire of 1308.

It may fairly be said, however, that until about 1300 there was no clear, consistent tradition of funerary monuments for the popes. The plain sarcophagi with inscribed epitaphs of the early centuries (to which many popes later were to return, desiring to be buried without pomp in empty urns (e.g. Marcellus II in 1555, at the height of the Renaissance) gave way gradually to substantial monuments. Over the centuries, however, these monuments were destroyed, leaving only a few stones with barely legible inscriptions.

These centuries, during which the Roman papacy slowly came to affirm its authority, were centuries of strife. Political and religious ambitions were virtually indistinguishable, and the supremacy of the Roman Church was continually challenged and reaffirmed. Popes and antipopes followed one another throughout a time of popular uprisings and conflicts between princes and potentates, until the Jubilee of 1300, the first in the history of the Church, proclaimed by Boniface VIII. Of Boniface the 'papophobe' Gregorovius could still write that he was the last great medieval pope, the last prince of the Church, with a vision of the papacy as universally triumphant.

BONIFACE VIII AND THE JUBILEE. ARNOLFO DI CAMBIO AND THE CHAPEL TOMB

Much controversy was aroused by the funerary chapel commissioned from Arnolfo di Cambio by Boniface to house the mortal remains of Boniface IV, and his own tomb when his time should come. Abutting onto the side of the basilica, it projected out from it, in the traditional manner of the day. Above the altar containing the body of Boniface IV was a baldachino or canopy, while Boniface

VIII's sarcophagus was against the back wall, surmounted by a mosaic depicting two saints (possibly Peter and Paul) presenting the pontiff to the Virgin. With the destruction of the old façade for the 'lengthening' of the basilica in 1605, this monument is known to us more through contemporary prints than through the few fragments now stored in the Grotte Vaticane (Vatican Grottoes).

On 22 February 1300 Boniface VIII issued a bull proclaiming the first Holy Year, granting pilgrims to Rome who performed the prescribed devotions the same indulgences and privileges as were earned by going on crusade. The commissioning of this monument from Arnolfo appears to have been one of a number of 'triumphalist' projects, along with the loggia of blessing at St. John Lateran and the bronze statue of St. Peter enthroned (this statue proved to be immensely important in the Jubilee: its peculiar fixed expression and iconlike rigidity enhancing its mystic forcefulness).

The funerary chapel, however, was not actually finished until 1300, and Boniface IV's body was translated there the following year. A still extant inscription which reads, *Hoc opus fecit Arnolphus architectus*, tells us clearly who built this monument even though no definitely recognizable traces of it now remain. Yet one need only look at the sarcophagus itself, with its recumbent figure sculpture, to recognize the characteristic style of Arnolfo at this point of his career. The face of the pope, conveying human emotion in visual terms through a kind of geometric purity, is a fine example of the way Arnolfo created portraits that are not merely descriptive, but are imbued with an inner life of changing individual emotion.

This work may even be seen as representing a vital moment in Arnolfo's career, when he met his old disciple Giotto again in Rome. Work on S. Maria del Fiore in Florence was taken over by Giotto more than twenty years after Arnolfo's death, yet it is in this church that the now aged artist's new understanding of space strikes us most vividly, notwithstanding the subsequent major alterations.

The Jubilee, by setting pilgrimage to Rome on a par with pilgrimage to the Holy Land, reaffirmed and further exalted the medieval concept of papal theocracy, contributing to its ultimate, though far from easy rise to paramountcy; and in a similar way, Arnolfo's new conception of space, already implicit in the funerary monument for Boniface, as it matured and evolved in an interplay of gothic and classical elements, led towards that remarkable feel for spatial values that characterized the Renaissance.

With Boniface VIII the medieval papacy came to an end; at moments during this time the Church had dominated the whole of the Western world. The year 1305 saw the start of the 'Avignon captivity.' And when the popes returned to Rome seventy years later, a historic turning point was reached both for the city of Rome and for the Church. In Germany Huss and Jerome of Prague were developing theories that anticipated the Reformation, while in Italy the local democracies gave way to the tyrants and their families. Rome itself had become a city of ruins.

The tombs of the popes from these early years of the return to Rome were removed from the old basilica when rebuilding took place at the beginning of the 17th century, and several stone slabs now in the Grotte Vaticane (Vatican Grottoes) are still partially recognizable (e.g. the tomb of Innocent VII, 1404–6). The iconography is simple and conventional, with no artistic pretensions, serving as a record rather than a eulogy of a particular individual. Very different, however, is the bronze funerary slab of Martin V in the Lateran: by Simone Chini, a follower of Donatello, it highlights the new precepts of perspective in creating a marvelously lifelike image.

The 15th century, the century of artistic and cultural renaissance, also brought a new era for the papacy which embraced the new trends energetically, becoming the most munificent of patrons. During this period prelates and popes vied with each other in preparing splendid tombs for

themselves, commissioned from the most celebrated masters, initiating the custom (that was to continue down the centuries) of assuring one's own immortality in marble during one's lifetime. Sadly the two most magnificent tombs from this period (those of Nicholas V and Paul II) have both been virtually lost to us. Nicholas's tomb was made for him by followers of the Bregno school. All that remains in the Vatican Grottoes is the sarcophagus of the pope who promoted the study of Greek and the purchase of manuscripts from all over the world, who loved to talk with Filelfo, Valla, and Bracciolini, and who aimed to make the Vatican palace the city of the popes.

PAUL II – THE CONDEMNATION OF HUMANISM

Of Paul II's tomb Vasari wrote that it was then considered the richest sepulcher, in terms of ornamentation and sculptures, ever made for a pope. It has been described by Charles Seymour as the largest and in many ways the most

characteristic walled funerary monument of 15th-century Rome. In a niche or triumphal arch above a sarcophagus bearing a recumbent statue of the dead pope, we see a sculpture of the *Resurrection of Christ* by Dalmata; above, in the lunette, is a *Last Judgement* by Mino da Fiesole and his workshop. To right and left of the sarcophagus rise two columns and pilasters decorated with friezes; the tall base in the center features *Charity* by Mino da Fiesole, and on the sides *The Fall* and the *Creation of Eve* by Giovanni Dalmata; at either end, below the two large columns, are allegories of *Faith* by Mino and *Hope* by Dalmata. The plinth, consisting of two rectangular slabs decorated with putti holding garlands and lions' heads (taken from 2nd- and 3rd-century Dionysiac sarcophagi), is now in the Louvre. Finally, over the arch is a mandorla of *God in Glory*, with four angels at the sides – a collaborative work by Mino da Fiesole and Giovanni Dalmata.

This monument is a testimony to Paul II's strenuous defense of Catholic orthodoxy against the materialistic paganizing influence of such Humanists as Platina and Pomponius Laetus. It is thus a powerful contradiction of the generally accepted idea of this pope's patronage of the arts as completely Humanist, in the style of his 16th-century successors. At the same time it reveals the innovations occurring in Roman art at that time.

Paul II was followed by Sixtus IV, whose ambitious town planning and architectural projects — at once grandiose and demagogic — were a logical continuation of his predecessor's work.

SIXTUS IV — THE MAUSOLEUM

Francesco della Rovere, elected pope under the name Sixtus IV, a diplomat eager for power, was the first to create a princedom for one of his nephews, Girolamo Riario, thereby consolidating the material foundations of the papacy by means of a dynastic monarchic state.

Gregorovius called him the first true papal monarch. However, he was a highly complex character, and this his nephew Giuliano della Rovere (later Pope Julius II) well knew when he commissioned his

The impressive funerary monument to Sixtus IV (opposite) was commissioned by Julius II from Antonio del Pollaiolo. The allegorical representations of the Cardinal and the Theological Virtues (opposite below and right) are: Perspective, Astrology and Music.

uncle's tomb from Pollaiolo – who until then was best known as a goldsmith (e.g. the cross and silver altar frontal in San Giovanni in Florence). In choosing this artist and having confidence in his interpretative imagination, Giuliano showed the same aesthetic flair that made him later commission Michelangelo to finish the Sistine Chapel decoration. Indeed throughout the Renaissance, patrons were swayed more by an artist's personality than by his specialist genre.

The bronze tomb of Sixtus IV, today in the St. Peter's Treasury, can be described as a sort of low pyramid-type base, or tumulus, on a thin green marble plinth. On top is the portrait sculpture of the pope, with his insignia and the theological and cardinal virtues; the concave sides of the pyramid feature reliefs of the liberal arts, here used for the first time, derived from the Petrarchesque tomb of Roberto il Saggio (in Santa Chiara, Naples), in place of the *pleurants* of Burgundy. The figure of the pope, with the face given particular prominence, through the head being raised on two cushions, is stylistically reminiscent of that of Martin V, but dating from some sixty years later it is more realistic in its vigorous plasticity.

At each corner are the arms of Sixtus and Julius, while the panel above the pontiff's head contains an allegory of *Charity, Hope* and *Faith* flank it, and the *Cardinal Virtues* follow along the sides. Compared with the first figures, the style along the sides is distinctly more mature, and clearly reflects the influence of Ghiberti's *Door of Paradise* as well as classical inspiration, and close ties with the drapery of the angels on Verrocchio's Forteguerri monument (now in the Louvre). What is new here is the subtle interplay between the figures, which creates a sense of rhythmic movement around the tomb. At the same time the seven liberal arts (become ten, for reasons of spatial harmony) constitute a precise visual exposition of late-medieval ideas concerning human knowledge and divine revelation. This rather gives the lie to the normal vision of Sixtus IV as a Humanist in the mold of Pius II.

An ardent Franciscan in his youth, at the time of his election as pope, Sixtus adopted the Humanist mantle as a way of showing that he was culturally 'with-it.' Yet when he died his library was found to contain the *Decretals* and Aristotle's *Physics* and *Metaphysics*, and Averroes's commentary on Aristotle's *De Coelo*, and mainly works by Franciscan theologians; not a line of Plato's or of neoplatonist philosophy.

The tomb was first sited in the Choir Chapel, built by Sixtus himself on the south of the old basilica (but then demolished in 1605). The apse of this chapel had a fresco by Perugino, depicting the Virgin and Child, with Sixtus being presented by St. Peter; the pope, kneeling in adoration, was flanked on one side by St. Francis and on the other by St. Paul and St. Anthony of Padua. The inlaid floor and the walls were adorned with the della Rovere arms.

Thus the chapel, chosen by Sixtus as his last resting place, was in fact a veritable mausoleum, with the tomb in the middle, near the altar. Perugino's fresco established a convention of intercessional paintings, employed on numerous 14th- and 15th-century funerary monuments. Such a tomb, in a recently built chapel sumptuously decorated with the arms of the papal family, with imperial overtones suggested by the incorporation of two late-classical porphyry reliefs, was indisputably a monument to a man who considered himself as much a prince of this world as of the Church, and who combined the spirit of Scholasticism with typically Renaissance self-assertion. The reality represented by the sculptures carries the mind to Savonarola's *Apologeticus*: the della Rovere arms are the perfect realization of what the reforming friar preached in 1496 against the Florentines and the late 15th century generally: '... you will raise up your own arms, and for your own honor, not for the honor of God.'

INNOCENT VIII AND MANNERIST HUMANISM

According to Vasari, only two monuments passed from the old to the new basilica: those of Sixtus IV and Innocent VIII, both by Pollaiolo. Innocent died while work was still in progress on Sixtus's tomb, and his nephew commissioned the same Tuscan artists to make the new tomb, which was completed in 1498. This second monument is in a way more conventional. Pollaiolo here adopts the style of the Angevin tombs in Naples, with two figures, one seated, the other recumbent. Initially built into the east wall of the transept, the tomb was moved to its present position in 1621, at which date, by some curious working of the baroque mind, the sarcophagus (originally occupying the console projecting between the seated figure and the crowning lunette) was put underneath.

As the composition was conceived, the Virtues were divided into Cardinal (beside the pope on his throne) and Theological (in the lunette, watching over the sleeping figure on the sarcophagus). For the former, designs made for Sixtus IV's tomb were used (as was customary in Pollaiolo's workshop), consisting basically of a series of variants of the theme of a seated figure holding an object in each hand. There is greater concern for originality in the Theological Virtues, which acquire certain iconographical attributes normally associated with funerary lunettes such as representations of the Madonna and Child, with angels and saints hovering over the recumbent figure on the sarcophagus; hence *Charity*, in the middle, and *Faith* and *Hope* on either side are borne up on clouds supported by cherubs.

The key to understanding the monument, however, is in the marked contrast between the two portraits of the pope, alive and dead. The head of the pontiff enthroned is full of vitality and character, as if worked up from a drawing made in his lifetime; the other is rigid and immobile, and was probably taken from a death mask. To the traditional wall tomb Pollaiolo adds the equally traditional pontiff *in cattedra*, giving his blessing – a popular type of statue all over Italy since the end of the 13th century, erected to commemorate visits or special papal privileges.

In his left hand Innocent VIII holds a singularly precious relic: the spearhead of Longinus, which had pierced the side of Christ, and which he had received a few months before his death from the Sultan Bajazet, and had preserved until the last in his own private apartment. This relic, so triumphantly exhibited, leads one to reflect on the significance of the pontificate of Pope Innocent VIII (which saw the alliance of the barons, and the culminating victory of Ferdinand of Aragon over the Moors, the geographical discoveries of Dias, and the Inquisition). The evident conviction here is that the greater the temporal conquests, the greater the triumph of the Church as a whole. This assumption finds expression in the rehandling of traditional formats; and this new synthesis itself became the prototype for future monuments of the kind, from della Porta to Bernini and through to Canova – all confidently exalting the mission of the Church in the temporal world.

PAUL III – THE MONUMENT IN ECLIPSE

This Farnese pope was a representative of two distinct yet mutually related trends of his time: on the one hand that of temporal concern, the affirmation of the Church on earth, and above all the accession of his own family to earthly power; and on the other that of spiritual reawakening according to severe principles, entailing combat against heresy, both internal and external. And in exactly the same way his funerary monument, reflecting both worlds simultaneously, had from the very first aroused diametrically conflicting opinions.

While Paul III was still alive, Guglielmo della Porta had suggested an isolated, pyramidal tomb, almost a chapel in itself, to be placed proudly in the middle of the apse. However, the opposition of numerous culturally prominent people (including Michelangelo) led to a reduction in its size, with only two of the four originally planned allegorical statues being allowed to remain by the tomb. The other two were transported to the Palazzo Farnese

Under Michelangelo's supervision Guglielmo della Porta executed the mausoleum for Paul III which occupies the left-hand niche of the apse. The monument was originally in the right-hand niche, but was displaced by order of Urban VIII to make room for his own tomb which he had commissioned from Bernini. The original design included two other statues representing Peace and Plenty as well as the existing ones of Justice and Prudence, which are thought to have been modeled on, respectively, the pope's sister, Giulia Farnese, and his mother.

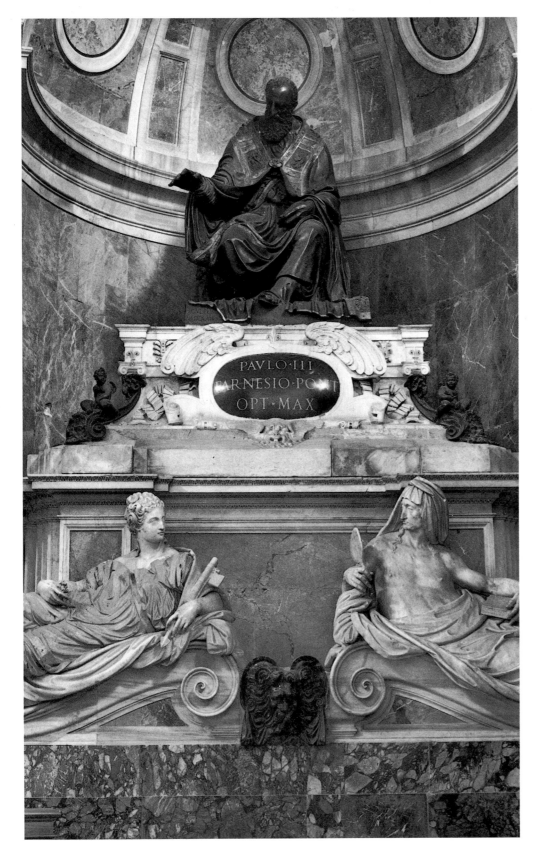

when the monument was moved in 1599.

Now in the alcove to the left of the apse in St. Peter's, where Urban VIII had it placed in 1628, Paul III's monument is a fine and important work even in its unfinished state. Elements borrowed from Michelangelo's Medici Chapel sculptures are fused into an anticipation of baroque sculpture. Similar in overall conception to Michelangelo's first plans for Julius II's tomb, which likewise was reduced (though with less trauma) to a mere hint of the complex original design.

Enthroned on the white marble sarcophagus, the bronze sculpture of the pope shows an old man, bowed by weight of years, wearing a cloak and pallium (though oddly, bareheaded), slowly raising his right hand in blessing. The inscription on a black background below reads simply: *Paulo III Farnesio Pont. Opt. Max.* The throne is decorated with the Farnese fleur-de-lys. On the sides are four bronze bas-reliefs: *Hope* and *Faith* on the left, and *Temperance* and *Strength* on the right, with, between them, swags and masks of obviously antique inspiration. Colored veins streak the dark marble plinth, and between this and the sarcophagus, on its sculpted scrolls, are two white marble allegorical figures, *Justice* and *Prudence* (the former, originally naked, like Michelangelo's *Dawn*, was clothed in a false cloak in 1595, an indication of a major point of tension between the Church and artists during the Counter Reformation: the respectability or otherwise of the nude, which Humanist assertion of man's dignity and archaeological discoveries had made generally acceptable).

This tomb seems intended as a deliberate point of reference: the self-control of gesture and expression appear almost cold and stiff compared with the expressive exuberance of Baroque, which was the product of the progressive rationalization of the human spirit and also of man's increased awareness of the Godhead without any external intermediary or guide, beyond the individual's capacity for rational thought. That capacity was the last fruit of Renaissance culture, yet it

The funerary monument of Gregory XIII, by
Camillo Rusconi, was commissioned by Clement
XI, Rusconi drawing his inspiration from
Algardi's tomb for Leo XI. The bas-reliefs on the
sarcophagus, flanked by the allegorical
representations of Religion and Courage, allude to
the reform of the calendar by Gregory XIII in
1582.

is here expressed, paradoxically, in a
manner we now think of as typically
baroque – through exploration of color
effects, and the accentuated realism of the
figure of the pontiff.

URBAN VIII – THE VITALITY OF DEATH

It is quite obvious that della Porta's tomb
of Paul III influenced the design of Urban
VIII's tomb by Bernini. As mentioned
above, the Farnese monument was posi-
tioned in the alcove to the left of the apse
at the same time as Borromini was working
on the application of the marble. This was
in 1629, during the first phase of Bernini's
grand project, when the master himself
must have been in charge. And the style of
Urban VIII's tomb clearly had to reflect
that of the monument with which it was
paired, rather than of the papal tombs in
Santa Maria Maggiore, which were
chronologically closer.

   Nevertheless, the differences between
the two tombs are enormous. Not only are
they unlike in construction (the two
Virtues reclining on the scrolls in that of
Paul III, while in that of Urban VIII they
stand either side of the setback sarcophagus almost outside the alcove), they
differ above all in a profound shift of
sensibility, which is particularly notice-
able in the respective treatment of the
borrowings from Michelangelo's Medici
tombs. Then again in the Bernini monument, the Virtues are no longer absolute
symbolic, and therefore abstract, entities;
they are alive spatially as well as morally,
and mediate between the pope and the
faithful. Even the choice of materials for
the various compositional elements:
bronze for the pope, the sarcophagus, and
the figure of Death, marble for the allegorical figures, enhances their separate value
in mutually beneficial effects of contrast.

   Taken as a whole, there is the same
fusion of commemorative monument and
personal tomb that Pollaiolo achieved, in a
completely different cultural context, in
the tomb of Innocent VIII. The 'supra-
personal memorial' (the triumph of the
pontiff) is indistinguishable from the
'personal tomb' (the weary gesture in-

179

dicating human weakness). The monumental becomes something everyday at the same time: the natural world intrudes, albeit with a certain element of the supernatural. Death writing the inscription – a vigorous, immediate vision replacing the somewhat banal epigraph plaque – is a triple allusion: to Fame, to History, and to the dead pope's own literary activities – Urban, meditating on the transitoriness of human existence, once wrote of a *nigra mors alata* (black-winged Death).

LEO XI – THE DYNASTIC MONUMENT

Algardi's first important work executed in Rome, the tomb of Leo XI, is by no means a mere duplicate of Bernini's tomb of Urban VIII watered down with classicism; it is immediately recognizable as a Medicean monument with its own iconography and stylistic traditions. Yet comparison with Urban VIII's monument is helpful in that it invites subtle criticism of the violently dramatic movement and constant echoing and doubling back of themes that typify Bernini's conception. And while Algardi's drawing in the National Gallery of Scotland (showing the pope making a more pronounced gesture, and incorporating two scrolls and a skull) makes it seem likely that Bernini influenced him, the inverse seems no less probable (i.e. that

Algardi influenced Bernini in his simplification of his original ideas for the monument to the Countess Matilda (*c.*1630); his influence seems even clearer in the base decorative motifs in the Capella Raymondi in San Pietro in Montorio).

Algardi was from the outset bound by his contract for the tomb of Leo XI (1634) to use white marble: the statue of the pope

Above left: the image of Urban VIII over his tomb, the work of Bernini. Center: Charity, a detail from the monument of Innocent XII, by Filippo Valle after designs by Fuga. Opposite: the marble statue from the tomb of Leo XI by Algardi.

giving his blessing, seated above the urn containing his body, with two figures beside the urn representing Magnanimity and Liberality; on the pedestals the pope's emblem in relief (a bouquet of roses), a relief depicting two scenes on the front of the urn, and two small putti holding up a curtain at the top of the arch above the alcove.

Identification of the left-hand Virtue with Athena is justified not only by Algardi's own restoration of the *Athena* now in the Museo delle Terme, but above all by Leo X Medici's identification of himself with the goddess Minerva as protector of the arts.

Panofsky links the allegory of Liber-

ality, one of this sculptor's finest works, following faithfully the iconography of Ripa, with the Medicean Generosity in the San Lorenzo tombs. The inclusion in the contract for the tomb of the two relief scenes depicting episodes in the pope's life would appear to have been prompted by the similar reliefs on the tombs of the Medici Popes Leo X and Clement VII, rather than by Bernini's use of relief on the Countess Matilda monument.

Iconographically the tomb only makes sense within the context of the traditional formulas used by the Medici family, to which it is essentially a tribute. Over and above this, however, it stands out as a fine work of art in its own right.

Algardi had studied in Bologna with the brothers Carracci, and he seems especially close here to Annibale's *Madonna and Child with St. John and St. Catherine* (Bologna, Pinacoteca Civica) in the uniform size of the figure and in the parallel compositional planes, equidistant between the classicism of Duquesnoy and the baroque dialectic of Bernini.

ALEXANDER VII AND THE VALUE OF PRAYER

Alexander VII's tomb in St. Peter's was commissioned by himself, but was not executed until after his death, between 1671 and 1678. The substantial differences that distinguish it from Bernini's tomb for

181

The tomb of Alexander VII Chigi. This monumental work was executed by Bernini between 1672 and 1678 with the help of various assistants. The figures of Justice, Prudence, Charity and Truth kneel in prayer at the feet of the pope, while Death holds up an hourglass at the same time lifting the edges of the rich shroud, as if to invite the dead man to enter into eternal life. Opposite: two details from the monument to Clement XIII by Canova, executed between 1787 and 1792. Left: the praying pope; and right: the spirit of death at the entrance to the sacellum.

Urban VIII are summed up in the figures of the respective popes. Where Urban was triumphant, Alexander VII, *servus servorum Dei* (servant of the servants of God), kneels in prayer.

If the religion of the early Bernini was, as Calvesi has described it, a religion of the imagination, imbued with the pantheistic ideology and cosmic naturalism of Giordano Bruno, which found in the words of Ignatius of Loyola the means of possessing God, then towards the end of the century it became a religion at once full of drama, yet informed with the total resignation of faith. His style became even more 'Spanish,' standing ground at the crossroads of popular taste and courtly invention, between the mystic experience of the initiate, and appeal to the mass.

Alexander VII, deep in prayer, no longer wears the *triregno* (papal diadem) that Urban VIII is shown wearing. The choice of materials underlines the living essence of the sculpture. The Virtues and the pope are in marble, and only the skeleton is in bronze. There is nothing supernatural about the pope, he is a living person surrounded by living beings (the Virtues), of whom there are now four rather than two; their function being to give movement to the composition, so that it changes according to the angle from

which it is seen; yet at the same time they also simply represent a crowd around the figure of the pope. Where the Virtues on Urban VIII's tomb represent the idealized characteristics of his pontificate, here they appear as the characteristics of the individual human being to whom they turn with interest and gratitude.

Death belongs to another world, it issues from the tomb and is separated from Life by a shroud. Rising up, hourglass in hand, it seems to assume the conventional role of destroyer, rather than vindicator as on the Urban VIII monument. On Alexander's tomb the group of the virtues of Charity and, at their side, Justice and Prudence, are accompanied by Truth who, though not strictly a Virtue, is according to Thomas Aquinas *objectum vel finis virtutis*, the object or end of virtue. Panofsky sees the prominence of Truth (originally further emphasized by her being naked, unlike the Virtues) as a personal reference to the latter years of the pope's life, which saw the dashing of his hopes of asserting the authority of the Holy See over Louis XIV, and of an alliance of all the Christian nations against the Turks.

The figure of Death, so intriguingly placed at the same level as the sun of Truth, can also be interpreted in the same

light. The hourglass now therefore becomes an allusion not only to time as mortality, but also to time as the discoverer of Truth. The yellow shroud covering Death's head is to be understood, not as contemporary biographers of Bernini saw it (shame at having deprived the world of so great a pope), but as the banishment of death itself, though not its hourglass, to obscurity, just as the moon is driven into invisibility by the sun, by a power even greater than that of the Virtues, by the sun of Truth.

This solemn monument thus also carries a prophetic message: the tomb remains triumphant. Fagiolo is right in insisting on the portrayal of prayer as the sole way to salvation. The door of the grave yawns wide in the foreground, and Death itself has become entangled in the very shroud it seeks to raise. But raising our eyes we see the catharsis of prayer, and the heavens, like an apsidal vaulting, in which the golden stars of the Chigi pope's crest proclaim the final salvation of the just man.

After Bernini, according to Panofsky, tomb sculptors found themselves on the horns of a dilemma, or rather a 'trilemma': how to steer a passage between pomposity, sentimentality, and deliberate archaism.

PIVS · VI · BRASCHIVS · CAESENAS
ORATE · PRO · EO

for the figure of the pope. However, a totally new and brilliant innovation is the oblique stance of the figure within the pyramidal composition.

Here the pope is no longer on the central axis, and the allegories do not follow the usual iconographical scheme. The tomb was obviously designed to be seen as a complete entity from the side; the orientation of the realistic dragon (from the Boncompagni crest) further confirms this.

Courage lifts the pallium covering the sarcophagus with a broad gesture, creating a diagonal line linking the allegory with the pope. This composition, suggested to the sculptor by the restricted space available for a frontal view of the monument, is a deliberate attempt to achieve a sort of 'glancing impact' in a genre that would at first sight appear better suited to full-frontal, meditative reflection. As a synthesis of various classically 'corrected' baroque devices, this work was something of a turning point. With the tomb of Gregory XIII a new assumption of the attitude of the faithful to such monuments appears; at the same time the allegorical figures have acquired life of their own, beyond that of their significant placing about the deceased pope.

During the course of the 17th century the political power of the papacy had gradually declined. And in that respect this remarkably coherent assembly of sculptures takes on political hues – here too the process of decline shows up. The imperiousness of the pontiffs' gestures lessens progressively, so that with Filippo della Valle's tomb of Innocent XII (1691–1700), realized in 1746 according to a design by Ferdinando Fuga, we are shown a frail old man, hardly more than a symbolic head of the Church, inspired by the dramatic forcefulness of Bernini's Alexander VII, yet rendered stiff and immobile in an all too 'genteel' rococo serenity.

Alexander VII's tomb also influenced another pupil of Rusconi's, Pietro Bracci, who in 1759 sculpted the tomb of Benedict XIV (1740–58). A new and slightly curious feature here is that the pope is shown

GREGORY XIII – CLASSICISM AND BAROQUE

Throughout the 18th century the papal tombs provided the clearest and most important sculptural evidence of the profound spiritual and cultural changes that were occurring in society. Pierre Etienne Monnot's tomb of Innocent XI (1676–89), erected in 1704 in the alcove opposite Algardi's tomb of Leo XI, combines aspects of the styles of both Algardi and Bernini; in its manipulation of different colors and materials it turns to Urban VIII, while in its 'narrative' quality and handling of allegory it turns to Leo XI. The difference between the early and the later phases of Baroque is here evinced by the extra importance given to the decorative elements, at the expense of the figures.

Observations of a similar kind apply to

the tomb of Alexander VIII (1691–1725) by Angelo De Rossi which, while it copies the basic format of the Urban VIII monument, introduces a tall pedestal for the sculpture of the pope; this pedestal bears an elaborate relief, thus considerably reducing the scale of the figures and completely altering the equilibrium of the architectonic and decorative features.

Camillo Rusconi's monument to Gregory XIII, which stands in the right wing, symmetrically in line with Monnot's work (after a design by Maratta), reveals the profound influence of Bernini while also incorporating common elements from Algardi and Monnot. The allegories and their positioning on scrolls derives from the tomb of Innocent XI, while echoes of Leo XI's are discernible in the exclusive use of white marble, the trapezoidal sarcophagus, and the absence of a pedestal

standing, leaning with his left arm against the arm of the throne, his right hand raised in blessing. The treatment of the base is unmistakably Berninian: in its division into two sections by means of a portal and the urn constituting the pedestal for the statue of the pope. By contrast, the symmetrical arrangement of the three figures in the niche, forming a rhythmic bilateral composition, reveals an imaginative world very different from that of Baroque; and though the erect figure of the pope gives a new longitudinal uplift to the conventional pyramidal format, nevertheless overall, with the figures of Holy Wisdom and Selflessness, a certain faltering is detectable: the balance between baroque impulse and classical restraint, evident in the best works of this period, is no longer sure.

CLEMENT XIII – THE EMERGENCE OF NEOCLASSICISM

The funerary monument of Pope Clement XIII Rezzonico, commissioned by his nephew from Canova, came slowly into being between 1787 and 1791. A classical version of the traditional pyramid composition, it is in white Carrara marble throughout, except for the travertine lions of the base and the fire-marble plinth. Canova was here clearly interested less in the *chiaroscuro* play of masses than in pictorial effects: the subtle color values of the sculpture (for which he actually executed a painted model directly on site). Initially he had thought of a circular tomb with a central doorway; in the end, however, he settled on this linear composition, with its constant striving after a 'geometrical absolute' (typical of Canova's work) representing the abstract dimension of eternity and the mystery of death.

His use of allegories is very different from the baroque conception of allegory. Faith Triumphant and the Angel of Death are closer to the lions of the base than to the pope, and both in feel as well as in composition seem to inhabit a completely different sphere. The baroque convention of conveying abstract concepts by means of figures has completely disappeared.

What we find now is a by no means 'heroic' statue of the pope, the guardian of the Faith, sunk in prayer. Again now, there is no longer any attempt to give a historical account of the man. Canova does not record the past, he conveys it symbolically through a realistic depiction of the pontiff at a precise, significant moment.

Even the basic religious assumptions are profoundly different. The baroque sculptor's certainty of resurrection is replaced by Canova's own conviction that a believer can do no more than hope and pray. In the Alexander VII monument, Death is made less frightening by being caught up in a thoroughly real shroud, and for Bernini, salvation and eternal life are certainties. Canova accepts death with melancholy Christian resignation. Clement XIII is no blessed being already ascended into heaven, but a man praying at the threshold between the earthly world and the world beyond. Bernini had done his utmost to abolish the distinctions between these two worlds; Canova insists that the Kingdom of Heaven cannot be represented through the language of space and time, and tends to make clear that in the next world such concepts of time and space have no validity.

This last conjunction of the figurative arts with Roman Catholicism in the specific field of papal tomb sculpture is really a return to first sources. For it was in the Greco-Roman artistic idiom (now rediscovered by Neoclassicism) that the repertoire of Catholic iconography originated. Canova's sculpture represents one of the most typical and most explicit aspects of this 'rediscovered' style.

FROM PIUS VII TO PIUS XII – THE AGE OF MEDIOCRITY

In his will the Secretary of State, Cardinal Consalvi, stipulated that in the event of Canova's death the tomb of the Chiaramonti pope should be sculpted by Thorwaldsen. This monument, placed *in situ* in 1831, cannot be said to be one of its creator's best works. Despite no fewer than thirty-seven preparatory sketches, the bust of Pius VII (also by Thorwaldsen)

has far greater spontaneity and human warmth than the pope giving his blessing on his funerary monument. Perhaps due to miscalculation of the size of the area where the monument was to be placed, the composition appears decidedly 'bitty,' lacking in overall unity. The allegories of Divine Wisdom and Divine Strength are aridly stereotyped, without even a trace of that down-to-earthness that frequently redeems such statues.

Once the possibilities of the neoclassical revival had been exhausted (a process intimately affected by the state of European politics, alternating from moral renewal according to the tenets of the Enlightenment to the propaganda mentality of Napoleon's 'return to order'), the gap between the Roman Catholic Church and the mainstream of artistic developments widened even further. The art of the society formed by the French Revolution was preeminently secular.

Religion of course continued to find authentic artistic expression even in the vastly altered society of the 19th century; yet what disappeared entirely were the Judaeo-Christian assumptions as formulated in the Counter Reformation. Roman Catholic art meanwhile refused to participate in the increasingly varied and complex evolution of the aesthetic consciousness, thus lagging behind 'history' and shutting itself up in academic formulae that reveal ever greater paucity of real motivation or genuine interest in the artistic imagination. The result was a kind of collage of different principles and theories, none of them related to anything that could remotely be termed 'real life.'

In the present century this gap between the Church and the visual arts has continued to deepen, notwithstanding certain extremely sincere efforts to remedy the situation, e.g. the architect Di Fausto and the sculptor Astorri's collaboration on the monument to Pius X (1903–14), or the calculated professionalism of the very able Pietro Canonica in the monument to Benedict XV (1914–22), completed in 1928, where the banality of the symbolism in the great bronze relief at the bottom is in no way relieved by the

The bronze statue of Pius XII by Francesco Messina.

cold figure of the kneeling pope. The book on the cushion, a reference to the promulgation of the Codex of Canon Law, is yet one more erudite allusion that, far from enlivening the composition, gives it a frigid didacticism. What lacks here is an overall vision and presentation of this individual pope's personality.

An important feature of these recent funerary monuments is that the actual tomb – a simple sarcophagus or urn with a recumbent figure of the pope – is situated in the crypt (the Grotte Vaticane), hence making the monument in the basilica merely commemorative. There is therefore a certain split here: between recollection and prayer in the Grotte on the one hand, and on the other the gratification of earthly homage in the splendor of the historic basilica.

This specifically 'memorial' function of the more recent monuments in St. Peter's perhaps in the end accounts for some of the best of the modern work. With the directly religious function safely out of the way, Popes Pius XII (by Francesco Messina) and John XXIII (by Emilio Greco) are once again just men – men of faith, indeed even of symbolic nature, but not the incarnations of a 'universal' power beyond distinctions of spiritual and material reality.

Messina's monument to Pius XII actually embodies this change of attitude, as the marble and the *triregno* of the first project were transformed into the more taxing medium of bronze and the less grandiose symbol of the cardinal's hat. It is as though the sculptor wished to complement Pius's attempts to revive the 'spiritual monarchy' of, say, Urban VIII or Sixtus V with explicit recognition of the events of history and the traumatic experiences of an entire generation.

Zeri indeed rightly observes that the somberness of this bronze and its ambitious, free composition, supported by a rigorously formal discipline, express the violent contradictions between paternalistic intentions and proud aristocratic rejection: the gesture of blessing, and the contracted hand through which it is conveyed.

THE PALACES AND GARDENS
The Vatican as a secular palace

Two events in the Carolingian era secured the Vatican's position as a politico-religious center and citadel: the coronation of Charlemagne in 800 and the response to the sack of the city by the Saracens in 846, in the construction of the Leonine walls.

Previously the Vatican had been almost exclusively a spiritual center, as the shrine or Trophy (*Trofeo*) of Peter and at the same time the 'great hall' of Christ. The basilica was originally a commemorative building rather than a place of worship, built around the tomb (the altar was not raised until c.600). Like St. John Lateran, St. Peter's was dedicated to Christ the Savior, as a *monumentum* for the victory of 312; in the mosaic of the triumphal arch, Constantine, presented by Peter, offers a model of the basilica to Christ (*Quod duce te mundus surrexit ad astra triumphans / hanc Constantinus victor tibi condidit aulam*, that the world might be raised to the stars under your command, the victor Constantine on this triumphant occasion has founded this hall in your honor).

The foundation ceremony was lofty and edifying in character. According to the *Liber Pontificalis*, the 'thirteenth Apostle,' Constantine, took the founding shovel and shifted twelve loads of earth in honor of the twelve Apostles. The work of filling in the already existing necropolis and leveling the hillside were to be seen as a symbol of the stupendous task of founding the Church on the Petrine Rock: even materially, the basilica was built on the ruins of the former civilization, and it is significant that the only remaining momento of the buried necropolis should be the Trophy of Peter.

Above the tomb Constantine had a baldachino erected, for which he donated the columns (decorated with a vine motif, they were said to have come from the Temple of Solomon). This canopy or *pergula* was at once a symbol of imperial

protection, an evocation of the vault of heaven (a lamp in the shape of a golden crown was hung over the tomb, like the sun in the sky), and an image of the mystic vine of Christ.

At times the Vatican had served, and would continue to do so, as an alternative site or place of refuge, sometimes as the seat of antipopes or popes assailed either from within or without, or simply as a retreat away from the more populous sections of Rome. The Vatican was also eminently suited for the reception of a Frankish king and his court: situated at the end of the *ruga francigena* or *rue de France*, it was appropriately placed to welcome pilgrims to the tomb of the Apostle, without their having to cross the Tiber or wend their way through a city that had so often been entered by armed bands and opposing factions. Contemporary sources mention a *palatium* or palace of Charlemagne in the Vatican, possibly on the site of the present Camposanto Teutonico. This could have been a preexisting building used as a temporary lodging for prelates and illustrious guests.

When in 846 the Saracens reached the very gates of Rome, and sacked the Vatican basilica, previously spared by the 'barbarian' Alaric, Leo IV deemed it no longer possible to delay building the defenses which one of his predecessors had already planned at the beginning of the century (this was Leo III, the pope who crowned Charlemagne). The walls were to enclose the whole area on the other side of the Tiber, from Castel Sant'Angelo to the Vatican: A small independent city, the *Civitas Leonina*, emerged as a result. The walls (which had four gates) were begun in 847 and solemnly consecrated on 27 June 853. Thus the Vatican became a fortress of the Faith.

On the military front meanwhile, the infidel Saracens were driven back at the battle of Ostia (849), and in 880 a second citadel was created around the tomb of the Apostle Paul, and named Giovannipoli ('Johnopolis') after John VIII. Only now did it become possible to create a stable residence at the Vatican. The *Civitas Leonina*, however, was to remain isolated

from Rome proper for some centuries.

Major building work was carried out during the 13th century, of which Redig De Campos has made a reconstruction. Records dating from 1208 reveal that Innocent III erected new buildings for the Curia as well as service facilities. Part of the work must have been a *palatium*, with a turreted precinct added to the Leonine walls (one tower is still traceable by the chapel of Nicholas V). This strongly fortified center, conceived by the same pope who ordered the building of the most powerful of medieval fortresses, the Torre dei Conti, protected the Vatican basilica which now began to outshine the Lateran in terms of primacy. Attesting to this fact is the mosaic in the apse of St. Peter's, which shows Innocent III conferring upon the Vatican basilica the title hitherto reserved for San Giovanni, 'Mother and Glory of all Churches.'

Another pope from one of the great Roman families, Pope Nicholas III Orsini (1277–80), was responsible not only for major new buildings, but also for the decision to take up permanent residence in the Vatican (only during the summer months did he move to the Lateran).

With the *Civitas Leonina* thus securely fortified, the palace became more and more the focal point, as to deserve the title, a 'palace in the form of a city.'

Among the architects who worked in the Vatican at this time were the Dominicans Fra Sisto and Fra Ristoro, the builders of Santa Maria Novella in Florence, who were called to Rome for the construction of the mother church of the Minerva.

Now, as extra protection, the *palatium* was joined up with the mausoleum of Hadrian and the Leonine defense wall became a bridge passage (*passetto*), a safe corridor linking the Vatican and the castle. Everywhere imposing buildings arose, recalling the splendors of the ancient city, their interiors of a breathtaking magnificence: the *aula secunda* (part of the Sala Ducale) and the *aula magna vel prima* (later the Sala Regia). A new Palatine Chapel was built on the site of the future Sistine Chapel.

The obelisk and a section of Bernini's colonnade against the background of the apostolic palace.

Among other outstanding new structures were the Logge (later either incorporated into or pulled down for the Bramantesque Logge di San Damaso), perhaps the first Vatican 'belvedere,' the pope's answer to the buildings of the old Capitol (the galleried *Tabularium*) and of the modern Campidoglio (the logge of the Palazzo Senatorio). Such a gesture may have been felt necessary because the pope had taken over the office of senator for life, uniting in his own person not only the powers spiritual and temporal, but also the 'third power,' the municipal. The senator-pope thus manifested his authority in the three key points of Rome's sacred axis: the Vatican, the Capitol (where successive senator-popes restruc-

First story

3, 4 Borgia Rooms
5 Museo Sacro
6, 7 Vatican Library
9 Museo Profano
12 Egyptian Museum
13 Museo Pio Clementino
14 Museo Chiaramonti
15 Galleria Lapidaria

Second story

1 Sistine Chapel
2 The Raphael Loggia
3, 4 Raphael Rooms
3 Cappella Niccolina
4 Hall of the Immaculate Conception
6 Gallery of Maps
8, 9 Gallery of Tapestries
10 Sala della Biga
11 Pinacoteca Vaticana
12, 13 Etruscan Museum

Cortile della Pigna

Cortile della Biblioteca

Cortile del Belvedere

Cortile di San Damaso

Corridore del Bernini

St. Peter's Square

St. Peter's

1 Charlemagne's statue
2 *Navicella* mosaic
3 Constantine's statue
4 Porta del Filarete
5 Cappella della Pietà
6 Monument of the Stuarts
7 Innocent XII's monument
8 Chapel of the Blessed Sacrament
9 Gregory XIII's monument
10 Innocent VIII's monument
11 Leo XI's monument
12 Cappella Clementina
13 Cappella Gregoriana
14 Clement XIII's monument
15 Alexander VII's monument
16 Paul II's monument
17 St. Peter's Chair
18 Urban VIII's monument

Porta Santa

Scala Regia

Above: plan of present-day St. Peter's with some of the chapels and monuments. Left: overall plan of the Basilica, Vatican buildings, museums, etc. Below: showing the modern link up between St. Peter's and Castel Sant'Angelo. Opposite: general ground plan of the state within a state – the Vatican City – a mixture of the glories of the past and the marvels of the present.

St. Peter's

1 Sistine Chapel
2 Cortile della Sentinella
3 Cortile del Maresciallo
4 Cortile dei Pappagalli
5 Cortile di San Damaso
6 Cortile Triangolo
7 Museums
8 Cortile Ottagono
9 Pinacoteca Vaticana
10 Casina di Pio IV
11 Fontana dell'Aquilone
12 Fontana del Sacramento
13 Palazzo del Governatorato
14 Cappella di Santa Marta
15 Seminario etiopico
16 Grotta di Lourdes
17 Vatican Radio
18 Railway station
19 Church of St. Stephen
20 Palazzo del tribunale

21 Palazzo San Carlo
22 Palazzo Santa Marta
23 Sacristy and Treasury
24 German College and Cemetery
25 Audience chamber

Cortile della Pigna

Cortile del Belvedere

St. Peter's

St. Peter's Square

Borgo Pio

Castel Sant'Angelo

St. Peter's Square

Piazza Pio XII

Via dei Corridori

Borgo Sant'Angelo

Piazza Pia

Via della Conciliazione

Lungotevere Castello

Lungotevere Vaticano

Ponte Sant'Angelo

Borgo Santo Spirito

tured the Ara Coeli as a palatine church), and the Lateran (where Nicholas III rebuilt, among other projects, the Sancta Sanctorum chapel).

Besides the fortress-city aspect, there must also be mentioned the garden aspect when, across the Tiber, beside St. Peter's, a villa-palace began to take shape; and in later centuries the Vatican was to become, so to speak, another Domus Aurea, Nero's Golden House, (the Circus and the Naumachia had kept the memory of Nero alive in the quarter).

In the view of Rome by Fra Paolino da Venezia (1323), Nicholas III's *hortus conclusus* in fact appears to be represented through archetypes of the Domus Aurea and the Circus. The elongated open area, similar to a classical circus in shape, has a row of buildings in the middle, around which animals were pursued on foot or from horseback, the whole tableau resembling a hunting scene from antiquity. This is the first illustration of the Vatican park, or 'wood' or 'belvedere,' which extended to the northern edge of the hill, where Innocent VIII was later to build the villa-belvedere, looking out across the Roman *campagna*, and repeating the loggia style

introduced by Nicholas III.

To arrive at the next major period of development in the history of the *palatium* we must now jump almost three centuries, to the projects (not all of them carried to fruition) of three great popes between the middle of the 15th century and the beginning of the 16th: Nicholas V, Sixtus IV, and Julius II, all of whom coincidentally came from Liguria, from whence also came Innocent VIII.

After the 'Babylonian captivity' of Avignon, the first decades of the papacy's return to Rome were far from easy, and it was against a background of schisms, sedition, and political wrangling that the ambitions of Nicholas V (very few of which were ever realized) invested the papacy with an imperial mentality.

According to one of the pope's biographers, the *palatium* on the Vatican Hill 'would have sufficed for one of those Roman emperors who ruled the whole world.' The vastness of the buildings actually constructed, and even more of those that never got beyond the drawing board, would, according to the panegyric of Giannozzo Manetti, have exceeded the seven wonders of the ancient world

(which included two Roman buildings: the Capitol and the Temple of Hadrian at Cyzicus), and measured well with the two wonders of the Bible, the temple and palace of Solomon. Indeed the same biographer, in lauding the 'objective' superiority of Nicholas's complex, goes on to say that the sublimity of St. Peter's compared with the temple of Solomon, was as great as that of Christianity over the religion of the Old Testament.

Nicholas V was also the first pope to 'profane' the venerable basilica of Constantine with designs for enlarging and perfecting it: the image and proportions of the human body were to take the place of the Cross as the measure of all reality and a reflection of the macrocosm (thus to the apse was added a *caput* by Rossellini), and a dome was designed to rise over the cross vault.

The stylistic touchstone of human proportions then led to the archetype of Noah's Ark, itself based on anthropomorphic ideas and furthermore interpreted by the Church Fathers as a prefiguration of Christ and the wood of the Cross, and hence signifying the death and rebirth of the human race through the Resurrection. The *Civitas Nicolina* was imbued with an atmosphere of regeneration after the deluge: a clean slate after all the crises and storms. The Ark was the *Navicella* of the Church which had now reached a safe haven after a rough voyage. (It will be remembered that Giotto's mosaic of the *Navicella*, the Barque of the Church, too seemed to carry a plea for the popes to return to Rome from Avignon.)

Nicholas V aimed to consolidate the state by means of fortifications in order to introduce a new era of peace based on security. Thus he reinforced the Aurelian walls and built new towers to guard the Vatican citadel. The great tower at the Porta di San Pietro was almost two hundred feet high, on a par with the largest buildings of the *palatium* and the never realized bell towers of St. Peter's.

While Constantine received a vision of the Cross, the *signum* of Nicholas V was the 'Fortress,' and this he tried to drive home to the cardinals assembled around his

The Scala Regia, the entrance to the Vatican palace which is reserved for ceremonial occasions. Its marvelous play of perspective was created by Bernini in the years 1663–66 as an imposing approach to the papal apartments. Above the arch, angel figures hold up the tiara, keys and the coat of arms of Alexander VII.

Opposite: the coffered ceiling of the Sala Regia, with stuccoes by Perin del Vaga after designs by Antonio da Sangallo. This was conceived by Paul III as an audience chamber for royalty, hence the name. Right: two views of the Sala Ducale, designed by Bernini.

deathbed: 'The Roman pontiffs would never have had to suffer the persecutions, either in time of old or more latterly, had they been protected by up-to-date, impregnable fortifications, especially within the walls of the *Urbe*; then neither external nor internal enemies, even had they wished to upset the whole social order, would have been mad enough to stake their very lives on an enterprise that was doomed to failure. Then, whatever the boldness of their hearts, all their offensives would have come to naught. Protected in this fashion, safe and sound, the popes might have enjoyed uninterrupted peace in the Apostolic See, acquiring the greatest authority, supreme power, and immense dignity.'

The preservation of *pax romana* did indeed have to be guaranteed by the new network of massive fortifications, by which the prestige of the Castle and the *Civitas Leonina* was enhanced, the Vatican becoming an unassailable artificial mountain, impressive enough to wipe out the memories of the *Arx Capitolina* or the *palatia* on the Palatine. The Barque was thus in the process of becoming a powerful vessel.

Several times over the following centuries, however, it almost came to grief in its quarrels with the new monarchies, until eventually in 1870 it was stripped of its temporal power. On a medallion of Nicholas V we see the pope at the helm of the barque *Ecclesia*; again, another medal, *Felix Roma* (apparently restricted to the Vatican), carries the outline of a ship. 'At the time of the Deluge,' Boniface VIII had proclaimed, 'there was only one Noah's Ark. And this Ark prefigured the only one Church, with Noah alone at its helm steering it. And, as we read in Holy Scripture, all living beings outside the Ark were destroyed.' So the ship of the Church was presented as the sole means to salvation, the ship, ever more soundly built on the 'rock,' anchored in St. Peter's and entrusted wholly to the successor of Peter, the Vicar of Christ.

Apart from any ecclesiastical symbolism, however, Nicholas sought to create an organic 'city,' functioning in all respects as the *caput* of a modern state. The cosmopolitan Borgo thus had to be re-moulded into a court, to become the quarters of the Curia (*vicus curialis*). Three new straight streets were planned to form the backbone of this area, linking the castle with three points of prime importance: the access to the basilica, the new canonical residences to be built to the left of St. Peter's, and the entrance to the *palatium* to the right.

It took two centuries to solve all the problems raised by these projects. In front of the basilica a colonnaded piazza was laid out, in an elongated, curved 'circus' shape (100 × 500 *braccia*, roughly 200 × 1000 feet, in a ratio of 1:5). In the center of the piazza was then placed the obelisk from the Circus of Nero, a symbolic *summa* of the New Testament. Sun symbol and ancient image of the arts and wisdom, it was to have been supported by four bronze statues of the Evangelists (after the manner of Roman spiral columns or the column at Constantinople) and surmounted by the supreme sovereign, Our Savior, bearing a golden cross.

The allegorical equation of St. Peter's with the temple of Solomon and the *palatium* itself with Solomon's palace was in the direct tradition of Christian secret places being seen as descended from their biblical archetypes, and especially from the temple, whose construction was said to have been inspired by God Himself. Even more interesting, though, and complementary to Rome's claims to be the new Jerusalem, was the desire to recreate the total context of the Solomonic complex: hence, in its *conjunctio* with the *palatium*, the great basilica assumed the status of a court chapel, despite its size and far more wide-reaching significance, and despite the completely independent palatine chapel of Nicholas III.

The primacy of the basilica tended to be associated with the primacy of the apostolic palace. The kingship of Solomon had indeed been taken as the ideal of joint political and sacred power by the 'Byzantine' emperors (from Constantine to Justinian, who, at the consecretation of Santa Sophia, exclaimed, 'I have beaten you, Solomon!') as well as by Charlemagne, whose court at Aachen was structured – according to one biographer – 'after the example of Solomon.' A century later, Philip II of Spain, 'King of Jerusalem,' erected the temple-palace of the Escorial as a reconstruction, or rather a reincarnation, of the palace of Solomon.

Manetti somewhat inflatedly refers to the apostolic palace as a *laberynthus* or *paradisus*. The latter description was most probably prompted by the 'paradisial' beauty of the palace and basilica (the courtyard of which, with the *fons salutis* of the Pigna, the famous sculpted pinecone, was in fact called the *Paradiso*), than by any specific intuition of the *civitas* of the elect. Meanwhile the beauty of the palace was enhanced not only by Nicholas III's *hortus conclusus*, but also by courtyards with dancing fountains, as described by Manetti, and by the gardens and orchards adjoining Nicholas's Logge.

Of greater interest is the reference to the labyrinth, in the use of which term no negative implications were intended: *pulcherrimus et distinctus, et non intricatus, ac involutus, ut a poetis fingebatur* (most beautiful and ever-varied, and not a

Opposite above: the third-floor loggia of the Cortile of San Damaso as illustrated in *Decorations des palais et des églises en Italie* by Louis Gruner, published in 1854.

Below: staircase of a square tower, built by Bramante in the early part of the 16th century. Rising over five stories, it leads to the Etruscan Museum; the columns are of granite.

complex warren, as poets have claimed). Thus the labyrinth in its distinctive beauty had a kind of heavenly splendor. The labyrinthine element did not so much reflect torture of mind and complexity of experience (as was the case with the mosaic mazes on cathedral floors, representing *chemins de Jérusalem*) as the more basic notion of the Daedalian fortress-palace of Minos – a great architectural archetype, sometimes included as one of the wonders of the world. It is also worth noting that labyrinths are occasionally depicted as towered citadels, in certain cases similar in iconography to the Heavenly Jerusalem. The idea of the labyrinth-palace, possibly evolved by the school of Alberti, was further developed and varied in the strange fantastic pictures of Filarete, showing rocks and castles amid mazes.

The grand, main approach to the *palatium* was through a new triumphal gate. This was a reworking of the old Roman gate set between circular or polygonal towers.

There was something of a fashion for monumental gates in the Middle Ages, and that of Frederick II at Capua may well have influenced both Nicholas's in Rome and others such as the Arch of Alfonso of Aragon in Naples, and also possibly the 'façade of turrets' of the palace at Urbino.

It is well to remember too the classical significance of the gate as symbol and epitome of the *palatium*, or the city, or the power of the state (one thinks of the 'Sublime Porta'). This fact is attested by the evidence of numerous monuments over the centuries and by representations, as on coins of both classical and medieval cities. Rome itself was portrayed in medieval iconography as a 'Porta' or gate; Charlemagne's imperial seal showed 'Rome' as a gate crowned with a cross, with the inscription *Renovatio Roman. Imp.*, while Charles IV's seal depicted a gate between two round towers framing the inscription *Aurea Roma*.

Certain cathedral fronts were similarly conceived, with imperial gates, or *Janua coeli*, set between their twin towers. The front elevation of the Vatican basilica would appear to have been thought of in these terms, with Nicholas's two tall towers flanking it (Manetti consents unwillingly to the use of the colloquialism *campanile* [literally, 'bell tower'] when describing these *turres e pulchris marmoribus*, these towers of beautiful marble).

Among the new additions to the palace Manetti mentions a *Capella maxima*, a large room reserved for ceremonial occasions, a theater *super columnis marmoreis fornicatum* (an arched structure on marble columns), a library, and various service facilities. In his will addressed to his cardinals, the pope says: 'I exhort you in the Name of God to proceed with and bring to completion the building work we have begun, that our successors, free from all danger of external aggression or internal persecution, may attend to Our Lord's flock with greater diligence and in greater tranquility, leading them on the way to eternal salvation.'

He thus entrusted completion of his *opus* to his successors. The 'Vatican City' as he conceived it was to be a collective creation, not the work of one man, in the higher interests of the See of Peter. Sixtus IV, the second Ligurian pope, is linked not only with the Sistine Chapel, the definitive court chapel, but also with the founding of the first complete 'sanctuary of learning,' the Palatine Library, modeled on that of Augustus and housing the precious manuscripts of Nicholas V.

The Sistine Chapel, somewhat crude in its design, is yet recognized as the *Sancta Sanctorum* of Humanist art. At first sight the Chapel resembles a tower, as high as it is long, a part of the Vatican fortifications, and therefore a symbol of the Fortress (*Castrum Fidei*), the Church Militant (*Ecclesia militans*) and the Tower of Ivory (*Turris eburnea*), the Virgin of the Assumption to whom it was solemnly dedicated in 1484. Its architect was certainly a military engineer, possibly Baccio Pontelli, and it was built at a time of considerable tension both at home and abroad. A chapel-cum-tower, it harmonized well with the tall towers put up by Nicholas V, and was in turn the model for the Torre Borgia built nearby by Alexander VI.

A squared prism topped by a platform of crenellations, it also evokes the iconography of the ark of Noah, the emblem, as we have said, of the basilica and the Vatican of Nicholas V. Nor can a certain analogy with the *Curia Senatus* be denied, when one considers the uses of a chapel reserved for the popes and the 'senate' of cardinals.

Eugenio Battisti has also shown that it too was inspired by the archetype of the temple of Solomon, both in its internal dimensions: ground plan approx. 44 feet × 132 feet, height approx. 68 feet, and in its role as court chapel (adjacent to the Chapel, and similar in its proportions, is the *aula major*, the Sala Regia as it is now known). With the idea of the temple of Solomon (possibly already envisaged in Nicholas V's plans) was also perhaps associated the vision of the New Temple described by Ezekiel, with its superimposed levels and turreted east elevation (the Sistine Chapel has two floors beneath it, and a large area above reserved for the papal guards).

The frescoes in the Chapel (1481–83) present a concise *summa* of religion and history, covering the two 'dimensions' of past and future. The past is depicted in the 'parallel lives' of the Old and New Testaments (Moses and Christ) and in the 'prehistory' of the popes up to the time of Constantine and before the victory of 312 (the last pope portrayed is the Roman Marcellus I, 308–9). The present is implicit in the palatine functions of the Chapel itself. And the future, clearly eschatological in conception, is shown on the ceiling firmament: a blue sky spangled with gold stars.

An overall understanding of the 'meaning' of the Chapel may perhaps be gained by pondering its dedication and function as a bastion and 'Fortress of the Church.' The Virgin of the Assumption can be taken as an allegorical reference to the Church, 'assumed up into heaven' and, so to speak, *consecrata* among the stars: this was a possible interpretation of the 'woman clothed with the sun, with the moon under her feet, and on her head a crown of twelve stars' in Revelation. The absence of any scenes relating to the post-Constantinian Church implies a consecration of the early Church. Though only thirty of the first fifty-four popes are portrayed, all of them are deemed saints. In all probability the first two figures of the series, above the altar, on the wall that was later to be painted with the *Last Judgement*, were Christ and Peter, representing in visual terms the concept of the *traditio legis* and the foundation of the Church, which the cycle of frescoes further develops.

Nicholas V's projects were continued almost to the letter even under Alexander VI, the great enemy of Cardinal Giuliano della Rovere, the future Julius II, nephew of Sixtus IV and *éminence grise* to Innocent VIII. The ten-year pontificate of the Borgia Alexander (1492–1503) saw dramatic outbursts of open rivalry and ruthless infighting. There was the opposition of the Curia faction, polarized around the della Rovere family, the conflicts with the other great families of Rome, and finally the occupation of Rome by French troops under Charles VIII.

Hence therefore the double need for order and strength to reestablish papal authority, at least in the Vatican, according to the wishes of Nicholas V. The main town-planning schemes embarked on in this period were concentrated on the castle and the Borgo quarter, with the work on the Porta San Pietro and the Porta Cavalleggeri, and the opening of the Via Alessandrina.

Castel Sant'Angelo was further protected by a ditch, and additional outworks put up guarding access to the bridge. The Castle, the key point in Rome's defenses, and the hinge between the two cities either side of the Tiber could qualify as a 'tyrant's castle' in the sense described by Leon Battista Alberti: '... a Tyrant should have rather a Castle than a Palace, and it should stand in a Manner out of the City and in it at the same time. ... The Tyrant must have his Castle entirely separated from all other Buildings ... nor the Castle so close and so crampt up, as to look more like a Jail than the Residence of a great Prince ... the Ancients used to consecrate their Fortresses to Religion, upon which Account they were called *Auguriales*, and that in them a certain Sacrifice used to be performed by Virgins, which was extremely secret and entirely remote from the Knowledge of the Vulgar. ... But Tyrants afterwards usurped the Piety and Religion of the Place, converting it to their cruel and wicked Purposes ...'

The history of the castle was not dissimilar. Initially a tomb, a consecrated place, it then became a kind of ziggurat temple dedicated to the Archangel Michael, eventually being transformed into a palace-cum-prison-cum-fortress. Alberti could have had Castel Sant'Angelo in

mind, when he went on: 'The Fortress will be ... neither within nor without the City ... it might perhaps be not amiss to say that it is the Back-door to the City strongly fortified on all Sides.' The castle is indeed in a sense a gate guarding Borgo, and Alexander VI went to great pains in reconstructing the principal means of access to the quarter, the *Porta Sancti Petri*.

The Via Alessandrina, or Borgo Nuovo, opened on the eve of the Jubilee of 1500, the only street planned by Nicholas V which was actually built, linked the *castrum* and the entrance to the *palatium*. A thoroughfare open to all, it was in symmetry with the raised corridor passage

of the *passetto*, which was reserved exclusively for the court (and which Alexander VI also restored).

The street was opened on 24 December 1499, the inaugural day of the Jubilee. Another noteworthy event that took place on the same occasion was the conferring of the supreme role previously fulfilled by the Porta Santa of St. John Lateran on the new Porta Santa of St. Peter's. This sudden decision was prompted not only by perfectly acceptable religious and strategic reasons, but also by the urgent need to find a suitably 'magnificent' symbolic entrance to the Via Alessandrina.

The Courtyard of the Pigna or Pinecone (below left and center) is so-called after the colossal bronze pine cone of the Roman period found near the Baths of Agrippa. Having been used to adorn a fountain, it was placed in the atrium of Constantine's basilica. Its present position is in the center of the large recess built by Pirro Ligorio in 1560 along the lines of an exedra, a suggestion by Bramante, later modified by Michelangelo. The Cortile della Pigna is the northern part of the Cortile del Belvedere – planned by Bramante – between the Palazzetto of Innocent VIII to the north and the pontifical palace to the south, and which extends for nearly three hundred and thirty yards, with three sloping terraces. At the end of the 16th century, the courtyard space was reduced by a new side wing to the Library, built by Domenico Fontana; later, at the beginning of the 19th century, another wing was built parallel to the first: thus the courtyard was divided into three parts which were called the Cortile del Belvedere, the Cortile della Biblioteca and the Cortile della Pigna. Below: a detail of the Cortile del Belvedere.

The inaugural ceremony for the opening of the new street as the gateway to the Vatican, following the demolition of the old buildings which stood in the way, was closely similar to the inaugural ceremony for the Porta Santa: the pope with a hammer symbolically demolishing the wall blocking the entrance. The new street therefore led not just to the gate of the *palatium*, but also to the one true *Janua coeli*, the Holy Gate which for centuries to come would sustain the role enunciated by Christ: '*Ego sum ostium: per me si quis introierit salvabitur,*' ('I am the door; if anyone enters by me he will be saved.') (John 10, 9).

During the pontificate of Julius II (1503–13) the projects of Nicholas III and Nicholas V were brought to full fruition with the achievement of a *palatium* 'in the form of a city' (at once modern and ancient), and it was these years that saw the apogee of that brand of imperialism that we have come to call caesarism-papism.

The pope's adoption of the name Julius has more than the ring of coincidence about it: on the commemorative medallion celebrating the victory of Bologna the inscription reads *Julius Caesar Pontifex II*. In the light of this, Bramante's idea of turning the façade of the new St. Peter's round 90 degrees, to point towards the obelisk that was said to contain Caesar's ashes, takes on new meaning.

We cannot here discuss the rebuilding of St. Peter's, begun in 1506 with the sacrifice of the ancient basilica of Constantine, under the direction of Bramante, the labyrinthine yet open-minded architect of the New Vatican. Nevertheless it should be emphasized that the buildings Julius chose as his models were predominantly pagan: he is traditionally seen as having taken as exemplars two of the greatest monuments of ancient Rome: the circular Pantheon and the great vaulted *templum Pacis* (as contemporaries called the Basilica of Maxentius).

As well as these models, there were two other archetypes. The first was the Heavenly Jerusalem, to which allusion was made both in the square shape of the building and in the enclosure-piazza, modeled on the Roman baths, with the fatidic twelve doors, three for each cardinal point according to the description in Revelation (reechoing the Constantinian ritual, Julius also placed twelve medallions in the foundations).

The second was the mausoleum of Hadrian, the idea of a magnificent tomb

that would outshine the ancient wonder of Halicarnassus and its other peers throughout the centuries. In particular the dome, with its great circular drum surrounded by columns, derived from the desire to emulate the one building in Rome which represented the incarnation of death, deification, and strength: the tomb of Hadrian, which had been reconstructed with just such a dome, the square base of which can still be seen.

Alongside the tomb of the Apostle, was to have been placed that of the emperor-pope, an eventuality best summed up in

the Michelangelesque 'tragedy of the tomb.'

The cupola of the new St. Peter's has come to be seen as the greatest of its kind, the roof of the dome representing the heavens (the mosaic decoration, executed under Sixtus V, consisting of symbolic golden stars on an azure background, radiating from the center, as in the Sistine Chapel, while the great cuboid base represents the Earth. The cube, however, is at the same time the rock, the cornerstone of Peter and Christ, to which there would appear to be echoes in the massive semiworked hewn block in Raphael's *Disputation on the Sacrament*.

The studies of Ackerman and Bruschi have thrown fresh light on the courtyard of the Belvedere (begun by Bramante before his work on St. Peter's), as an *exemplum* of a palace at once modern and classical (according to Vasari, Bramante also designed a completely new façade for the *palatium*). The courtyard has been described as the first permanent outside theater of modern times, the first museum, and the first attempt to integrate gardens and architecture.

The simple need to link with a corridor or *passetto* the *palatium* and Innocent III's villa (enlarged with a museum-courtyard, and possibly intended as an artist's studio) became transformed into a grandiose enterprise on the lines of imperial Rome. Thus, to the north of the Vatican appeared a structure that recalled both the Palatine stadium (e.g. the garden-stadium on the Palatine, or the Circus Maximus at the foot of the same hill) and the circus of Nero.

The 'circus' theme was also a feature of another architectural genre: the classical villa. Antiquarians have spoken of the Tuscan villa of Pliny the Younger, described by himself as having a hippodrome-garden, and this provided a constant source of inspiration for villa architecture in the 16th century, from Raphael's Villa Madama to the 'amphitheater' of Boboli. In its turn, the Cortile del Belvedere, with its stepped gardens and terraces, provided inspiration for villa and urban architecture until the coming of Baroque.

The 'corridor' on the west of this Cortile starts at the Logge di San Damaso (also designed by Bramante as a 'stage-set' façade, but altered perhaps when Settizonio designed the upper logge), and extends to the Belvedere villa with its winding staircase, on which Bramante tried out the five architectural orders, with mixed results.

In the satirical dialogue *Simia*, by Andrea Guarna da Salerno (1516), Bramante ascends the lofty, precipitous mountain of Paradise, which is perhaps modeled on the old Vatican, with *muri magnifici, turres excelsae, palatia incomparabilia*. St. Peter, in greeting him at the gates of Paradise, reproaches him for the demolition of the venerable old basilica. Bramante's answer is to offer a design for a total reconstruction of Paradise, obviously along the lines of his design for the new St. Peter's. 'I would like to remove this road leading from earth to heaven, it is hard and wearisome to climb; I shall build another, a spiral one, so wide that souls will be able to come up on horseback. Then I would tear this Paradise down and put up a new one where the blessed could dwell in greater elegance and comfort.' Seeing the perplexed look on the face of the prince of the Church, the terrible 'destructive genius' (*mastro ruinante*) threatens to go down and redesign Hell.

Still incomplete on the death of Julius II (St. Peter's was in a similar state, and for the next few decades was said to have looked more like a ruin than a construction site), the Cortile del Belvedere was eventually finished in stages in the course of the century. The most decisive contribution was that of Pirro Ligorio under Pius IV (1559–65), when the Cortile was designed to fulfil more uses than ever before. First and foremost, a theater in the round was constructed at the foot of the *palatium*, the first stone reconstruction of a classical-style theater; on the opposite side, Bramante's portico was transformed into the *nicchione* (literally, 'large niche'), a mixture of the sacred and the secular, the semicircular loggia modelled on the sanctuary of Praeneste, prefiguring the Berninian colonnade.

Pius IV was also responsible for the completion of the Vatican defenses, e.g. the finishing of the bastioned perimeter walls around the Hill and the bottom slopes of the Janiculum, begun by Paul III. Meanwhile the Borgo had doubled in size with the 'addition' of the *Civitas Pia*, which formed a sort of radial urban sector around the castle: this was in fact the first expansion of modern Rome, and was to remain the only one up until 1870 if one discounts Urban VIII's new fortifications on the Janiculum and in Trastevere. The castle itself was modernized by the addition of a bastioned pentagonal citadel. Nicholas's dream of the 'Fortress' had found its supreme moment of realization.

Nicholas's idea of 'Paradise' similarly came to its most perfect fruition in the hands of Pius IV and Pirro Ligorio in the exquisite little Casina of Pius IV. This curious architectural complex, comprising the 'little house' itself, the loggia, and the two atriums, centers on an oval courtyard that pays homage to the ancient Vatican Naumachia (or to the *stagnum* (pond) of the Domus Aurea, which antiquarians describe as having been oval shaped), and which at the same time is a symbol of the city or the citadel (the mind harks back to the reconstructions of ancient Rome and the Capitol, and also the oval Piazza del Campidoglio built in the time of Pius IV); it is an emblem of the cycle of time and the seasons, a 'theater of memory,' and a visualization of a culture at once sweeping and encyclopaedic.

The Casina, like the villa of Innocent VIII, is both an academy and a museum: a temple and refuge of the Muses, on the

The Casina of Pius IV in the gardens of the
Vatican, built by Pirro Ligorio with the assistance
of Sallustio Peruzzi; it is a small ensemble of two
distinct buildings which face each other across an
elliptical piazzale with an encircling chaplet of
stone seats.

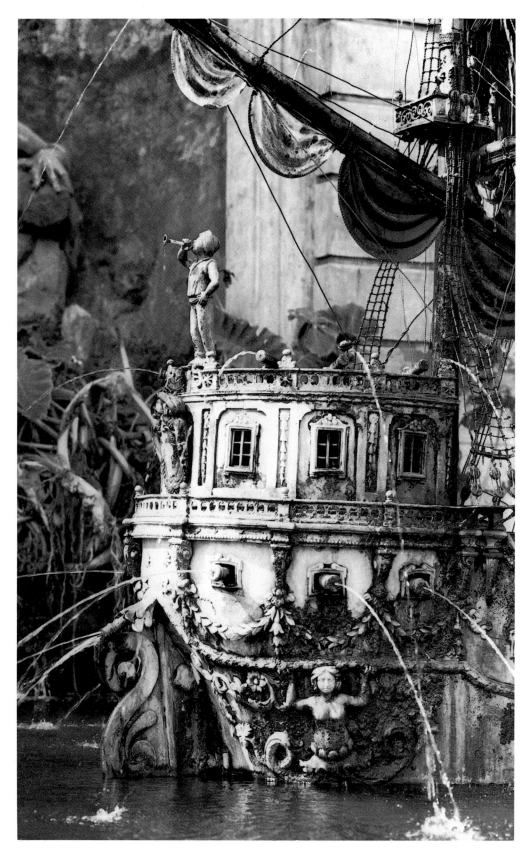

Vatican Hill which has become Parnassus. Sixtus IV, the founder of the Palatine Library, had already been hailed as *pastor Apollo*; Julius II had rejoiced in the titles *alter Apollo* and *Apollo magus*; Leo X had been eulogized as Apollo reigning over the Vatican Parnassus. Now Pius IV, a Medici from Milan, took up where the last Medici pope had left off, seeing himself as *Apollo Medicus* and *Sol pacifer*, the promoter of a new golden age and of the return to earth of Astrea, the dawn of a new world.

All these themes are represented here, in the bas-reliefs of the sun, Aurora-Astrea, and Zeus being suckled by the goat Amalthea. In an elevated position at the center of the Vatican 'sacred grove,' the Casina also contains other classical-style bas-reliefs developing the Parnassus theme. Apollo and the Muses appear on the loggia, while in an *aedicula*, in the middle of the choir, is shown the mythical Mount Pieria in Thessaly, where Zeus met with Mnemosyne and the Muses were conceived. Pieria is an ambiguous, feminine form, identifiable perhaps with Memory (Mnemosyne). The prominence given to this mountain (one might rather have expected to find Parnassus or Helicon, the reference to the Pierids or 'false Muses' is puzzling), is perhaps attributable to its very name a *nomen-omen*, since 'Pierius' was the Humanist rendering of the name 'Peter,' and is hence also an allusion to the Vatican as *Mons Pius* in homage to the pope.

The *palatium* became settled in its definitive layout during the pontificates of Sixtus V (1585–90) and Paul V (1605–21). Sixtus V, apart from finalizing the completion of the dome of St. Peter's, also initiated on the one hand the building of the Palazzo Nuovo (the Vatican's first 'modern' residential building, inspired in shape and dimensions by the Palazzo Farnese), and on the other the somewhat insensitive intrusion on the Cortile del Belvedere of a new transversal wing of the Sistine Library, a temple of knowledge that fulfilled an important wish in Nicholas's will. With the further reduction of the Cortile by the new wing built under Pius VII, the northern part of the

A corner of the Vatican gardens with the dome of the basilica as backdrop. Below left: the Fontana dell'Aquilone by the Jan van Santen.

Vatican then became, once and for all, a museum. Paul V finally completed the *opus magnum* of the basilica and enriched the Vatican *Paradiso* with new buildings and fountains; at the same time he also completed another of Nicholas's project: the gate of the *palatium*.

Beside Maderno's new façade for St. Peter's there arose (if only to remain for a few decades) a curious bell tower-cum-loggia-cum-clock tower intended to echo the Quirinal and Campidoglio towers, and serve simultaneously as a monumental *sublime porta*. It disappeared in Bernini's replanning of St. Peter's square, the great all-enveloping colonnade setting the ultimate seal on the 'palace that is a city.'

The colonnade is a portico, a covered walkway, evoking memories of the *porticus Sancti Petri* (or Portica), the street joining the castle and the Vatican basilica. The 'corridor' of the colonnade is in effect no more than a covered extension of the

Three views of the Casina of Pius IV. On the right, the smaller building, and below left, a detail of the latter. Below right: the group of buildings which make up the Casina, the smaller with open loggia and balcony looking onto a nymphaeum with fountain and statues.

Via Alessandrina, embracing the entrance of the palace and concluding the vista of the *via triumphalis* with the Scala Regia, which may be thought of as an upward sloping colonnaded street.

The piazza was conceived as a 'forum,' as the use of classical monuments, both real and reproduction, demonstrates. This concern with staying close to old models, stylistically as well as in purely intellectual terms, makes it the last imperial forum: the *forum christianum* in front of the 'temple of the *divus* Peter' and the *palatium*. Furthermore its oval shape makes it not simply a palatine square, but also a palatine stadium.

In fact this connection between the stadium and the *palatium* (which we have already observed in the Cortile del Belvedere) was a recurrent theme of 16th- and 17th-century neoimperial cultural thought. One thinks for instance of the Piazza Navona, in a sense the 'courtyard'

On these pages are shown the fortifications of the Vatican at different periods and the close connection between the basilica, the palazzi and the Castel Sant' Angelo. From top to bottom: a view of the city in the 15th century; at the end of the 15th century (from the *Chronica* of

H. Schedel, Nuremberg, 1493); and in 1600, the year of the Jubilee of Clement VIII.
Opposite: the narrow passage or *corridore*, a pathway hollowed out along the top of the Leonine walls in order to join the pontifical

to the palace designed by Giuliano da Sangallo for Leo X, or Innocent X's 'Pamphili courtyard' (here too, as in St. Peter's square, there is an obelisk).

Another way in which the colonnade may be seen is as a kind of garden or *'paradiso,'* in both reproducing the porticoed courtyard of the Constantinian basilica and hinting at a garden world through 'the beauty of those two famous fountains whose waters, leaping up into the air, provide such delight, together with glimpses of green gardens caught between the columns of the portico' (C. Fontana).

The enfolding arms of the colonnade then form a *portus salutis*, the haven of salvation for all mankind, in the same way that the basilica itself had been seen as a barque or *Navicella* and Ark. Oval like the Colosseum, but larger, the colonnade is literally a *theatrum urbis*, able to accommodate twice the population of baroque Rome. In style, it was partially inspired by the theatrical architecture of the Naumachia and the circus: its most direct model was the Circus Maximus, capable of holding 385,000 spectators, the population of the entire city. But the colonnade is also *theatrum orbis*, the theater of the world.

It was also, however, a *theatrum Ecclesiae*, a reflection on earth of the Christian Olympus, with its statues of saints resembling the celebratory columns of the ancient world. A 'theater of the Sun,' here too space and time could be measured, with the obelisk intended as both a gnomon and *axis mundi*. With the solar symbol of the obelisk therefore and the piazza itself seen as the 'palace of the sun' in honor of Alexander VII (a Sun King like his contemporary Louis XIV in France), there was here in effect a revival of the cult of Apollo and of the temple of Mars and the Sun which was said to have existed in the Vatican area.

Finally one might mention the verse from the Psalms chosen by Alexander VII for the medal struck to commemorate the colonnade: *Fundamenta eius in montibus sanctibus*. The psalm in question sings the glory of Sion, the capital of the world, and palace to Castel Sant' Angelo, built at the orders of Nicholas III between 1277 and 1280. The photograph (right) shows the stretch near the castle and the photograph (below) the part near the apostolic palace and Bernini's colonnade.

thus we can deduce that this Vatican-Jerusalem, founded on the pope's own heraldic hills, is symbolic – reflecting a new religious tactic – of Rome as the Heavenly Jerusalem. In the vision of Solomon this Heavenly Jerusalem was the habitation of all the world, the symbol of unity and reconciliation after the ruptures of earthly existence. It was the *communis patria*, at once the house of men and the house of God. The 'embrace' of the colonnade, prefiguring the Kingdom of Heaven, hence expresses reconciliation and universal rejoicing in the bosom of the Church that is both birthplace and place of rebirth and final regeneration.

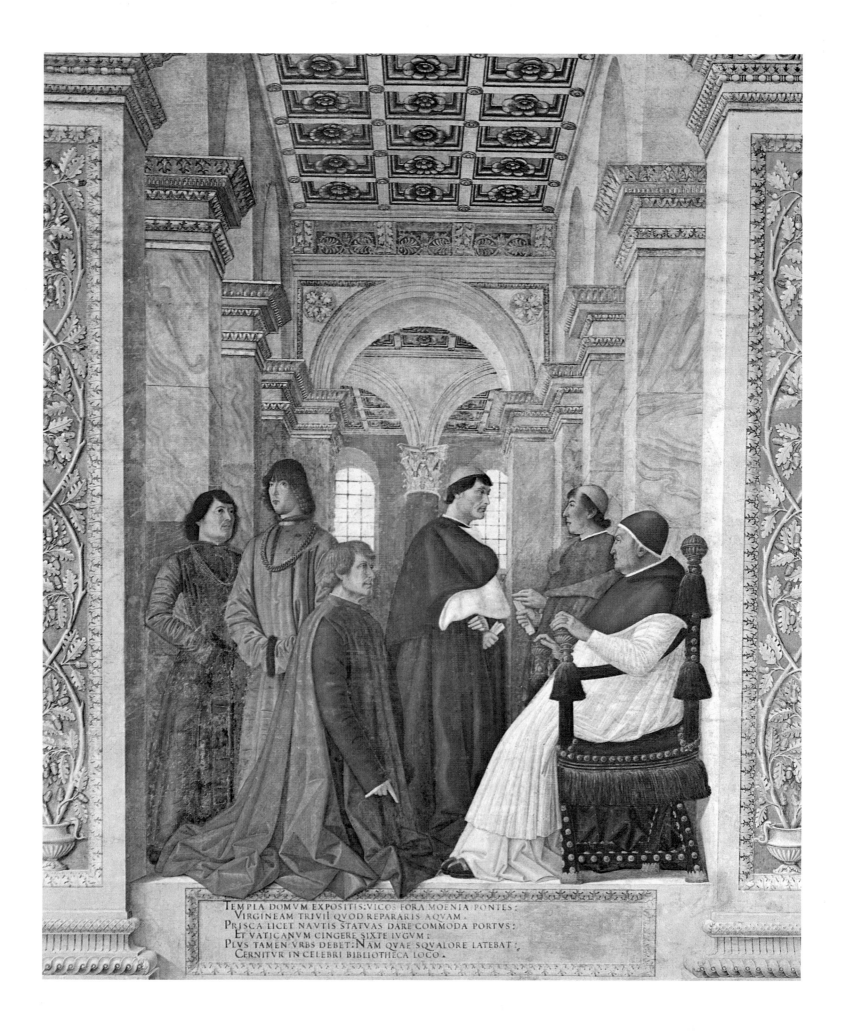

TEMPLA DOMVM EXPOSITIS·VICOS·FORA·MOENIA PONTES·
VIRGINEAM TRIVII QVOD REPARARIS AQVAM·
PRISCA LICET NAVTIS STATVAS DARE COMMODA PORTVS·
ET VATICANVM CINGERE SIXTE IVGVM·
PLVS TAMEN VRBS DEBET:NAM QVAE SQVALORE LATEBAT·
CERNITVR IN CELEBRI BIBLIOTHECA LOCO·

A STOREHOUSE OF THE ARTS
The Archives, Library and Museums

The pontiffs have over the centuries fulfilled a very particular role as 'custodians of the arts,' and in the conserving of individual works of artistic endeavor. The popes themselves were often private patrons and collectors, and once elevated to the See of Peter they set about enriching and exhibiting to the best advantage the collections of their predecessors, with enthusiasm and genuine competence. Certain popes have indeed been criticized for spending too much of the Holy See's resources on decorating the Vatican with works of art more beautiful than in any other princely residence. Yet how in fact have attitudes of the papacy changed over the ages?

Relatively little concern for things artistic marked the pontificates of the early centuries. However, the pontificate of Boniface VIII represents the culmination of a process, and indeed in a way also its reverse, for with the proclamation of the Jubilee of 1300, the pope busied himself with embellishing Rome with works of art, transforming the city into one gigantic worksite.

These initial creations: Giotto's fresco at the Lateran, the Loggia of Blessing, and all the other works dating from this period, were not so much an expression of love for these specific artistic phenomena, as a desire to flaunt, through them, the economic and political certainties of a power that had already sensed its foundations shifting under it. Through these works of art papal authority sought confirmation of its own power in both the spiritual and the temporal spheres. Disregarding the problems expressed by the individual artists in their works, Boniface aimed at creating an effect of magnificent security that would totally convince those who were to visit Rome in that special year.

The inauguration of the Vatican Library, fresco transferred onto canvas by Melozzo da Forlí. It shows Sixtus IV conferring the directorship of the Library to the Humanist Bartolomeo Platina who kneels in front of him. The other figures are, from right to left: Raffaello Riario, Guiliano della Rovere (Julius II), Girolamo Riario and Giovanni della Rovere.

The end of the Avignon 'exile' and the reestablishment of unity in the Roman Catholic Church after the Western schism in the years immediately following the return, created a climate of renewal and fresh enterprise which found a natural outlet in the Humanist culture that was beginning to emerge at that very time.

It was in this context that Nicholas V extrapolated his plans for the urban replanning of Rome and summoned numerous artists to enlarge and decorate the pontifical seat of the Vatican. It was this same general climate too that encouraged his interest in ancient manuscripts (Greek most of all). The transformation of the papal residence into a royal court was a natural outcome of the cultural changes during this time. Just as no one was shocked to see Julius II clad in armor, it seemed equally matter of course that he should be concerned with contemporary cultural developments, even of the most secular kind.

The basic assumption was that the prestige of the Roman Church should be upheld in all fields. In the first half of the 16th century the Roman popes were in certain respects undeniably worldly; yet even Gregorovius, no indulgent apologist for the Roman Catholic Church, was able to write that from that sudden liberty of spirit, that happy awareness of being alive, and that splendid sensuousness there had come a wonderful, exuberant flowering of all the arts at which mankind still marveled. The world should be grateful for the pagan tendencies of these popes; had they not done so who else would have supplied the necessary counterweight to the severe, arid Protestant spirit? Who else would have poured out upon humanity that refreshing wellspring of the beautiful, without which the Reformation would have stifled the other side of life? In the Stanza della Segnatura this cultural atmosphere is captured with vivid immediacy; while outside, St. Peter's square conveys almost tangibly the new spirit of Baroque.

The popes of the Counter Reformation were still very interested in the arts, but their interest was more ambiguous, with a clear distinction between form and content. The love of beauty was now only acceptable if enveloped by love of truth. Nevertheless, art was still a valuable instrument of authority, as the pressures brought to bear on Bernini to persuade him to go to the Sun King in France reveal. In proportion to the decline in real political power of the Roman Church, the papal attitude to the arts (their promotion and conservation, with no ulterior purpose) became more open and enlightened.

No longer a tool of power, protection of the arts became an intellectual and moral imperative for the learned popes of the 18th century, from Clement X to Benedict XIV. The broader understanding of the social usefulness of archaeological and documentary research into the past is reflected in the severely restrictive regulations controlling the export of works of art promulgated by Pius VI and Pius VII (though in fact various edicts from the end of the 17th and early in the 18th century, had anticipated these restrictions).

Gregory XVI and Leo XIII's long-overdue reordering of the various collections, and the opening of the Library and Vatican Archives to an ever wider public (continued to the present day) bear witness to the explicit desire of the popes to represent a cultural reference point: a fixed point of orientation, remaining constant through all political and ideological crises, not just for Roman Catholicism, but for Western culture generally; and a storehouse of research material available to all who seek a clearer understanding of human history.

THE ARCHIVES

The Vatican Library and Archives started life together in the early centuries of the Roman Church, when in the 6th century an archive-library was made available to scholars in the Lateran. At the same time further collections of manuscripts were being assembled at the *confessione* in the basilica of St. Peter's, in the *chartularium*, the erstwhile Byzantine *juxta Palladium* on the Palatine Hill near the Arch of Titus.

Until the beginning of the 13th century

the papal archives would appear to have remained in the Lateran, then to be totally destroyed in the bloody fighting that was such a feature of Roman life at that time. Transferred to the Vatican in the early 13th century, together with the Papal See, the archives then became an integral part of the 'treasure' which the popes took with them whenever they had to leave Rome.

With the move to France, all the Vatican documents were also transported to Avignon. Meanwhile the successive schisms of these years resulted in the creation of other archives, so that in the end there were three different pontifical archives, in Avignon, in Pisa, and in Rome. Martin V it was who, at the beginning of the 15th century, initiated the transfer to Rome (which had once again been recognized as the sole Papal See) of all these dispersed manuscripts, an undertaking that was to continue in phases up until the 19th century. Very soon, however, much of the material kept in the Vatican had to be transported to Castel Sant'Angelo for security reasons; in this way it survived the sack of Rome in 1527 (when the Sistine Chapel was used as stables).

A no less violent upheaval for the Roman Catholic Church was the Protestant Reformation; and it was amid the religious turmoil of the Roman response to this inescapable tragedy that Pius IV, on 15 August 1565, officially commissioned Cardinal Mula to create a central Vatican archive by arranging the return to Rome of material still in Avignon. Two years later, Pius V adapted certain rooms in the Vatican to serve as a secret archive for vital documents, though once again practical difficulties meant that his original plans were never fully realized.

In the end Paul V, at the beginning of the 17th century, founded the new secret Archive of the Holy See. This was created by bringing together various collections, which were then housed alongside the Vatican Library, in the long wing of the papal palace giving onto the gardens. All the documents collected here were ordered and numbered, an index was made, and (on 2 December 1614) strict security measures were introduced.

The assertions of the Counter Reformation (or, as it is sometimes called, the Catholic Reformation) required official sanction; irrefutable proof had to be given for the supremacy of the Roman papacy, to substantiate its confident claims to being the only judge in matters of faith. To this end the very earliest documents were invaluable. And it was surely with these considerations in mind that in 1630 Urban VIII separated the Library administration from that of the Archives, founded the Consistory Archive (acts of the consistories and records relating to the appointments of bishops) and the Urban Archive (acts of the Roman notaries), and instituted a systematic collection of all diplomatic documents of the Holy See.

On conclusion of this great schismatic battle, or rather, as the modes of confrontation evolved, the papacy seems to have become less interested in its heritage of books and documents, which was by now correctly organized, then with its own independent dynamic for progress.

A new era began for the Vatican Archives at the close of the last century and in the early years of this, under Pope Leo XIII, who brought them into new prominence, appointing a cardinal in charge, opening their doors to researchers, and founding the palaeographical and diplomatic schools around them. The archives themselves were then further enriched with material hitherto dispersed in different religious establishments, con-

gregations, and papal embassies, and larger premises were provided to accommodate them.

The reaffirmation of the spiritual centralism of Rome in the Catholic world (an all too obvious compensation by the Church for its loss of temporal authority over the city) resulted in an ever greater influx of documentary material from numerous different sources, while the availability of this incomparable store of records to researchers soon brought about the creation of cultural institutes and national organizations, as focal points for national studies. Finally it should also be mentioned that the Vatican Archives contain, as well as written material, a huge number of drawings by the greatest artists

Rare treasures from the Vatican Library. Below left: a drawing by Botticelli to illustrate the *Divine Comedy*; and (right) a caricature by Gian Lorenzo Bernini. Opposite above: two views of wall cabinets designed by Louis Valadier at the end of the 18th century for the rooms of the Museo Profano della Biblioteca. The cabinets are used to store valuable antique objects. Below: a neoclassical table in one of the Library rooms.

of all periods, relating to papal and private family commissions (either bequeathed or bought over the centuries). And this very considerable collection has still not been properly explored, though by any standards it ranks as one of the Vatican 'treasures.'

THE VATICAN LIBRARY

The Vatican Library is traditionally reputed to have been started by St. Peter himself. All we know for sure is that Clement V took certain manuscripts to Avignon with him in 1305 (these were then recovered by the Vatican with great difficulty, from 1417 on). However, the nucleus of material around which the library was to grow dates from the end of the Eastern Empire. When Constantinople fell in 1433, Nicholas V welcomed to his court the Greek scholars who fled west with their precious manuscripts.

A Humanist completely convinced of the value of the study of antiquity, Nicholas took translators and copyists with him to Fabriano, where he had to go in 1450 to escape the plague, unwilling that they should interrupt their work on the manuscripts. In the collection of manuscripts he managed to assemble, theology was indisputably the best represented subject. Soon the richest and, qualitatively, most valuable library of the period, instituted explicitly *pro communi doctorum virorum commodo*, it thus from the outset bore a predominantly ecclesiastical stamp.

This first nucleus, outstanding and priceless as it was, was then partially split up by successive popes who, in their struggle against the Turks, sold the valuable bindings dating from Nicholas V's pontificate, along with some of the manuscripts themselves.

In the end the real moving force behind the definitive foundation of the Vatican Library was the Humanist Francesco della Rovere, Pope Sixtus IV (1475). This pope enriched the collection with numerous volumes, on works of theology, philosophy and patristics, rather than classical texts. He also had many works translated into the vernacular. Most importantly, however, it was now that the need for this particular institution was officially recognized, with the assignment of regular funds, the appointment of the eminent Platina as librarian, together with three separate assistants for the Greek, Latin, and Hebrew manuscripts respectively, and a bookbinder, and the provision of special premises, three rooms decorated with suitable frescoes by artists such as Ghirlandaio, Melozzo, and Antoniazzo Romano. Intended for use by scholars, this institution was also very generous in loaning valuable books, in keeping with the all-round concept of culture of the age.

The theological confidence of 15th-century Humanism was succeeded by the disillusioned detachment of the late Renaissance. At the beginning of the 16th century the Medici pope Leo X, who as a cardinal had already been a collector of manuscripts (mostly illuminated) and books, brought the Medici and Vatican libraries together; and in the new importance he put on the classics he became symbolic of the 'secular' trend in contemporary culture, protecting the printer Manutius, yet at the same time also accepting dedications of works hardly appropriate to his office.

Saved by being hurriedly moved to the castle just before the imperial troops entered Rome, the Vatican Library became (like the Archives) one of the weapons of the 16th-century Counter Reformation. The intelligent and informed policies of the Farnese pope Paul III reflect the special importance it acquired thereby. He was responsible for the cataloging of the Greek and Latin manuscripts and their indexing with serial numbers, for the appointment as chief librarian of a cardinal (underlining the importance of the post), and for the loaning of a great many manuscripts to scholars and the granting of printing concessions. Significant too is the fact that of the many works dedicated to him, most were theological.

Except for certain periods of particular narrow-mindedness (as, for instance, when Paul V forbade the copying of any works that were considered suspect), the Vatican Library on the whole remained fairly easily accessible. Montaigne in his letters describes the unique rarity of the collection, and mentions that the Library was open to scholars almost every day.

The spirit of the Counter Reformation, which inevitably permeated every aspect of the Roman Catholic Church both during and after the Council of Trent, is clearly to be detected in the magnificent building constructed by Sixtus V especially to house the Vatican Library, which had recently been expanded by the addition of further manuscripts and printed material. Next to this building the same pope also erected the Vatican state printing house (*Tipografia*), with the specific aim of publishing works for the defense and propagation of the Catholic Faith.

It must be conceded, however, that it was precisely its autonomous location that allowed the Library to evolve throughout the centuries, up to our own day, since it was possible, situated as it was, to add on to it as needs dictated. The lavish decoration of the *salone* designed to house the Library itself, and the magnificence of the cupboards in which the books were stored (with strikingly 'modern' security sense) were, in some scholars' opinions, a major incentive behind the bequests through which the Library was enriched in the 17th century. Included among these new additions were the Heidelberg court library (which Gregory XV had wished to acquire, 'to employ in reverse that arsenal of knowledge hitherto used to attack the papacy') and Queen Christina of Sweden's collection of manuscripts, for which Alexander VII fitted out a special room.

Further material and rooms in which to store it were added later in the 18th century, under Popes Clement XI, Clement XII, and Benedict XIV. During these years of enlightened patronage the collections of books and documents were complemented by ever richer collections of antique vases, lead seals, and above all coins and inscriptions from the most famous private collections such as the Albani and the Carpegna.

The progressive narrowing of cultural horizons in the second half of the century, the fortunes of the papacy between the end of the 18th and the beginning of the 19th century, and the need for a reaffirmation (even if purely superficial) of its sovereignty resulted in greater restrictions on the use of the Library; and it was not until the pontificate of Leo XIII at the end of the 19th century that it was once again – indeed even more liberally – made available to scholars, in new prem-

MVSEVM · CLARAMONTANVM
PIOCLEMENTINO · ADIECTVM

Opposite above: the Museo Pio Clementino, showing (left) the Graces, and the Aphrodite of Cnidos; and (right) the Gallery of Statues. Below: the Sala della Biga and the Gallery of Busts. Right: the *Wounded Amazon*, a copy of a lost work by Polyclitus.

ises to cope with the ever increasing requests for consultation (still in Sixtus V's building cutting across Bramante's Cortile, but on the floor below the *salone*).

Today the Vatican Library is unique both for the sheer quantity of ancient manuscripts and printed material it possesses, but also especially for the successful way in which the actual premises facilitate working there. An irreplaceable institution for the study of the 'Queen of Sciences,' it is also a priceless treasury of source material for the Humanities in general.

THE VATICAN MUSEUMS

The resurgence of the papacy after the exile in Avignon and the Western schism in the middle of the 15th century came clearly on the wave of a new spirit very much in harmony with the Humanist cult of classical antiquity (though for all this 'harmony,' cultural enthusiasms were always in the end used to shed fresh light on Christian doctrine). Pope Nicholas V, the Humanist Tommaso Parentucelli, in addition to his radical rethinking of the pontifical palace of the Vatican (creating a holy city that was at the same time a fortified citadel), also laid the foundations of the Holy See's two most 'secular' institutions (afterwards consolidated by Sixtus IV), the Library and the Museums.

The Vatican Museums can trace their beginnings to the collection just housed in the Cortile del Belvedere, where Julius II placed some of the most highly prized works of classical sculpture. The inspiration behind Bramante's design of the Cortile del Belvedere was its ultimate function of linking together the papal palace and Innocent VIII's palazzetto, where in 1512 the pope put the most valuable of his 'antiquities,' other exhibits being displayed in various rooms of the palace itself.

These original mythological marbles comprised: the *Belvedere Apollo*, the *Venere Felice* (a Venus), the *Tiber*, fragments of a group with Hercules and Antaeus, the *Sleeping Ariadne* (at the time thought to be Cleopatra), and the only

Below: the Animal Room in the Museo Pio Clementino. Opposite above: the Gallery of Statues in the same Museum. Below: the Gallery of the Candelabra.

recently discovered and 'snapped up' *Laöcoon*. Chattard speaks of niches built for these precious sculptures, with wooden frames also designed by Bramante. Connoisseurs, scholars, and artists all had free access to these sculptures, to which successive popes added others, ever more overtly secular, gaining the Cortile the nickname of the 'atrium of pleasure.' An epigraph by Virgil placed over the entrance warned, *procul este, prophani*, which translates as, 'Let not the impious enter here.'

Very different in mood was the pontificate of Pius V, one of the most thorough and morally severe representatives of the spirit of the Counter Reformation. Though aware of the universal value of these works of art, he was so determined to restore the due decorum of the papal court that he donated to the Senate and the People of Rome (i.e. the Capitoline collection) thirty of the more 'pagan' sculptures

with which Pirro Ligorio had adorned the Cortile and the Villa Pia (likewise in the Vatican). Indeed it would appear that it was only due to concerted opposition from the cardinals that the famous masterpieces of the Belvedere were permitted to remain – 'on condition that they are not seen.'

The spirit of the following century continued faithful to the same Counter-Reformation mood. Antiquity was as greatly loved as ever, and new laws were passed to protect collections that were in process of formation; yet at the same time antiquity was 'appropriated' and molded to suit contemporary tastes and requirements, creating a slanted picture of classicism which is one of the distinctive features of Baroque. In fact there were relatively few acquisitions between the second half of the 16th century and the first half of the 18th. Some authorities have interpreted this hiatus in the development of the Vatican collections as the

first, distant stirrings of a new understanding of classicism: no longer through immediate aesthetic response, but (though the basic 'apologetic' motivation still persisted) through a more obviously art-historical, archaeological approach.

While increasing concern over the gradual dispersal of Italy's artistic heritage led, in the 17th century, and even more so in the 18th, to a series of directives and edicts restricting exports, nevertheless it was not until 1734 that an institutional museum was set up by the Corsini pope Clement XII. In the third Capitoline palazzo, finished under Innocent X, Corsini established the Gallery of Statues, the first great public museum in Europe displaying works of art from antiquity; he then continued to add to it with more statues, inscriptions, and reliefs, and complemented it with a collection of pictures which, under the next pope, Benedict XIV Lambertini, grew in size

with acquisitions from the Sacchetti
collection and that of Cardinal Pio da
Carpi.

When still a cardinal, Benedict had
written to Bottari: 'The duty of a cardinal,
the best service he can offer the Holy See,
is to attract scholarly and honest men to
Rome. The Pope has no weapons or armies,
he has to maintain his prestige by making
Rome a model for all other cities.' During
his pontificate the Capitoline Museum was
also enlarged, and Ridolfino Venuti drew
up a first catalog. In 1748 the same pope
founded an Egyptian Museum on the
ground floor, with Roman works taken
from the Canopus which Hadrian had
reproduced from the Egyptian original for
his magnificent villa at Tivoli.

The Capitoline Museum, conceived
essentially as a collection of models for the
students of the Accademia di San Luca,
was open to all and sundry, and among
those who took advantage of this
privilege, it suffices to mention Winckel-
mann, whose ideas must have been
influenced by his studies there. At the
same time as recognizing the importance
of enhancing the public collections (this
museum was under the aegis of the city of
Rome), the Holy See, within the Vatican
walls, continued to collect objects that
would 'heighten the splendor of the *Urbe*
and help confirm the verity of religion,
through the holy monuments of Christianity,' i.e. early Christian treasures: bulls,
seals, cameos, inlaid work, gilded glass,

and inscriptions. Once again it was private
collections that formed the nucleus of
this museum of Christian art which was
annexed to the Vatican Library in 1756.
Meanwhile under the same pope the
lapidary collection came into existence in
the Library corridor.

Today the manner in which these
collections were assembled is considered
quite unacceptable: inscriptions were
removed from churches, and the carvings
sawn off sarcophagi, without even any
record of provenance. Such procedures
exemplify the cultural attitude of the
papacy during these years, which was at
once propagandistic (aimed at showing the
venerable antiquity of Catholic dogma and
Church discipline) and informed by a

serious concern to foster archaeological studies. Some ten years later another gallery was set up next to the Library, the Museo Profano (Museum of Pagan Antiquities), brought into being by the recognition of the need to conserve monuments of Roman antiquity.

It should be remembered that up until 1770 such monuments and works of art (apart from the important, though small, Belvedere collection), discovered in the course of excavations or bought at the popes' orders, went to the Capitoline Museum. Then in 1770, prompted by a sudden 'buying spree' of important works, the Treasurer General, Cardinal Braschi (later Pope Pius VI), suggested to Clement XIV that the new acquisitions be housed in the Vatican, in Innocent VIII's palazzetto of the Belvedere. The work thereby necessitated (executed by the architect Alessandro Dori) was financed by a lottery. Depicted in a fresco of 1774 by Mengs in the Sala dei Papiri, the entrance from the courtyard was retained, while the courtyard itself was rendered octagonal by an internal portico, creating individual 'rooms,' with the doors of the niches removed, and an appreciably larger display area achieved thereby. This new design successfully fulfilled all the required practical demands, while at the same time not betraying the original concept of Julius II's 'nucleus' of statues.

With the election of Giovanni Angelo Braschi to the Papal See in 1775, the entrance to the museum was once more moved to the Vestibolo Quadrato, at the end of the Library corridor; this change was due to further enlargements of the museum as well as substantial alterations of a more general nature. In 1776 Pius VI resolved to 'complete this important building by adding two more wings, ending in a curved atrium of eighty handsbreadths giving access to the Library, and itself containing other fine monuments.'

All this entailed the demolition of the Belvedere chapel (with frescoes by Mantegna), and the addition of five extra arches to the arcaded Gallery of Statues on the lower floor of the palazzetto, with the subsequent building, within the space of

Opposite: the *Apollo Belvedere*, a copy or reworking of a Greek original of the 4th century BC attributed to Leochares (Museo Pio Clementino). On this page: from the Treasury of the basilica. Above left: the reliquary cross of Pope Paschal I, which dates from the 9th century. Below left: the *crux vaticana* which was given to the city of Rome, according to an inscription on the crossbar, by the Emperor Justin. Below right: the so-called *Dalmatic of Charlemagne*, a masterpiece of Byzantine embroidery, dating from the 13th or 14th century.

only a few years, of a series of rooms featuring classical (original or modern but of classical inspiration) styles of architecture and decoration. Thus were born the Gabinetto delle Maschere, the Sala degli Animali, the Sala delle Muse, the Sala Rotonda, and the Sala a Croce Greca (the Mask Room, the Animal Room, the Hall of the Muses, the Circular Hall, and the Hall of the Greek Cross), which the museum visitor today still sees, though in somewhat different order.

The architect here (Simonetti) did a remarkably skillful job of harmonizing the styles of different periods of building in the rooms he had to link together. The spirit of the age is eloquently manifest in the contrast between the plain brick exterior of these new sections and their sumptuous, bright, colorful interior decoration: neoclassical severity of form did not necessarily mean a shying away from the splendid and sumptuous. The predominant concerns of architecture had changed from a sense of overall design and the manipulation of volume, to a more purely visual conception inside and out. Emphasis was given to the entrance, but the rest of the museum building was declaredly just a 'container' for the treasures within, which, however, had to be seen in a fittingly ornate and sumptuous decorative setting.

The new entrance stairway, commonly called the Scala Simonetti after its architect, is a final testimony to this love of lavish decoration and somewhat theatrical architecture. Simonetti's successor, Giulio Camporese (who designed the Quattro Cancelli lobby and the Sala della Biga), was rather more coldly academic, however, despite a rigorous respect for classical models, especially as reinterpreted in the 16th century.

The sarcophagus of Junius Bassus, 4th century, with scenes from the Old and New Testament, in the Vatican Grottoes.

Roman sculptures in the Museo Profano della Biblioteca. Right: detail of a sarcophagus with a figure tentatively identified as Plotinus, c. 270. Below: a relief from the altar of the Vicomagistri, early 1st century.

Begun by Simonetti, but completed by Camporese, the Galleria dei Candelabri (Gallery of the Candelabra) housed the numerous sculptures unearthed during the excavations undertaken during these years. The additions to the papal collections acquired in this period in fact came largely from excavations organized directly by the Camera Apostolica or conducted under licence from it (a third of the finds having to go to the Vatican). In just five years, between 1775 and 1780, one hundred and thirty sites were excavated. Subsequently Pius VI created the Picture Gallery (Pinacoteca Vaticana), joining up with the Gallery of Maps (Galleria delle Carte Geografiche), and closing off a last section of still open loggia), hanging one hundred and eighteen canvases there between the years 1785 and 1792. These paintings, now dispersed, were all of sacred subjects, and included Guercino's *Incredulity of St. Thomas*, Vanni's *St. Cecilia*, Reni's *Crucifixion of St. Peter*, and Poussin's *Martyrdom of St. Erasmus*.

A series of displays on the upper floor

229

echoes the magnificent perspective of the lower (created in 1793), with the division of the Gallery of Clement XIII into five spans, leading to the Museo Sacro (Museum of Christian Art).

Historical events at the turn of the century temporarily interrupted the evolution of the Vatican Museums. By the Treaty of Tolentino the despoilment of the Museums and Library was officially sanctioned, and during the Franco-Neapolitan occupation the Museo Profano (Museum of Pagan Antiquities) lost its collection of gems, coins, and medallions for ever. A survey of 22 April 1800 presented a dismal picture of the museum created by Pius VI over twenty-five years of unceasing research and labor, one of the first public museums in the world, and one of the most advanced in terms of professional facilities to its users.

With the restoration of the Papal States, Pius VII arranged the return of much of what had been removed (though this was more thanks to the diplomacy of Canova and Gaetano Marini than as a result of any clauses stipulated at Vienna). Many of the works returned to Rome at this juncture, for instance Raphael's *Transfiguration*, which had originally been in San Pietro in

Montorio, now went to the Vatican, rather than back to the places from which the French had removed them. As a result, extra space was needed to store and display them; at the same time more space was also needed to accommodate the material coming in from the resumed archaeological excavations.

Between 1807 and 1810 Canova had already directed the setting up of the Museo Chiaramonti, as a continuation of the reorganized Galleria Lapidaria. Now, given the further need for space, Pius VII ordered the building of the Braccio Nuovo (New Wing), parallel with Sixtus's *Salone*, and traversing the end of Bramante's cortile. This New Wing was designed by Stern and finished by Belli. It was finally opened in 1822. Comparison of this new gallery (approximately 230 feet long by 25 feet wide, and well lit by skylights in the barrel vault ceiling, with an apsidal room facing north in the middle) with those of Pius and Clement reveals immediately the improved understanding of what a museum should be. While in the earlier galleries, with their lavishly decorated yet solemn grandeur, the works exhibited were essentially part of an overall decorative scheme, in the Braccio Nuovo the exhibits stand out individually, and overall structure has taken second place to the separate works displayed.

On 7 April 1820 an edict signed by Cardinal Pacca established the bases for the modern laws governing conservation of the artistic heritage, regulating excavation work and the sale of antiques, introducing strictures even on private owners, asserting the state's 'right of first refusal' on works of art offered for sale, and stressing the need for a comprehensive survey and record of this heritage.

The Stefaneschi Triptych by Giotto and his pupils, kept in the Pinacoteca Vaticana, is painted on both sides. The work was commissioned for Constantine's old basilica by Cardinal Jacopo Stefaneschi, who is shown on one side with angels adoring the enthroned Christ, along with the martyrdom of SS. Peter and Paul. On the other side, St. Peter is shown bestowing benediction, with angels, saints, the donor, the figures of St. Andrew, St. John the Evangelist and SS. James and Paul. Opposite: detail of the predella of the triptych.

One of the first consequences of this new legislation was the immediate acquisition of numerous finds from the major Etruscan archaeological sites in central Italy, as a result of which Gregory XVI ordered the creation of the Etruscan Museum, opened in 1837. Two years later the Egyptian Museum opened, in a climate of renewed interest in Egyptian civilization prompted by the deciphering of the hieroglyphics on the famous Rosetta Stone.

In the years immediately after this, further display space was created in the Lateran, with Gregory's Museo Profano, the Pinacoteca Laterana, and the Pio-Christian collection. The proclamation of Rome as the capital of Italy, marking the end of the Papal States, brought freedom from numerous restrictions and duties. The Vatican Museums continued the work of recording and researching into their amassed treasures, but now concentrated specifically on the Roman Catholic Church's role in the world (in so doing, also actively reflecting contemporary 'modernism'). Thus in 1926 Pius XI founded the Ethnological Missionary Museum, while in 1973 the Gallery of Modern Religious Art was inaugurated.

Meanwhile in 1932 the Vatican collection of Old Masters was finally settled in a building specially designed for the purpose by Luca Beltrami, after years of being moved from one wing to another. This new picture gallery brought together the Lateran collection, the Byzantine works, and the 'primitives' from the Vatican Library, alongside the Vatican's own

Opposite above: the *Birth of St. Nicholas of Bari* (detail shown right). Opposite below: detail from the predella of the Perugia Triptych showing St. *Nicholas Meeting the Emperor's Messenger and the Miraculous Rescue of the Sailing Ship* (below, detail from same), all by Fra Angelico.

collection. Then in 1960 new rooms of original Greek sculpture were opened, displaying works definitely identifiable as Greek rather than Roman copies.

With the building of a new wing by the Passarelli firm of architects in 1970, the Lateran Museums – Pagan Antiquities (Museo Profano), Pio-Christian, and Ethno-logical Missionary – were transferred to the Vatican. The purpose of this transfer was to make the Lateran available for the running of the diocese of Rome, as well as to house all the papal art treasures in one place. Today most of the work carried on in the Vatican Museums consists of critical assessment of the material stored there, reorganization and refurbishment of the galleries, and the provision of up-to-date guide commentary for the visitor. At the same time, as well as the restoration of individual pieces, whole sections of the actual palace itself are being restored to their ancient decor (a most recent example being the Torre dei Venti – the famous Tower of the Winds).

What we have been talking about is a conglomeration of museums and galleries without parallel in the world, whose every stage of development is a matter of facinating interest.

The central concern of this outstanding cultural institution remains today what it was in the days of the early Humanist popes: the conservation of an artistic heritage acquired over centuries of histor-ical and cultural upheaval. Organized to exploit to the maximum the treasures contained in the Museums, Library, and Archives, the Vatican today continues to adapt and respond to new advances in the sphere of art conservation and restoration.

On the following pages, left: detail of the *Miracles of St. Vincent Ferrer* by Ercole De' Roberti, a predella from a now dispersed polyptych in the Pinacoteca Vaticana. Right: three reliefs attributed to Matteo del Pollaiolo, which once adorned the marble baldachin of the old basilica, now kept in the Vatican Grottoes.

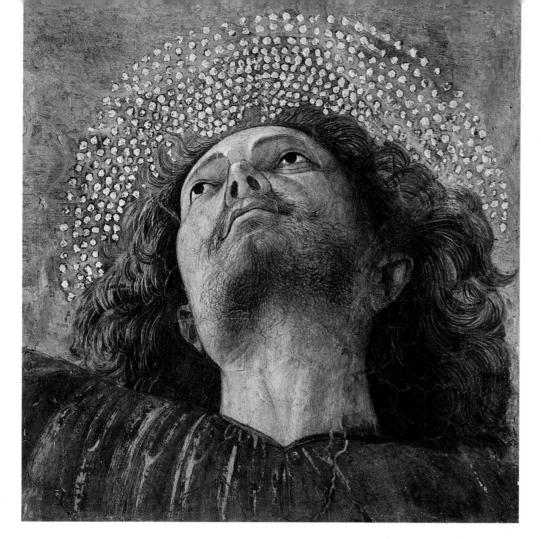

Apostle's head and (below and opposite) angels making music, fragments of a fresco by Melozzo da Forlí from the church of the Holy Apostles, preserved in the Pinacotica Vaticana.

On the following pages, left: the tabernacle from the old basilica, attributed to Donatello, now used to frame a Madonna who is the subject of popular veneration; kept in the Treasury of St. Peter's. Right: Leonardo's *St. Jerome*, from the Pinacoteca Vaticana.

Opposite: *Lament over the Dead Christ* by
Giovanni Bellini. Right: the *Coronation of the
Virgin* by Raphael; both preserved in the
Pinacoteca Vaticana.

Below: the *Magdalen* by Guercino.
Center: the *Burial of Christ* by Caravaggio.
Opposite: *Clement IX Rospigliosi* by Carlo
Maratta; all in the Pinacoteca Vaticana.

On the following page, above left: *Benedict XIV* by Giuseppe Maria Crespi; above right and below left and right: Mars, the Sun, and Saturn from Donato Creti's *Astronomical Observations*; all in the Pinacoteca Vaticana.

A JOURNEY ROUND THE VATICAN

'If the common faith is reinforced and consolidated by great buildings, looking as if they might almost have been raised by God Himself as an imperishable testimony to it, in such a way as to be able to survive as a sacred tradition in those who witness them, both now and in the future, then the world will embrace the Faith with the most profound devotion.'
Nicholas V (1447–55)

ST. PETER'S SQUARE

St. Peter's square is reached from the Via della Conciliazione. This street was begun in 1936 and finished in 1950. Designed by Marcello Piacentini and Attilio Spaccarelli, it was the realization of a street project in the area of the Borghi first conceived in 1350.

This square is one of the most superb in the world. Its main feature is the brilliantly designed colonnade (Gian Lorenzo Bernini, built 1656–67), which in a sense repeats the handling of space within the basilica itself. The basilica of St. Peter's was conceived by Michelangelo (and, before him, Bramante and Peruzzi) as a central plan building, giving maximum importance to the dome. Carlo Maderno, who completed the building in 1614, upset the balance of the design by the addition of a triple nave extending out towards the square.

THE BASILICA

Let us go farther back in history, however. St. Peter's dates back to *c.* 322, when the Emperor Constantine decided to build a church over the tomb of the Apostle Peter. It was then completed by Constantius in the middle of the 4th century. At this point it was similar in plan to the basilica of St. John Lateran.

According to Alfarano's reconstruction of this great complex, a stairway led up to a porticoed rectangular entrance porch, in the center of which stood a fountain (for ablutions) with a huge sculpted pine cone enclosed under a canopy. The façade was decorated with mosaics, as is depicted in an 11th-century manuscript now at Windsor. Sadly, as Cerrati already laments, these mosaics were lost when the new building was erected in the 16th century. Five doors opened into the basilica.

Inside there were five naves and a floor. The shrine of St. Peter (*Confessione*) consisted (as shown in a representation by Sebastiano Verro dating from 1581) of a small temple-like structure (*tempietto*) with a small dome supported on four columns, and was covered with sheet gold (Galassi Paluzzi). A mosaic decorated the apse, while the central nave was adorned with frescoes (possibly dating from the pontificate of St. Leo the Great, 440–61) showing scenes from the Old and New Testaments. The narthex was decorated with episodes from the life of St. Peter. The crypt dates from the time of St. Gregory the Great (590–604), when the altar was constructed on top of the tomb.

Ideas for a new basilica began to germinate in the 15th century, and Nicholas V (1447–55) commissioned the Tuscan architect Bernardo Rossellino to make a design for it. The initial plan was for a Latin cross shape, but the pope died, and the project was shelved. Not until the beginning

of the 16th century did work start. Julius II (1503–13), out of several proposed plans, chose that of Bramante, which had a Greek cross design. Work started on 18 April 1506.

After Bramante's death in 1514, Raphael took over, with Sangallo and Fra Giocondo as assistants. The design was altered to a Latin cross again. On Raphael's death in 1520, direction of the work was entrusted to Baldassarre Peruzzi, who returned to the Greek cross design, while his successor, Antonio da Sangallo the Younger once again reverted to the Latin cross.

Sangallo died in 1546, and Michelangelo once and for all established the Greek cross ground plan, in a design of great tautness in which the dominant feature was the dome. Michelangelo was followed by Vignola and Pirro Ligorio, until the eventual appointment by Gregory XIII (1572–85) of Giacomo della Porta in 1573 (della Porta enjoyed the patronage of the powerful Tommaso Cavalieri and the cardinal vice-chancellor Alessandro Farnese). By this stage, as we know from an engraving of 1574 by Cartaro, work had not progressed beyond the transept or higher than the drum of the dome.

Della Porta completed the Cappella Gregoriana between 1574 and 1584. On 12 May 1590, in the pontificate of Sixtus V, the vaulting of the dome (begun in 1586) was finally finished. Partly for technical reasons, della Porta had in fact altered Michelangelo's design for the dome, making it higher and more pointed. Three years later the lantern was added.

Immediately afterwards della Porta began on the Cappella Clementina, which was completed in 1601. Now, however, came the great alteration to Michelangelo's design: Paul V, with the backing of a committee of cardinals, decided for liturgical reasons to adopt the Latin cross design after all. Carlo Maderno was chosen as architect (the competition included architects of the caliber of Giovanni Fontana, Flaminio Ponzio, Orazio Torriani, and Domenico Fontana).

The following quote from Mucantius, mentioned by Galassi Paluzzi, explains the motivation behind this decision: *Est enim Templum novum divi Petri parum aptum ad celebrandum, nec secundum ecclesiasticam disciplinam fuit constructum, unde numquam aptum erit, ut in eo huiusmodi sacrae functiones decenter et commode celebrari possent* (The new temple of St. Peter is in fact not convenient to celebrate in, and was not built according to ecclesiastical discipline, and will thus never be a suitably dignified and commodious setting for the celebration of these sacred functions).

The remnants of the old basilica were therefore demolished, and work continued until 1614, when the façade was finally completed.

Basilica of St. Peter.
Equestrian Statue of Constantine
(1670) in the portico of the basilica.
Gian Lorenzo Bernini.
Bottom: detail from the *Door of Death*.
Giacomo Manzù.

Basilica of St. Peter. *Monument to Matilda of Tuscany.*
Gian Lorenzo Bernini and his school.

Urban VIII (1623–44) consecrated the new edifice on 18 November 1626. Three years later Bernini's plan for two bell towers above the façade had to be scrapped: cracks having appeared on the first, it was pulled down (the other was never built). In the 18th century the façade acquired its two clocks (by Valadier), while the statues of SS. Peter and Paul on either side of the steps up to the entrance (the work of Giuseppe De Fabris and Adamo Tadolini) are 19th-century replacements of those executed in the 15th century for Pius II (1458–64) by Paolo Taccone and Mino Del Rame, which had been moved to the former Museo Petriano.

The portico retains the five entrances of the old basilica. On the right is Bernini's *Equestrian Statue of Constantine* (1670), and on the left that of *Charlemagne* by Cornacchini (1725). Of the doors into the basilica the most noteworthy are that of Filarete, made for Eugenius IV (1431–47), showing scenes of the lives of SS. Peter and Paul, and events of Eugenius's pontificate, and that by the modern sculptor Giacomo Manzú. The mosaic over the central bay of the portico is the remnants of the mosaic by Giotto made for the old basilica.

In the far right-hand nave is Michelangelo's wonderful marble *Pietà*, an outstanding early work (1498–99), and the only one he signed: it was made for Cardinal Jean Bilhères de Lagraulas, governor of Rome, and was originally intended for the church of Santa Petronilla; however, it was moved from there in about 1515 and placed in St. Peter's sacristy; from there it was moved to the altar of SS. Simon and Jude, and again in 1626 into the choir; it was eventually sited in its present position in 1749. Already once restored in the 18th century, it was attacked with a hammer by a mentally deranged man in 1972. In the course of its restoration after this damage – by

means of painstaking copy work, and reuse of the various fragments, which had all been systematically cataloged – the imperfections of the 18th-century restoration work (on the left hand) were also smoothed out.

The fresco of the *Triumph of the Cross* over the altar is by Giovanni Lanfranco, while the mosaic in the oval dome is by Cristofari, after a cartoon by Pietro da Cortona and Ciro Ferri.

After this chapel we come to the *Monument to Christina of Sweden*, who is buried in the Vatican Grottoes. This monument was commissioned by Innocent XII (1691–1700) and finished in 1702

under Pope Clement XI (1700–21). Designed by Carlo Fontana, the bust and bas-reliefs were executed by Jean Baptiste Théodon and the putti by Lorenzo Ottoni. Opposite, over the entrance to the *Chapel of Relics*, is the *Statue of Leo XII*, sculpted by De Fabris in 1836 for Gregory XVI (1831–46).

The *Cappella del Crocifisso* is by Bernini, with details by Vanvitelli. Noteworthy here is the 14th-century *wooden crucifix*, formerly on the altar of SS. Simon and Jude. In the *Cappella di San Sebastiano* the altar is by Bernini. And here we encounter for the first time a common feature of St. Peter's from the 16th century on: a mosaic copy of paintings (on altarpieces, ceiling and lunettes) removed elsewhere. In this case the mosaic, by Cristofari, depicting the *Martyrdom of St. Sebastian*, is copied from an unfinished oil mural by Domenichino, moved by Nicola Zabaglia (who transferred it to canvas) in the 18th century to Santa Maria degli Angeli. The dome is decorated with scenes from the Old Testament.

The *Monument to Pius XI* (1922–39) is by Pietro Canonica; that to *Innocent XII* (1691–1700) by Filippo Valle and Ferdinando Fuga. Facing, is the *Tomb of Matilda of Tuscany*, whose body was translated to the basilica from the monastery of San Benedetto di Polirone by Urban VIII (1623–44). The commission for the monument went to Bernini. Begun in 1633 and finished in 1644, it was, however, mostly executed by his workshop. According to Fagiolo dell' Arco, Bernini only made the drawings and the models for the decoration and the figures, and added the finishing touches.

Through a gate (designed by Borromini), we now come to the *Cappella del Santissimo Sacramento*. The arch at the front is decorated with mosaics by Abatini after cartoons by Pietro da Cortona, depicting Old Testament scenes. The mosaics in the lunettes, show-

ing the *Mystery of the Eucharist*, are by Manenti. On the drum of the dome are four carved angels.

The bronze *ciborium* on the altar was cast between 1673–75 to a design by Bernini, who had received the commission for this work in 1629–30. Actually made by Lucenti, with assistance of Mattei, it has lapis lazuli decoration by Geri. Pietro da Cortona's altarpiece of the *Trinity* dates from between 1628 and 1631, according to Briganti.

The altar on the right has a mosaic by Tomberli, Cerasoli, and Cocchi, depicting the *Stigmata of St. Francis*, copied from

Domenichino's painting in Santa Maria della Concezione.

Leaving the chapel, on the right is Camillo Rusconi's grandiose *Tomb of Gregory XIII* (1572–85), sculpted in 1723. The bas-relief on the sarcophagus, illustrating the reform of the Julian calendar (worked out by this pope in 1582) is the work of Cametti and Melloni. The two statues represent Religion and Wisdom. On the pilaster opposite is the simple *Tomb of Gregory XIV* (1590–91): the two statues by Antichi in the niches formerly decorated the monument to Gregory XIII which stood here. On the first of the great piers supporting the dome is

249

Basilica of St. Peter.
Altar of the Cappella del Santissimo Sacramento. Gian Lorenzo Bernini.

Plaster model for one of the angels of the *Cappella del Santissimo Sacramento*. Gian Lorenzo Bernini.

Cristofari's mosaic depicting the *Communion of St. Jerome* (a copy of the painting by Domenichino painted in 1614 for the church of San Gerolamo, and now in the Pinacoteca Vaticana).

To the right is the *Cappella Gregoriana*, begun by Michelangelo towards the end of 1561 and continued by Vignola between 1567 and 1573, and finished eventually by Giacomo della Porta in 1584. The mosaics are after cartoons by Girolamo Muziano. On the marble altar stands the *Madonna del Soccorso* (Our Lady of Succor), placed here in 1580 by Gregory XIII (1572–85). On the right is the *Monument to Gregory XVI* (1831–46) by Luigi Amici. Towards the transept, on the right, is the *Monument to Benedict XIV* (1740–58) by Pietro Bracci, who also sculpted the statues of the pope and Wisdom, while the statue of Selfishness is by Gaspare Sibilia. Opposite, is a mosaic copy of a painting commissioned for Santa Maria degli Angeli from Pierre Subleyras in 1745, showing the *Mass of St. Basil with the Emperor Valentius*.

In the right-hand transept we first come to the *Altar of St. Wenceslas* in mosaic, by Cesare Caroselli. Next is the mosaic by Fabio Cristofari of *SS. Processus and Martinian*, after Valentin's

painting in the Pinacoteca Vaticana. Immediately after this comes the *Altar of St. Erasmus*, a copy in mosaic by Cristofari and Ottaviani of Poussin's canvas in the Pinacoteca Vaticana. The niche sculptures are: *St. Jerome Emiliani* by Pietro Bracci, *St. Joseph of Calasanza* by Innocenzo Spinazzi, *St. Cajetan* by Carlo Monaldi, and *St. Bruno* by Michelangelo Slodz.

In the next passage, to the right, is Canova's *Monument of Clement XIII* (1758–69), dating from 1788–92. To the left is the statue of *Religione Crucifera*; on the right a spirit of death leans against a torch (appropriately upturned and extinguished); the bas-reliefs on the sarcophagus represent Hope and Charity; at the bottom are two lions. In front is Cristofari's mosaic of *St. Peter Walking on the Water*, after a painting by Lanfranco.

Entering the *Chapel of St. Michael*, on the right is an 18th-century mosaic by Regoli and Fiani of *St. Michael*, a copy of Guido Reni's painting in Santa Maria della Concezione, executed for the cardinal of Sant'Onofrio.

On the next altar is Cristofari's mosaic of *St. Petronilla*, a copy of the magnificent painting by Guercino now in the Capitoline Gallery, commissioned by Gregory XV and dated by Barbieri to 1623.

In the left-hand passage now

stands the *Monument of Clement X*. Dating from 1760, the mosaic in front is by Fiani, Ottaviani, and Regoli, and shows *St. Peter Raising Tabitha from the Dead* (after the painting by Placido Costanzi in Santa Maria degli Angeli).

The monumental *Chair of St. Peter* in the apse was fashioned by Bernini between 1656 and 1665 for Alexander VII (1655–67), and is of gilded bronze. This baroque creation is an outstanding example of Bernini's highly theatrical genius, and supremely captures the 17th-century love of immediate, explosive effects. To help him on this truly great work, Bernini employed various members of his workshop: Ferrata, Artusi, and Morelli produced the statues; Schor the throne; Morelli, the two Sassi, and Naldini the stuccoes; and Schor the painted window with the *Dove of the Holy Spirit*.

To the right of the Chair is the *Monument of Urban VIII* (1623–44), executed by Bernini between 1628 and 1647, with limited collaboration from Pietro and Luigi Bernini, Morelli, Balsimelli, and Sale. On the left is Guglielmo della Porta's *Monument of Paul III*, sculpted between 1551 and 1575 for Cardinal Alessandro Farnese. This monument, which had four statues initially, was reduced in size when it was moved from the Capella Gregoriana into the apse; the two remaining statues symbolize Prudence and Justice.

The four statues in the niches here are of *St. Francis*, *St. Benedict*, *St. Dominic*, and *Elijah*; dating from the first half of the 18th century: the work of Monaldi, Montauti, Legros, and Cornacchini.

Proceeding into the left transept, we come to the *Monument of Alexander VIII* (1689–91) sculpted by Arrigo di San Martino in 1725; the statues of Religion and Prudence are by Angelo De Rossi. Opposite, is the mosaic of *St. Peter Healing the Paralytic* by Ottaviani, Cocchi, Palat, and Embau.

In the dome of the *Cappella della Colonna* are 18th-century mosaics of the Litanies of Loreto; those in the pendentives, of the *Doctors of the Church*, dating from the first half of the 17th century, are by Giovanni Calandra (after cartoons by Lanfranco) as are also the lunettes, in which Abatini also assisted, from cartoons by Giovanni Battista Romanelli. Over the *Altar of St. Leo the Great* is the great relief showing the Saint meeting Attila at the gates of Rome. By Algardi (with the collaboration of Domenico Guidi), this relief is a fine example of the classical school of 17th-century Roman art. The work was commissioned in 1646 by Innocent X (1644–55), but only completed in 1652, two years after the Holy Year for which it was intended.

On the left is the *Altar of the Madonna of the Column*, designed by Giacomo della Porta.

Going towards the Cappella Clementina, we find the *Tomb of Alexander VII* (1655–67), a magnificent allegory of death, produced by the school of Bernini, under the master's direction, between 1671 and 1678. *Charity* is by Mazzuoli, *Truth* by Morelli, *Prudence* by Baratta, and *Justice* by Cartari, while the decorations are the work of Cartari and Baciadonna. *Alexander VII* is by Maglia and

Basilica of St. Peter.
Below: *Monument to Christina of Sweden* (1702). Jean Baptiste Thédon and Lorenzo Ottoni, after the design of Carlo Fontana.
Bottom: a detail from the *Monument to the Stuarts* (1817–19). Canova.

Basilica of St. Peter.
Below: *St. Longinus.*
Gian Lorenzo Bernini.
Bottom: the *Loggia della Lancia* (1633–40).
School of Bernini.

Sante, and *Death* by Lucenti; Morelli and Renzi collaborated on the shroud. Others, however, also worked on the monument: as well as Bernini's own son, there were Rinaldi, Santi, Balestra, Sicurati, Mattei, and Carcani. Innocent XI (1676–89) later had the figure of Truth covered with a metal drape made by Lucenti after a design by Carcani. Opposite, is Muccioli's mosaic of the *Sacred Heart*.

In the left transept is a mosaic by Vincenzo Camuccini depicting the *Incredulity of St. Thomas*. The altar opposite has a mosaic with the *Crucifixion of St. Peter* by Tomberli, Cerasoli, and Roccheg-

giani, a reproduction of the painting by Guido Reni now in the Pinacoteca Vaticana. The central altar has a painting of *St. Joseph* by Funi, placed here in 1963. The sculptures are 18th-century, by Bracci, Campi, and Valle.

In the next alcove we find the *Monument of Pius VIII* (1829–30) by Pietro Tenerani, with, opposite, a mosaic depicting *Ananias and Sapphira Deceiving Peter*, executed by Adami after a painting by Pomarancio.

Next we come to the *Cappella Clementina*, which was finished in 1600 by Giacomo della Porta at the instigation of Pope Clement VIII (1592–1605). The decorative mosaic work in the lunettes and pendentives is by Provenzale and Rossetti, after cartoons by Pomarancio. On the altar, where the relics of St. Gregory are kept, is a mosaic by Cocchi and Castellini, after a painting presented to this chapel in 1627 by Andrea Sacchi, now in the chapter room of the Canonica di San Pietro. Opposite is Thorwaldsen's *Monument of Pius VII* (1800–1823), commissioned by Cardinal Consalvi; the two statues symbolize *Strength* and *Wisdom*, while flanking the throne are the spirits of *History* and *Time*.

Returning into the nave, we find the 18th-century mosaic of the *Transfiguration* by Monosilio and collaborators – a copy of Raphael's painting now in the Pinacoteca Vaticana.

In the following alcove is the *Tomb of Leo XI* (1605), a fine monument by Alessandro Algardi and his school, dating from between 1634 and 1650, commissioned by Cardinal Roberto Ubaldini. Algardi himself sculpted the figure of the pope, the reliefs, and the putti supporting the coat of arms; *Strength* and *Abundance* are by Ferrata and Peroni. Opposite is the beautiful *Monument of Innocent XI* (1676–89), by Pierre Monnot, after a design by Carlo Maratta. The two statues symbolize *Religion* and *Strength*.

We now pass into the *Cappella del Coro*, built by Carlo Maderno, who, along with Giovanni Fontana, in January 1603 succeeded della Porta as official architect of St. Peter's. Completed in 1614, it was then decorated after designs by Bernini. The altar mosaic of the *Immacolata* is after a cartoon by Pietro Bianchi.

In the next passage stands the *Monument of Pius X* (1903–14), by Di Fausto and Pier Enrico Astorri. Then we come to the *Tomb of Innocent VIII* (1484–92) by Antonio del Pollaiolo, finished in 1498. Taken from the Old Basilica, it was sited here in 1621.

We now come to the *Cappella della Presentazione*, where the Biblical mosaics are by Cristofari, Ottaviani, and Conti, from cartoons by Carlo Maratta; the altar mosaic by Cristofari is after an 18th-century model by Gian Francesco Romanelli. On the left is the *Monument of Benedict XV* (1914–22), by Pietro Canonica.

Returning into the passage, we come to the *Monument to Maria Clementina Sobieska*, an exquisite rococo work completed in 1745 by Pietro Bracci and Filippo Barigioni. Opposite, stands the *Monument to the Stuarts*, by Antonio Canova. Dating from 1817–19, this monument was commissioned by the Prince Regent of England, later George IV, in honor of James III, Charles III, and Henry IX (the Old Pretender, Bonnie Prince Charlie, and Henry Stuart, Cardinal York).

Next door is the *Baptistery*, with Cristofari's mosaic of the *Baptism of Christ* (1722), after an original by Maratta; on the sides are *St. Peter Baptizing the Centurion Cornelius* and *SS. Processus and Martinian*, after paintings by Andrea Procaccini and Giuseppe Passeri. The splendid *font* is by Carlo Fontana, completed in 1698.

Most of the statues in the center nave are 18th-century. The bronze *St. Peter Enthroned*, on the right just before one enters the octagonal central area of the crossing, is attributed to Arnolfo di Cambio.

The interior of the dome is decorated with mosaics. In the medallions are the four Evangelists: Giovanni De Vecchi produced the *St. John* and *St. Luke*, while *St. Matthew* and *St. Mark* are by Marcello Provenzale after cartoons by Cesare Nebbia. Also by Provenzale (with the help of Abbatini, Serafini, Torelli, Turchi, and Rossetti), after cartoons by the Cavalier d'Arpino, are the *Figures of the popes*, of *Christ, Mary, St. John the Baptist*, and *St. Paul*, together with the *Angels* and *Apostles* in the sixteen link ribs

The Vatican Grottoes.
The facade and portico of Constantine's old basilica.
Fresco from the 16th century.

between the drum and the lantern.

Four logge were made (by the school of Bernini) in the main piers between 1633 and 1640, dedicated to the 'Sacred Relics' of Christianity. Below, in four niches, are statues of *St. Helena* by Andrea Bolgi, *St. Veronica* by Francesco Mochi, *St. Andrew* by François Duquesnoy, and *St. Lawrence* by Bernini. These statues reveal clearly the various stylistic trends, between the two poles of Classicism and Baroque in Roman sculpture during the first half of the 17th century. Conceived by Urban VIII (1623–44), the project was entrusted to the respective artists in 1628. Duquesnoy finished his sculpture in 1639, Mochi in 1640, Bernini in 1638, and Bolgi in 1639.

The canopy (*baldacchino*) over the tomb of St. Peter is one of the supreme masterpieces of baroque art. Made between 1624 and 1633 by Bernini, with the assistance of other artists, notably Duquesnoy and Borromini, the latter designing the dolphin-back curves of the top (*coronamento*), it incorporates bronze taken from the Pantheon.

THE SACRISTY AND TREASURY

Various architects including Carlo Fontana, Antonio Canevari, and Filippo Iuvara worked on plans for St. Peter's sacristy, but in the end the design accepted by Pius VI (1775–99) in 1776 was that of Carlo Marchionni. Work began that very year, and the building was finished in 1784. To make way for it (it was joined to the basilica by means of two small bridges) the Porta Fabrica and the church of Santo Stefano degli Ungari were pulled down. The entrance is situated below the *Monument of Pius VIII*. A gallery leads to the octagonal *Sagrestia comune*, at the entrance of which stands a *Statue of Pius VI* (1775–99) by Penna, Sibilia, and Franzoni. Inside are four columns from Hadrian's Villa at Tivoli. The altar mosaic is a copy

of Caravaggio's *Deposition* (now in the Pinacoteca Vaticana). A symbolic bronze cockerel adorns the clock. Proceeding to the *Sagrestia dei Canonici*, the *Saints in Glory* above the door are by Federico Zuccari.

In the adjoining chapel is a *Madonna and Child with Saints* by Penni, a *Madonna and Child with the Young St. John* by Guilio Romano, and two canvasses by Antonio Cavallucci with scenes from the lives of SS. Peter and Paul. Afterwards we come to the *Sagrestia dei Beneficiati*, with the *Delivery of the Keys* by Muziano and *Quo vadis?* and *St. Peter*

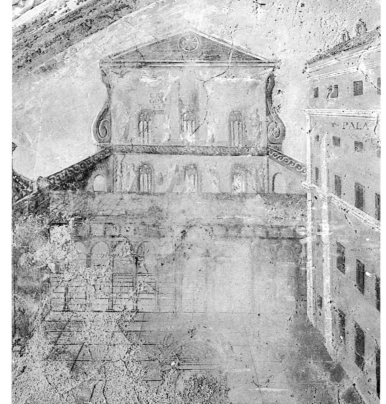

Presented to Jesus both by Cavallucci. The carved *shrine* is by Donatello and dates from 1432–33. In the *Sagrestia dei Chierici Beneficiati* it is worth noting Guidubaldo Abatini's painting of *St. John Chrysostom*.

Next we come to the *Treasury* whose history dates back to the

4th century. On the one hand treasures were donated to the basilica, while on the other it was raided and plundered at intervals from the early Middle Ages down to the Napoleonic invasion (e.g. the sack of Rome in 1527, and the Treaty of Tolentino in 1797). The donations were from kings as well as popes – even certain barbarian kings. Thus Theodoric presented two silver candlesticks weighing sixty pounds; Clovis a votive crown set with jewels; and Charlemagne various items, including a round silver shield (*clipeus*) and a gem-studded gold crown. When Charlemagne was made emperor in

800, he also had the Cappella della Confessione decorated with gold.

Among the objects lost, it is enough to mention the 14th-century silver busts of SS. Peter and Paul, set with pearls and precious stones, works of the 14th century by Giovanni di Bartolo; Julius II's tiara; and the cope stud

made by Cellini for Clement VII (F. S. Orlando).

Let us here note some of the exhibits in the Treasury today, the majority, crosses, monstrances, reliquaries, and liturgical ornaments dating mostly from the 17th–19th centuries.

The *Dalmatic of Charlemagne* is the traditional description of a dalmatic of Byzantine origin (probably 13th or 14th century), that in fact has no historical connection with Charlemagne. Against a background of little Greek crosses are represented the Transfiguration and Christ in Judgement surrounded by choirs of angels, embroidered with gold and silver thread on silk.

The *Crux Vaticana* is a reliquary cross with four stone *pendentifs* (dating from the second half of the 6th century) containing fragments of the True Cross. The cross itself is made of copper plated with silver, engraved with an account of the Crucifixion, and set with precious stones along the arms. The actual reliquary casket is in the middle, where the arms intersect.

The back is richly decorated with floral motifs, while in roundels at the ends are Christ holding the Book, giving his blessing, and the Emperor Justin II and his wife Sophia; in the middle is the Mystic Lamb. The cross was donated by Justin II, and his empress had some of her own jewels set into it. Always a famous piece, it was the subject of an essay by the eminent scholar and collector Cardinal Stefano Borgia in 1779 entitled *De Cruce Vaticana*.

The *Bernini monstrance* is a miniature reproduction of the *baldacchino* in the basilica, signed by Eugenio Bellosio, and dating from the latter two decades of the 19th century. Made in silver, it is lavishly decorated with gilding, enamels, pearls, and precious stones. At the bottom are Christ and the Eucharistic Table, and the four Cardinal Virtues; the shaft

The Vatican Grottoes.
Below: *John VII*. Fragment of an 8th-century mosaic.
Center: *Figure of an angel* – fragment of a mosaic from the *Navicella* series by Giotto.

Below: the *Bathing of the Infant Jesus*, a fragment of an 8th-century mosaic from the Oratorio of San Giovanni

contains four niches with the four Theological Virtues; while the actual receptacle for the host is in the *baldacchino*, supported by angels. This piece was a gift of expiation offered by a number of catholics to Leo XIII (1878–1903), after the discovery in April 1889 of the monument to Giordano Bruno in the Campo dei Fiori (F. S. Orlando).

The *Farnese Cross*, included in a set of six candlesticks, was made in Rome by Antonio Gentili of Faenza, in the second half of the 16th century. A beautiful silver gilt piece, it is decorated with rock crystal medallions attributed to Valerio Belli. The base is irregular in form and is engraved with the Farnese coat of arms. The detailed scrollwork, floral motifs, masks, niches with fluted columns and broken up spandrels, caryatids, and allegorical figures are all typical of late 16th-century ornamentation, reflecting very strongly the influence of Michelangelo.

The *Stuart Chalice* is so known because it belonged to Henry Stuart, Cardinal York, the son of James III, the Old Pretender, and Maria Clementina Sobieska, and bishop of Frascati. Of sculpted gold and silver, set with diamonds, it came into the Treasury in 1807, on the cardinal's death. The marks reveal that it was made by Louis Valadier in the second half of the 18th century; in style it reflects the neoclassical preference for decorative sobriety over late-baroque richness of detail.

Among the other pieces in the Treasury it is worth mentioning the neoclassical *bust of Henry Stuart, Cardinal York*; the 19th-century ornaments for the bronze statue of St. Peter in the basilica; the *gilded bronze ring* set with rock crystal belonging to Sixtus IV (1471–84); the *reliquary bust of Blessed Barbarigo* (gilt bronze with silver decoration); the 18th-century *silver and glass monstrance* donated by Cardinal Albani; the

10th- or 11th-century gilt and enamel *stauroteca* (cruciform receptacle for fragments of the Cross) standing on a 19th-century base; the *'palaeo-slav' icon* of SS. Peter and Paul and a scene of baptism, dating from the end of the 18th century; the two great 16th-century *candlesticks* in the Sala delle Reliquie; the statues of *SS. Peter and Paul* attributed to Sebastiano Torigiani, restored by Cardinal Francesco Barberini in 1962; the *candlesticks and altar cross* of Gregory XIII (1572–85) dating from the last quarter of the 16th century and attributed to Sebastiano Torrigiani; and finally the *reliquary of St. Peter*, with a little *aedicula*, Bramantesque in style, a typical example of late 17th-century Roman craftsmanship.

THE VATICAN GROTTOES

The crypts or grottoes under the basilica were first 'tidied up' under Gregory XIII (1572–85), a work which was to continue under Clement VIII (1592–1605).

The *Grotte Vecchie* (Old Grottoes) built by Gregory XIII, with pillars and cross vaulting and three naves, are situated beneath the eastern arm of the Bramante-Michelangelo Latin cross section of the basilica; these are adjoined by other crypts under the two symmetric Clementina and Gregorian chapels. Clement VIII's *Grotte Nuove* lie beneath the cross vault of the basilica. During the pontificate of Pius XII (1939–58) surveys were conducted, and the floor level was lowered by just over thirty inches to make the *Grotte* more functional. In the process the floor of the old basilica of Constantine and a Roman necropolis were discovered (Schiavo). A new entrance was also opened.

As Alfarano records, the first ancient Roman finds were made during the Gregorian excavations; more came to light in Paul V's pontificate (1605–21), however,

when the support for Bernini's *baldacchino* were sunk. The graves discovered during the excavations of 1940–50 belonged to various Roman families: Matucii, Caetenni, Valerii, Aelii, Tullii, Fannii, Popilii. Some extremely beautiful mosaics were also found, including that in the *Cella del Pescatore* (cell of the fisherman) depicting Christ as the Sun and as the Good Shepherd and Jonah.

Of the *sarcophagi*, that featuring a *Procession of Bacchus* (2nd–3rd century) and that of *Valerianus Vasatulus* (3rd century), depicting a lion hunt, are worthy of note. Of exceptional interest are the highly refined *stuccoes of the Valerii tomb*. From this hypogeum (underground chamber) we ascend to the third room. In the first two are various *tombstones*, among which one might mention those of Fra Raimondo Zacosta, Grand Master of the Knights of Jerusalem, who died in 1467; of Cardinal Pietro Rodriguez (Pietro Ispano), the faithful follower of Boniface VIII (1294–1303), who died in Avignon in 1311. In the second room are the *tombstones* of Cardinal Rinaldo Orsini the Younger, who, as arch-priest of the basilica, was present at the abjuration of John V Palae-ologos in 1369; of Cardinal Francesco Todeschini Piccolomini (later Pius III), who distinguished himself as a diplomat; of Jean Bilhères de Lagraulas, governor of Rome, who commissioned Michelangelo's *Pietà*; and finally of Bishop Theobold de Rougemont, who worked to repair the Western schism, and who witnessed the dismissal of the antipope John XXIII.

The third room contains various fragments from old St. Peter's. In the fourth are *mosaics* from the apse of Constantine's basilica and from the oratory which John VII had had built inside the basilica including an *angel* attributed to Giotto, but probably in fact a product of the late 13th-century Roman school. The fifth room

The Vatican Grottoes.
Passageway in the preconstantinian
necropolis with doorways leading to
the tombs.

The Vatican Grottoes.
Sarcophagus with spiral fluting, from
the 4th century, which was once the
tomb of the Emperor Otto II.

contains *funerary monuments* of: Benedict XII (1334–42), attributed to Paolo da Siena and dating from 1341 (Filippini); Cardinal Pietro de Fonseca, Roman school, first quarter of the 15th century; Cardinal Cristoforo Maroni, archpriest of the basilica; the apostolic protonotary Giacomo Caetani, from the end of the 15th century; Cardinal Ardicino Della Porta, 15th-century; and Cardinal Berardo Eruli, the eminent Humanist, attributed to Giovanni Dalmata and his workshop.

In the sixth room is the *Monument to Sixtus IV* (1471–84), with the pope shown lying surrounded by reliefs, with four coats of arms, two topped by cardinal's hats, and the other two by papal diadems (*triregno*), and with the Cardinal and Theological Virtues, as well as Geometry, Music, Grammar, Perspective, Rhetoric, Logic, Astronomy, Philosophy, and Theology. It is the work of Antonio del Pollaiolo and his brother Piero. Antonio's signature and inscribed date show that it was completed in 1493; originally intended for the Capella dei Francescani, it was moved to the sacristy in the 17th century, then into the Capella del Coro, and thence to the Cappella del SS. Sacramento, in the Museo Petriano, and finally the Grottoes.

In the aisles are situated the *Monument of Calixtus III* (1455–58), commissioned from Paolino di Antonio di Benasco for the Rotonda of Santa Maria della Febbre by Calixtus's nephew, Cardinal Rodrigo Borgia (later Alexander VI); with the demolition of the Rotonda to make way for the transport of the Vatican obelisk, the tomb was transferred to Santa Maria di Monserrato, and then eventually to the Grottoes.

Turning left, we see the *Tomb of Urban VI* (1378–89), the pope under whom the Western schism began; removed from the old basilica, it is of the late 14th-century Roman school. Immediately following is the *Tomb of Innocent XIII* (1721–24). Next is the *Tomb of the last Stuarts*: James III, Charles III, and Henry IX (the Old Pretender, Bonnie Prince Charlie, and Henry Stuart, Cardinal York). Then follow those of *Rafael Merry del Val* and *Pius XI* (1922–39). The mosaic is by D'Achiardi, and the statue by Castiglione.

In the center aisle is the *altar of Christ the King* (Roman school, second half of the 15th century), then reliefs and mosaics. Noteworthy is the *Madonna della Bocciata*, a Roman-school fresco of the early 14th century. The *Cappella di San Pietro* follows, then a number of reliefs from the *tabernacle of Sixtus IV*, attributed to Matteo del Pollaiolo, but more probably of the Roman school of

the mid-15th century, and statues of the Apostles attributed to Giovanni Dalmata, Matteo del Pollaiolo, and Mino da Fiesole. After a relief *reliquary of St. Andrew* (ascribable to the workshop of Isaia da Pisa), from a shrine commissioned by Pius II (1458–64), we come to the *Cappella di San Colombano*, built in 1954.

Further on is the *Monument of Paul II* (1464–71), of which the original triumphal arch derives from a design by Ciacconio (Galassi Paluzzi); commissioned by the pope's cousin, Marco Barbo, it is by Giovanni Dalmata (the statue of the pope the Father and Angels, the Resurrection, the two angels supporting the tablet, the Evangelists Mark and Matthew, Hope, and the Creation of Eve) and Mino da Fiesole (the lunette of the Last Judgement, Charity and Faith, and the Fall). It was probably produced in 1474–77. The original base, with masks, putti, and garlands, is now in the Louvre.

Next follows the *Tomb of Pius VI*, consisting of a scored palaeochristian sarcophagus and a relief dating probably from the 4th century. Now appears a marble monument of the *Madonna, SS. Peter and Paul, and two donors*, originally from the Orsini family Cappella di San Biagio; the two kneeling figures have been variously identified as John XXII (1316–34) or Eugenius IV (1431–47) or the cardinals Giovan-

ni or Gaetano Orsini or Latino Orsini; Bürger convincingly ascribed the work to Isaia da Pisa.

In the chapel containing the *Tomb of John XXIII* (1958–63) is a fine relief of the *Madonna and Child and Angels*, of the 15th-century Lombard school. The next tombs are of *Queen Charlotte of Savoy* and *Queen Christina of Sweden*; then of *Benedict XV* (1914–22), by Giulio Barbieri, and *Innocent IX* (1591). Next to these is the *Tomb of Marcellus II* (1555), a 4th-century sarcophagus, while the next chapel contains a 15th-century Tuscan relief of the *Madonna and Child and two Angels*. The *Tomb of Julius III* (1550–55) follows, an early Christian sarcophagus, while the *Tomb of Innocent VII* (1404–06) is of the 15th-century Roman school.

After these come the *Tombs of Nicholas V* (1447–55) and *Boniface VIII* (1294–1303), the latter a masterpiece by Arnolfo di Cambio (though the two angels lifting the curtain are of his school).

Next is a fine 4th-century sarcophagus, the *Tomb of Nicholas III* (1277–80), and the *aedicula* with a 15th-century Sienese fresco of the Madonna. In the middle is a 3rd-century *Statue of St. Peter* (the head and hands resculpted in the 13th century), originally in the portico of the old basilica. The following chapel contains *4th-century sarcophagi* serving as the *Tombs of Gregory V* (996–99) and the *Emperor Otto II*; also a *stone inscribed with the text of Matilda's donation of Canossa* and a 9th- or 10th-century *mosaic of Christ and SS. Peter and Paul*. The last two *Tombs* are of *Hadrian IV* (1154–59 – the only Englishman ever to have become pope) and *Pius III* (1503).

On the right of the Grottoes, in the last rooms before the exit, are *fragments* from different periods and *early Christian sarcophagi*.

THE GARDENS

One of the loveliest, but at the

The Vatican Grottoes.
The Tomb of Pope Nicholas V.

The Gregorian Museum of Egyptian Art.
Antinous, the favorite of Hadrian, dressed in Egyptian fashion. 2nd-century sculpture, from Hadrian's Villa at Tivoli.

same time the least well known features of the Vatican complex are the gardens. Divided by the long street running from the Piazza della Zecca to the Cortile delle Corazze, on the right is the Cortile della Pigna and that of the Belvedere, designed by Bramante (the recess for the Pigna itself was designed by Pirro Ligorio, while the Belvedere proper is the work of Giacomo da Pietrasanta); and on the left is the park with Pius IV's Casina or summerhouse.

The garden is 16th-century in origin, and contained within the Leonine walls. Apart from a number of recent constructions, such as the *tempietto of the Madonna della Guardia*, built for Benedict XV (1914–22) and the *Casina di Leo XIII* (1878–1903), there are also certain outstanding buildings, such as the *Torre leonina* (the Leonine Tower, 847–55) and the 16th-century *Torre dei venti* (Tower of the Winds) by Ottaviano Mascherino, built as an observatory for Gregory XIII (1572–85) and partially modified by Urban VIII (1623–44), with a sundial by Ignazio Danti in the Salone del Calendario.

Of quite exceptional interest, however, is the *Casina di Pio IV* (1559–65), in front of which is an elliptical square, with two side staircases leading up, curving in the opposite direction. It was built for Paul IV (1555–59) between 1558 and 1561 by Pirro Ligorio, assisted by Sallustio Peruzzi.

Together with its Italianate garden, its is one of the finest examples of late-Renaissance villa architecture. The somewhat cerebral sensitivity of the time finds beautifully harmonious expression in the direct borrowing from and reworking of classical models. This form of classicism is evident above all in the handling of the exterior: the building is no longer simply a 'receptacle' seen from the outside; the walls are sectioned up in light, graceful proportions and decorated with exquisite reliefs of mythological subjects, in which a free rein has been given to the 'fantastic' streak in the character of a great, somewhat bizarre architect, active just before the dawn of Baroque.

Inside, it is richly decorated with stuccoes and paintings inspired by either mythology or Holy Writ. The artists involved were Federico Zuccari, Lorenzo Costa, Santi di Tito, and the young Barocci, with Pierleone Genga as assistant, and Tommaso Boscoli da Montepulciano in charge of the stucco work.

The fountains are one of the most attractive features of the gardens, and were mostly the work of Maderno, Vasanzio, and Ferrabosco. Of particular note are the *Fontana degli Specchi* (Fountain of Mirrors) by the stairway of Paul V (1605–21); the *Fontana dell'Aquilone* (Fountain of the North Wind), abounding with mythological sea creatures; the

Fontana del Sacramento, a curious liturgical allegory commissioned by Paul V in 1608; and finally the *Fontana della Galera*, dating from the time of Paul V, but with Pius VI's (1775–99) arms on the bronze galleon in the pool.

THE VATICAN MUSEUMS

The sheer richness of variety in these museums makes them unique. At the same time it is a direct testimony to the concern of the papacy over the centuries in the fostering of the arts. The archaeological galleries first took shape in the 18th century, when interest in antiquity became intense as a result of excavation work that brought to light entire cities, as at Herculaneum and Pompeii. 'Antiquities' began to appear on the market in large numbers; and such finds were made even more widely known through albums of print illustrations. Collecting became a passion.

One consequence of this was the creation of different specialist private museum collections, e.g. those of Cardinal Albani, and Cardinal Stefano Borgia's Velletri collection, now in Naples. Of exceptional note here is the Pinacoteca Vaticana containing the finest works from all periods from the 11th to the 20th century (although recently a separate gallery was opened for modern religious works of art).

THE GREGORIAN MUSEUMS

These are situated in the apartment of Pius IV overlooking the Cortile della Pigna, on the same side as the Pigna itself, and were the brainchild of Gregory XVI (1831–46). Access is via the Scala Simonetti, which leads to the first floor, to the **Egyptian Museum**, which was set up between 1838–39 by Father Luigi Ungarelli (the Egyptian reconstruction in the first room is by Giuseppe De Fabris), with material from

Hadrian's Villa and the Capitoline Museum as well as the Vatican. There are ten rooms in all, displaying sarcophagi, mummies, and statues. Of particular merit are the *Head of Pharaoh Mentuhotep IV*, and the *Statues of Rameses II* and his mother *Tuaa*, the *Pharaoh Seti I*, and *Ptolemy Philadelphus with his wife Arsinoe*.

There is a number of copies of Egyptian originals dating from the 2nd and 3rd centuries AD (taken from Hadrian's Villa). The *fragment depicting a Roman galley* is from Praeneste. The fourth room (Sala del Naoforo) contains basalt *votive statuettes*, of which that of Udjeharresnet is particularly important.

In the next room (Sala dell'Emiciclo) it is worth mentioning the *Tombstone of the Official Iri*, from the 4th Dynasty, and the 6th-century AD *anthropoid sarcophagi*. The sixth room houses a collection of *statuettes of human and animal deities*, while in the seventh are various *funerary objects*. Rooms eight to ten have a collection of *papyri*, mostly funerary, together with various stone objects from prehistoric Egypt.

On the second floor we come to the **Etruscan Museum**, set up by Gaspare Salvi. This collection began to grow, under the supervision of Camuccini, Thorwaldsen,

Valadier, Grifi, and Nibby, after the great discoveries of Caere (Cerveteri). In 1836 the Vatican acquired the appurtenances of the Regolini-Galassi tomb.

The first room (there are seventeen altogether) contains *sarcophagi* bearing scenes from Greek mythology, a procession of lictors escorting a chariot, a wedding procession, and a bearded man. The second, with frescoes by Barocci and Federico Zuccari, houses the contents of the *Regolini-Galassi tomb* at Cerveteri, dating from the mid 7th century BC – one of the most complete examples of the culture of this intriguingly orientalized civilization.

In the third room, decorated with frescoes by Niccolò Pomarancio and Santi di Tito, are exhibited bronzes and an assortment of different finds; the most important object is the Umbro-Etruscan bronze statue called the *Mars of Todi*, from the 4th century BC.

The fourth room contains small *cinerary urns* decorated with mythological subjects. In the fifth is a collection of clay ewers (*buccheri*) and *vases* from the 7th–5th century BC, from the cemetery of Vulci.

The sixth contains *jewellery*; the seventh *terracottas*; the eighth *terracotta friezes*, *weapons*, *ivories*

and *bone carvings*, *lamps*, *incense burners*, *glassware*, and a 3rd-century AD *head of an emperor*. In the ninth is housed the Falcioni collection of *terracottas*, *bronzes*, and *gold objects*, while in the eleventh are the fragments of a *bronze statue* (probably Neptune) found at the port of Civitavecchia.

We next come to the room of original Greek sculptures, with classical Greek marbles, some from the Parthenon, of which the most outstanding are the *stele of Palestritas*, from a 5th-century BC Attic tomb, and the *Head of Athena*, from the 5th–4th century BC. A corridor then leads to a room containing Assyrian reliefs: *cuneiform inscriptions* and *scenes of war*. The last room contains *Italiot, Attic* and *Etruscan vases*.

MUSEO PIO CLEMENTINO

The Museum was originally stocked with objects from the Cortile del Belvedere and the Mattei and Fusconi collections, acquired in 1770. The rooms were laid out, and Innocent VIII's (1484–92) palazzetto adapted, by Alessandro Dori, under the supervision of Giambattista Visconti and Giovanni Angelo Braschi. The moving force behind the creation of the Museum was Pope Clement XIV (1769–74), whose enthusiasm was shared by his successor Pius VI (1775–99). The architects under the latter's patronage were Michelangelo Simonetti and Giuseppe Camporese.

The disposition of the sculptures was undertaken in 1772, while the rearrangement of the atrium that same year was entrusted to Simonetti (Pietrangeli), who worked on it until 1773. New work began in 1776 with the destruction of Mantegna's chapel and sacristy for an extension of the Galleria delle Statue (Gallery of Statues). The extension was completed by 1793 with the addition of Camporese's Atrio dei Quattro Cancelli.

Sculptures, sarcophagi, mosaics, and architectural fragments dating from various periods are housed here. As examples, one might mention the 4th-century *sarcophagus of Constantia*, Constantine's daughter, from Santa Costanza, with pagan and Christian symbolic decoration; and the 4th-century *sarcophagus of St. Helena* from Tor Pignattara, with depictions of Roman soldiers and barbarian prisoners. In the beautiful circular *Sala Rotonda* is the *Otricoli mosaic*, with water deities and a battle of centaurs; then there is the extraordinary *Otricoli Jupiter*, a Roman copy of a 4th-century BC Greek original by Bryaxis; especially beautiful are the *goddess with peplum* (copy of a 4th-century BC Greek sculpture) and the gilt bronze statue of *Hercules* (early 1st century), from the Theater of Pompey.

Next we come to the Hall of the Muses, decorated with mythological subjects by the school of Sebastiano Conca. Here are displayed various *herms* of characters from history and Greek literature, together with the Tivoli *Muses and Apollo* (copies of 3rd-century BC Greek originals). After this is the Animal Room, conceived by Pius VI (1775–99), in which are housed 18th-century animal sculptures by Francesco Antonio Franzoni; here

too is a representation of the mythological story of *Meleager and the Caledonian boar*, a fine Roman copy of a 4th-century BC sculpture by Scopas. Equally impressive are the 2nd-century *Mithras slaying the Bull* and the mosaics depicting genre scenes.

Of special note in the Gallery of Statues are: the *Eros of Centocelle*, after a 4th-century BC original; the *bust of a sea god*, of Hellenistic date; and above all the *Apollo Sauroctonus* (Apollo the lizard-killer, a Roman copy of a sculpture by Praxiteles), and the Villa Mattei *Amazon*, a replica of a 5th-century BC work by Polyclitus. Of interest also are the *Satyr resting* (after an original by Praxiteles), and a Hellenistic sculpture from the early 3rd century BC representing the *Sleeping Ariadne*.

There are also the *Barberini candelabra* (2nd century) from Hadrian's Villa, with decorative reliefs of various deities. In the Gallery of Busts it is worth mentioning the portraits of emperors (including the extremely fine *Julius Caesar, Young Octavian,* and *Caracalla*), and gods, e.g. the Palazzo Verospi *Jupiter*.

Pius VI's Gabinetto delle Maschere (Mask Room), with paintings by Domenico De Angelis, contains the *Venus of Cnidus*, and a Roman copy of the 4th-century BC Aphrodite by Praxiteles, from the Colonna collection.

The magnificent marble *Laöcoon* gives its name to the room in which it is displayed. The work of the Rhodian sculptors Agesander, Athenodoros, and Polydoros, it probably dates from the 2nd century BC. Having been discovered in 1506 in the Domus Aurea, it was restored soon afterwards by Montorsoli; and restored again recently to bring it closer to its original state.

A similar fate has attended the *Belvedere Apollo* which, after restoration also by Montorsoli in the 16th century, has now been re-

The Etruscan Museum.
The *Mars of Todi*. Umbro-Etruscan bronze statue, 4th century BC.

Museo Pio Clementino
Porphyry sarchophagus of St. Helena, the mother of Constantine. Beginning of the 4th century.

Museo Pio Clementino.
The *Belvedere Torso*, signed by the neoattic sculptor, Apollonius, son of Nestor.

stored. This superb work is one of the most famous examples of classical sculpture. It is a Roman copy, from the time of Hadrian, of an original by Leochares dating from about 320 BC.

Proceeding on, we now come to the Gabinetto del Canova, containing the statue of *Perseus* sculpted by Canova between 1797 and 1801 (of which a second version, made for the Countess Tarnowska, is owned by the Metropolitan Museum of New York). Finally we reach the Gabinetto dell'Hermes, named after a Roman *Hermes* of the 2nd century copied from a 4th-century BC original by Praxiteles. Traversing the circular vestibule, we next come to the Sala delle Iscrizioni, in which is displayed the *Apoxyomenos*, a Roman copy of the bronze made by Lisippus *c*. 320 BC, discovered in Trastevere in 1849. Next door is the *Belvedere Torso* (discovered at the beginning of the 16th century), signed by the Athenian sculptor Apollonios.

MUSEO CHIARAMONTI

The Museum is divided into three parts: the Museum itself, the Braccio Nuovo, and the Galleria Lapidaria. The new building, commissioned by Pius VII (1800–23), was built by Raffaello Stern, Antonio Canova, and Pasquale Belli.

The Museo Chiaramonti houses sarcophagi, herms, portraits, and statues representing different periods of Roman sculpture. As well as the sculptures, the Galleria Lapidaria contains a collection of Christian and pagan epigraphs from catacombs and cemeteries, arranged by Gaetano Marini. Noteworthy are the *Augustus of Prima Porta* (1st century BC), discovered in Livia's Villa in 1863, together with a statue of *Demosthenes*, a copy of a 3rd-century BC bronze by Polyeuctus; the *Wounded Amazon* (copy of a 5th-century BC statue by Polyclitus, the feet and arms

restored by Thorwaldsen); an *Artemis* from a 4th-century BC original; the Hellenistic *Nile* by Iseo Campense, discovered in 1513; the Giustiniani *Pallas Athene*, copied from a 4th-century BC bronze; the *Satyr in repose* after a statue by Praxiteles; and the exceptional *Spear Bearer*, after a 5th-century BC bronze by Polyclitus.

Ascending to the Gallery of the Candelabra, we find many sculptures of great interest: the *sarcophagus with the Orestes myth*; the sets of candelabra from Sant' Agnese and Santa Costanza; the *Ganymede* after a 4th-century BC original by Leochares; a fine *statue of an old man*, by a Pergamenian sculptor; a *sarcophagus with the Slaughter of the Niobids*; and a *candelabra from Otricoli*.

Next door is the Sala della Biga (Chariot Room), so named after the chariot reconstructed at the end of the 18th century by Francesco Antonio Franzoni, using ancient fragments. Very beautiful are a *Bearded Dionysius* (early 4th-century BC); a *Discus Thrower*, after an original by Myron; and three *sarcofagi with cupids driving chariots*.

Returning to the Gallery of the Candelabra, one then proceeds through to the Gallery of Tapestries, where ten tapestries by

Raphael used to hang; these are now in the Pinacoteca Vaticana, and have been replaced by ten *tapestries* made in the 16th century in Brussels by Pieter Van Aelst, after cartoons by Bernard Van Orley and Tommaso Vincidor, showing scenes from the life of Christ.

Proceeding further, we come to the Galleria delle Carte Geografiche (Gallery of Maps), set up by Gregory XIII, and so named after the thirty-six *perspective maps* of Italy produced in the latter half of the 16th century by the cosmographer Ignazio Danti. The ceiling, with stuccoes and scenes of Biblical history, is the work of Girolamo Muziano and Cesare Nebbia, jointly in charge of a whole 'workshop' of painters: Niccolò Circignani, Baldassarre Croce, Paul and Mathys Bril, Iacopo Semenza, Matteo da Siena, Giacomo Stella, Antonio Tempesta, Giacomo Palma, Giambattista Lombardelli, Marco Marchetti, and Ottaviano Mascherino.

THE VATICAN LIBRARY

The Library was founded by Nicholas V (1447–55) and subsequently enlarged, often with the acquisition of private collections: the Palatina in 1622, the Urbinate (1658), the Capponiana (1746), the

Ottoboniana (1748), the Borghesiana (1891), the Barberiniana and Borgiana (1902), and the Chigiana (1923). It also contains incunabula and manuscripts. It comprises the following rooms: the Galleria Clementina, built in 1732 for Clement XII (1730–40), containing a remarkable collection of maps of Rome; the Sala Alessandrina, built in 1690 for Alexander VIII (1689–91), containing *Maps of Rome* by Du Perac, Lafréry, and Maggi-Maupin-Losi; the Biblioteca Sistina; and the Salone Sistino, built for Sixtus V (1585–90) by Domenico Fontana, with decoration by Federico Rainaldi and Silvio Antoniano glorifying the role of the book in history, and recording Sixtus's various building projects.

The decoration of the Salone, which, as Redig De Campos comments, is particularly useful for an understanding of Counter-Reformation culture, was completed by a hundred artists under the supervision of Cesare Nebbia and Giovanni Guerra. The *Views of Rome* are the work of Antonio Tempesta and Paul Bril. The Library contains an immensely rich collection of codices and Latin manuscripts (four Virgils), miniatures (the exquisite illuminated *Book of Hours* of Jean Bourdichon; the *Breviary of Mat-*

thias *Corvinus*, 1487; and the
Divina Commedia illustrated by
Botticelli), and works of Latin and
Italian poetry of every period,
along with the 1499 Venetian
edition of the *Hypnerotomachia
Polyphili*. The last two rooms of
the Vatican Library are the Sala
Sistina and the Gallery of Urban
VIII (1623–44).

MUSEO PROFANO AND MUSEO SACRO

These Museums are at either end
of the long Library corridor. The
Museo Profano, built for Clement
XIII (1758–69) and Pius VI
(1775–99) is furnished with brazil
wood cupboards designed by
Louis Valadier, and contains small
exhibits of ivory and hard stone.
The Museo Sacro, built for
Benedict XIV (1740–58) in 1756

has ceiling decorations by Stefano
Pozzi depicting the *Theological
Virtues* and the *Triumph of the
Church*. It houses a variety of
exhibits dating from the 1st to the
17th century: glassware, incense
burners, enamelware, silverware.

In the next room is the fresco of
the *Nozze Aldobrandini*, a wedding
scene dating from the end of the
1st century BC, discovered on the
Esquiline in 1605 and conserved in
the Villa Aldobrandini, whence it
was moved to the Vatican in 1818;
the other wall frescoes show landscapes from the Odyssey and the
Esquiline, and a procession of
children from Ostia. The ceiling
frescoes, telling the *Story of
Samson*, were painted by Guido
Reni for Paul V (1605–21). In the
19th century they were detached
and transferred to canvas. We
then pass into the Cappella di San
Pio V (1566–72), with frescoes by
Jacopo Zucchi depicting episodes of
St. Peter Martyr. The last rooms of
the Museo Sacro contain *liturgical
ornaments* from various periods.

THE BORGIA ROOMS

We come now to the Apparta-
mento Borgia, between the courtyards of the Belvedere, the Borgia,
and the Pappagalli. These rooms
were decorated by Pinturicchio
(and workshop) for Alexander VI
(1492–1503), who had summoned
the artist to Rome while he was at
work on the cathedral of Orvieto.
The work was started at the
beginning of 1493 and finished in
the following year.

The rooms decorated by Pinturicchio and his assistants were
the Sala dei Misteri, the Sala dei
Santi, the Sala delle Arti, the Sala
del Credo, and the Sala delle
Sibille, together with small areas
in the west wing. Under Leo XIII
(1878–1903) they were restored by
Lodovico Seitz. The Sala dei
Pontefici was frescoed by Perin
del Vaga and Giovanni da Udine
during the pontificate of Leo X
(1513–21); the decoration was

embellished by six 16th-century
Flemish tapestries depicting the
myth of Cephalus and Procris.
Later a *bust of Leo XIII* by Guido
Galli was placed there. Small
carvings were then displayed in a
show case; these include Bernini's
terracotta models for Charity and
Truth on the tomb of Alexander
VII (1655–67), a 15th-century
bronze portrait of the Emperor
John Palaeologos, and a number of
small bronzes of different schools
and periods.

In the Sala delle Sibille, the
Prophets and *Sibyls* in the lunettes
and the ceiling frescoes (incorporating gilded reliefs) are by the

school of Pinturicchio; the decoration here was completed with
Flemish tapestries, a della Robbia
Madonna, and a 15th-century
wooden crucifix.

Weapons from various sources
of origin were displayed in the
Sala del Credo (decorated with
lunettes containing pairs of
Apostles and Prophets). The Sala
delle Arti, the pope's study, was
decorated mostly by Pastura, with
an allegorical cycle of *Logic*, *Grammar*, *Astrology*, *Music*, *Arithmetic*,
Geography, and *Rhetoric*; the ceiling is decorated with grotesques
and gilded reliefs.

In the Sala dei Santi is the
*Disputation of St. Catherine of
Alexandria with the Philosophers
before the Emperor Maximilian*, by
Pinturicchio; assistants helped on
the other scenes: the *Meeting of St.
Anthony and St. Paul the Hermit*,
the *Visitation*, the *Martyrdom of
St. Sebastian*, *Susannah and the
Elders*, and *St. Barbara*. The
wooden furbishings date from the
second half of the 15th century.
On the ceiling Isis, Osiris, Io, and
the bull god Apis appear amid
gilded stucco work.

Pinturicchio also worked on the
next-door room, the Sala dei
Misteri della Fede, where there is a
very fine portrait of the Borgia
pope at prayer in the *Resurrection*
scene. The other scenes depicted
here are the *Annunciation*, *Nativity*, *Adoration of the Magi*, the
Ascension, *Pentecost*, and *Assumption of the Virgin*. The old furnishings have been removed to make
way for the Gallery of Modern
Religious Art.

We now ascend to the Raphael
Rooms. Just before the Stanza
dell'Incendio di Borgo, however,
is the *Chapel of Urban VIII*
(1623–44), begun for this pope in
1631; the pictorial decoration is
by Pietro Berrettini da Cortona
(who received payment for a
Deposition as late as 1635), though
the *Passion of Christ* (ceiling and
lunettes) is by Cortona's school.

The nearby Sala dell'
Immacolata was restructured for
Pius IX (1846–78), and decorated
by Francesco Podesti with representations of the dogma of the
Immaculate Conception, approved
by the First Vatican Council on 8
December 1854. On the ceiling,
along with the pope's family arms,
are Biblical scenes and allegories;
while between the windows are
painted Sibyls.

Of note in the Sala del Sobieski
is the large painting by Jan Alois
Matejko dating from 1883,
illustrating John Sobieski's
repulse of the Turks from Vienna
in 1683.

THE RAPHAEL ROOMS

We now come to the first of the Raphael Rooms, that of the *Fire of Borgo*. These frescoes were first conceived when Julius II (1503–13) decided to make these rooms into his personal apartments, not wishing to take over the apartments of his predecessor, Alexander VI Borgia whom he held in abhorrence. Unfortunately the new Raphael frescoes – one of the consummate masterpieces of Renaissance art – entailed the destruction of (as Vasari attests) already preexisting frescoes by Piero della Francesca, Luca Signorelli, and Bartolomeo della Gatta.

Initially the pope had planned to have the frescoes painted by several artists, including Sodoma, Bramantino, Lotto, and Peruzzi; Raphael, however, agreed to take on the work himself, and came to Rome from Florence in 1508, and at once set about the task. He started on the *Stanza della Segnatura*, so named because it later became the seat of the courts of the *Signatura Gratiae* and the *Signatura Iustitiae*. The decoration was finished in 1511, as we gather from the inscription on the *Parnassus*. The themes developed in the frescoes (possibly suggested by Julius himself) where a glorifica-

tion of the concepts of the True, the Good, and the Beautiful.

These therefore were the subjects that inspired the *Disputation on the Sacrament*, and the *School of Athens* (revealed truth and rational truth), *Gregory IX's approval of the Decretals* and *Justinian delivering the Pandects* (canon and civil law), and the *Parnassus* (Beauty represented as poetry). On the ceiling, adorned with cornices and grotesques, were the same concepts personified by female figures in roundels, and rectangular panels with *Adam and Eve, Apollo and Marsyas*, the *Judgement of Solomon*, and *Urania*. The *Disputation* is on the entrance wall, the *Virtues*, the *Justinian* and *Gregory IX frescoes*, on the left, and the *School of Athens* opposite the entrance; finally there is the *Parnassus*.

In the first fresco (1508–09) we see depicted the symbolic function of the Eucharist, the link between the Church on earth and the Church celestial. We see here the full maturity of a great artist still only twenty-five years old. Refining and elaborating on the *schema* already used for the Trinity and Saints in San Severo (Perugia), Raphael has gone far beyond what his master Perugino had been able to teach him. Though still re-

sponsive to the achievements of his contemporaries, he has here managed to create perspective essentially through the handling of his figures by placing them in a unique milieu *en plein air*.

On the opposite wall is the *School of Athens* (the fresco was given this title by Bellori in 1695), in which the greatest philosophers and scientists of antiquity are represented alongside Plato and Aristotle, engaging in discussion with contemporary figures (a common device, already used in the *Disputation*). The architectural elements are in part classically inspired, certain details deriving from the Basilica of Maxentius, e.g. the hexagonal compartments of the coffered ceilings, and in part related to Bramante's design for the new St. Peter's. The fresco, through it glorification of philosophy, is a paean to Truth: Plato and Aristotle, holding the *Timaeus* and the *Ethics* respectively, represent between them speculative and a posteriori thinking, two antithetical philosophical systems that need not necessarily be self-excluding in the search for truth. Completed between 1509–10, this fresco is perhaps the single most important visual expression of the ideals of Renaissance culture. All previous and contemporary experiments in figurative painting are here synthesized into a veritable *summa* which, while offering a solution to the crisis of traditional values, brought to a head in the work of Michelangelo, also lays the ground rules for Italian figurative art.

The fresco of *Parnassus* is on the wall facing towards the Cortile del Belvedere. Here we see Apollo playing a nine-string lyre, surrounded by the nine Muses and various Latin, Greek, and Italian vernacular poets, amongst whom Homer, Dante, and Sappho are easily recognizable. According to an engraving by Raimondi, mentioned by Vasari, the poet's laurel wreaths were originally held by

fluttering cupids. Though generally agreed to be the work of Raphael, its authorship is contested by Copier, who attributes it to Sodoma. The window inscription gives the completion date of the work as 1511 (it was probably started at the end of 1509). The preparatory drawings are scattered throughout the world, at Windsor, Oxford, Lille, Vienna, Florence, and London.

The two monochrome paintings depicting Augustus refusing to burn the Aeneid, and Alexander the Great placing the poems of Homer in the tomb of Achilles, are attributable either to Penni or to

Perin del Vaga. On the opposite wall, facing towards the Cortile dei Pappagalli, are frescoes by Raphael of the *Virtues* (Fortitude, Prudence, Temperance) with other spirits which have been interpreted by Wind as representing the theological virtues. This wall can be dated to the latter half of 1511. The two scenes of the *Delivery of the Decretals to Raymond of Penafort* and the *Delivery of the Pandects to Trebonianus* are probably to be ascribed to Gianfrancesco Penni and Marcillat.

In chronological order, we next come to the *Stanza d'Eliodoro*, so named after the fresco of the *Expulsion of Heliodorus from the*

259

The Room of the Fire of Borgo.
Detail from the *Fire of Borgo*.
Raphael and assistants.

The Room of Heliodorus.
Detail of the monochrome decoration.
Polidoro da Caravaggio.
Below: the *Burning Bush*.
Attributed to Guillaume de Marcillat.

Temple, painted between the summer of 1511 and 1514. The iconographical themes for this room too were selected by the pope, and are a clear assertion of the Church's political and doctrinal authority under the guidance of divine intervention. Arabesques divide the ceiling into sections containing four episodes from the Bible: *God Appearing to Noah*, the *Burning Bush*, *Abraham's Sacrifice* and *Jacob's Ladder*. Variously attributed to Peruzzi, Penni, and Marcillat, they are most probably by the latter.

In the main arches are the *Expulsion of Heliodorus from the Temple*, the *Mass of Bolsena*, *Leo I Repulsing Attila*, and the *Liberation of St. Peter*. In the first scene (from the Book of Maccabees) Heliodorus, who has profaned the Temple, is being driven out by an angel; the fresco is given contemporary significance by the inclusion of Julius II and his various dignitaries, a clear allusion to the internal and external problems of the Church.

The hand of Raphael is detectable in the chair carriers and the portrait of the pope, while the rest of the fresco is largely by his school, with, notably in the figure of Heliodorus, certain Michelangelesque elements. The *Mass of Bolsena* depicts the miracle that occurred at Bolsena in 1263, when blood began to drip from the Host after the consecration.

It was following this that Pope Urban IV (1261–64) instituted the feast of Corpus Christi in 1264. Also in this fresco Julius II is depicted with various of his contemporaries, as if symbolically emphasizing the presence of the Church, a reemphasis given more concrete expression in the Lateran Council of 1512. This fresco is considered to be by Raphael, except for certain sections of architectural detail.

The theory that Sebastiano del Piombo or Lorenzo Lotto worked on it does not really hold water: the statuesque, aristocratic gravity of the chair carriers, each a definite portrait, thoroughly Raphaelesque in style, is undeniably similar to the parallel group in the Stanza d'Eliodoro. It was painted in 1512, after the removal of paintings by Bramantino.

Next to it (similarly replacing earlier works by Bramantino) is *Leo I Repulsing Attila*, the former being made to resemble Leo X (1513–21), who is also portrayed on the left as a cardinal. Almost all of the fresco is by the school of Raphael (notably Giulio Romano), the only exception being the portrait of Leo X, which is by the

master himself. The turbulent movement of the group on the right already anticipates the confused swirling mass of infantry and cavalry in the later *Victory of Constantine over Maxentius* by Giulio Romano.

Where we now see the *Liberation of St. Peter*, there were formerly frescoes by Piero della Francesca. The present work, illustrating an episode from the Acts of the Apostles, is one of the most brilliant night scenes in the whole of Italian art, and is wholly by Raphael, except for the section on the left where he was aided by assistants. Dating from 1514, it appropriately reflects the contemporary disputes between the pope and the king of France.

The *Room of the Fire of Borgo* was painted between 1514–17, and honors the papacy: the the-

matic content was probably decided on by Baldassar Castiglione. The ceiling still retains the tondi painted in 1508 by Perugino, depicting sacred subjects. The main frescoes were executed, after cartoons by Raphael, by his school. The monochrome works are by Giulio Romano.

The *Fire of Borgo* illustrates the occasion in 847 described in the *Liber Pontificalis*, when Leo IV quelled a great fire that was raging in the Vatican area (Borgo) by giving his blessing. Quite new here is the handling of the architectural elements, which give the scene a certain theatricality, actu-

ally enhancing the figures, which are deftly classicized as Aeneas, Anchises, and Iulus. Raphael himself was only responsible for the young man (second from the right) distributing the pitchers of water; the rest is by Giulio Romano, Gianfrancesco Penni, and Giovanni da Udine. The fresco dates from the latter part of 1514.

The arch with the *Victory at Ostia* illustrates another episode from the *Liber Pontificalis*, the naval battle of 849 between the papal and Muslim fleets. Leo IV (847–55) is again made to resemble Leo X. Raphael contributed only the portrait of Leo and the attendant cardinals, while the other figures are by Giulio Romano; Giovanni da Udine probably painted the architectural elements and the ships in the background. It was completed in 1514–15.

The Raphael Loggia.
Decoration of a pilaster.
Raphael and his school.

Stanza della Segnatura.
Urania. Detail from the ceiling.
Raphael.

The arch with the *Justification of Leo III* is once again derived from the *Liber Pontificalis*: Leo III (795–816) reasserts the dependence of the papacy on God alone in the face of attacks from the nephews of Hadrian I (772–95). The explicit reference here is to the papal bull *Unam Sanctam* issued by Boniface VIII (1294–1303), which the Lateran Council of 1516 confirmed. The artists were Gianfrancesco Penni and Giovanni da Udine. In the last arch we see the *Coronation of Charlemagne*, a reference to the treaty made at Bologna between Leo X and François I. This fresco is by Penni and Raffaellino del Colle, after drawings by Raphael.

The *Sala di Costantino* was frescoed after Raphael's death on 6 April 1520. His pupils endeavoured to remain faithful to their master's precepts in this glorification of the role of the Church among men. On the walls are figures of popes, angels, and allegories (Meekness and Justice are painted in oils), and grisailles of fake reliefs. The decoration of the window embrasures is by Perin del Vaga. Altogether, the sala is made to resemble a room hung with tapestries. It was finished in 1524, and is largely the work of Giulio Romano, with the assistance of Gianfrancesco Penni and Raffaellino.

Giulio Romano's *Apparition of the Cross to Constantine before the Battle of the Milvian Bridge* is inspired by classical models (the spiral column). The dwarf on the right is Gradasso Berettai, Cardinal Ippolito Medici's fool. The battle scene itself (also by Giulio Romano) is similarly inspired by classical works of art, and represents an important point of reference in the development of battle scenes (*battaglismo*) as a genre, which became so popular in the 17th century. The *Baptism of Constantine* is by Gianfrancesco Penni, with help from Giulio Romano; the two figures at either

end are, on the right, Constantine's son Crispus, and on the left Cavalierino, a gentleman at the court of Clement VII (1523–34). Meanwhile the *Donation of Constantine* is attributed to Giulio Romano, with the assistance of Raffaellino del Colle and Gianfrancesco Penni.

So we come to the *Sala dei Palafrenieri* or *Sala dei Chiaroscuri*, for which, according to Vasari, the drawings for the Apostles and Saints were prepared by Raphael himself, but actually painted by his pupils. These paintings were removed by Paul IV (1555–59), and new ones painted by Taddeo and Frederico Zuccari, Giovanni Alberti, the Cavalier d'Arpino, and others.

THE RAPHAEL LOGGIA

Raphael's Loggia, to which we now come, look out over the Cortile di San Damaso. Originally designed by Bramante, the Loggia was completed by Raphael in 1519. It is made up of thirteen arches, each with its own small frescoed ceiling, twelve of which depict Old Testament scenes, and the last, scenes from the life of Christ. Each ceiling has four frescoes as well as a variety of decorative elements (winged figures, grotesques, and caissons).

Both Vasari and Marcantonio Michiel record that the preparatory drawings were by Raphael, while the actual painting was carried out by his school: Giulio Romano, Perin del Vaga, Giovanni da Udine, Gianfrancesco Penni, Vincenzo Tamagni, Pellegrino da Modena, Tommaso Vincidor, Vincenzo da San Gimignano, Polidoro da Caravaggio, Raffaellino del Colle, Guillaume Marcillat, and Pedro Machuca. To the last two of these, Dacos convincingly attributes the scenes of *God Creating the Sun and Moon*, the *Burning Bush*, the *Annointing of David* (Marcillat), and *Isaac Blessing Jacob* (Machuca). The floor was the work of Luca della Robbia, who was paid two hundred and twenty-five ducats. Restoration work was carried out in 1546–47. The frescoes depict, in order:

1. *Separation of Light from Darkness*, by Giulio Romano; *Separation of Land and Water* (Penni); *Creation of the Sun and Moon* (Marcillat); *Creation of the Animals* (Giovanni da Udine).

2. *Creation of Eve* (Vincidor); *The Fall* (Pellegrino da Modena and Vincidor); *Expulsion of Adam and Eve from Paradise* (Vincidor); *Adam and Eve Toiling* (Vincidor).

3. *Building the Ark* (Giulio Romano and Penni); *The Flood* (Giulio Romano and Penni); *Exit from the Ark* (Giovanni da Udine); *Noah's Sacrifice* (Giulio Romano and Penni).

4. *Abraham and Melchisedech* (Giulio Romano); *God's Covenant with Abraham* (Giulio Romano); *Abraham and the Angels* (Penni); *Flight of Lot* (Giulio Romano and Penni).

5. *God Appearing to Isaac* (Penni); *Abimelech Spying upon Isaac and Rebecca* (Giulio Romano); *Isaac Blessing Jacob* (Machuca); *Isaac and Esau* (Penni).

6. *Jacob's Dream* (Giulio Romano); *Jacob and Rachel at the*

Well (Vincidor); *Jacob Asking Laban for the Hand of Rachel in Marriage* (Penni and Giulio Romano); *Jacob Fleeing to Canaan* (Vincidor).

7. *Joseph Recounting his Dream to his Brothers* (Giulio Romano, Penni and Giovanni da Udine); *Joseph Being Sold by his Brothers* (Polidoro da Caravaggio); *Joseph and Potiphar's Wife* (Giulio Romano); *Joseph Interpreting Pharaoh's Dreams* (Penni).

8. *Moses in the Bulrushes* (Giulio Romano); *The Burning Bush* (Marcillat); *Crossing of the Red Sea* (Giulio Romano); *Moses Striking the Rock* (Penni and Polidoro da Caravaggio).

The Sistine Chapel.
Detail from the *Journey of Moses into Egypt*. Perugino and Pinturicchio.
Center: detail from the *Temptation of Christ*.
Botticelli.

Bottom: detail from the *Trials of Moses*.
Botticelli.

9. *Moses Receiving the Tablets of the Law* (Perin del Vaga); *The Golden Calf* (Giulio Romano); *The Pillar of Fire* (Perin del Vega); *Moses Showing the Tablets of the Law to the People* (Giulio Romano).

10. *Crossing of Jordan* (Polidoro da Caravaggio); *Capture of Jericho* (Perin del Vega); *Joshua Halting the Sun and Moon* (Perin del Vega); *Partition of the Promised Land* (Perin del Vega).

11. *David Anointed King* (Marcillat); *David and Goliath* (Perin del Vega); *Triumph of David* (Perin del Vega); *David and Bathsheba* (Perin del Vega).

12. *Consecration of Solomon* (Tamagni); *Judgement of Solomon* (Pellegrino da Modena); *Building of the Temple* (Perin del Vega); *Solomon and the Queen of Sheba* (Perin del Vega).

13. *Adoration of the Shepherds*, difficult to identify the artist (though Vasari attributes it to Perin del Vega); *The Three Kings* (Machuca or Tamagni); *Baptism of Christ*, (possibly by Perin del Vega); *The Last Supper* (Tamagni or Vincidor).

The stucco work is mostly by Giovanni da Udine.

THE CAPPELLA NICCOLINA

The Cappella Niccolina (Chapel of Nicholas V) is sometimes confused with the Study of Nicholas V, which in fact was probably destroyed during the pontificate of Julius II. Built in the tower of the old palace of Innocent III (1198–1216), this chapel was frescoed by Fra Angelico for Nicholas V (1447–55), with scenes from the lives of SS. Stephen and Lawrence, taken from the Acts of the Apostles. The upper frescoes depict *scenes from the life of St. Stephen*, the lower frescoes *events from the life of St. Lawrence*.

The other frescoes depict Doctors of the Church and the *Evangelists*; the work around the windows is by assistants. Fra Angelico was aided by Benozzo Gozzoli, who

worked mostly on the *St. Stephen* cycle; the work was completed about 1450.

The present entrance was ordered by Julius II (1503–13), and the large inner window by Gregory XIII (1572–85). Modern restoration (1947–51) has given us back the trompe-l'oeil effect of the fake damasked drapes of the skirting, and also proved that the frescoes were touched up with tempera (Redig De Campos). Depicted in the *lunettoni* at the top are: *St. Stephen Receiving the Diaconate from St. Peter and Distributing Alms*; *St. Stephen Preaching and Arguing in the Sanhedrin*; and the *Martyrdom of St. Stephen*. While below are: *St. Sixtus Consecrating St. Lawrence Deacon*; *St. Lawrence Receiving the Treasures of the Church from St. Sixtus*; *St Lawrence Distributing Alms*; *St. Lawrence before Emperor Decius, and his Martyrdom*. On the pilasters: *St. Leo the Great, St. John Chrysostom, Pope St. Gregory, St. Athanasius, St. Ambrose, St. Thomas Aquinas, St. Augustine,* and *St. Jerome*.

These frescoes represent the apogee of Humanist visual art. Fra Angelico shows himself master of all the developments hitherto evident in Italian figurative art, from the primitiveness of Giotto to the realism of Masaccio – as is most strikingly borne out in *St. Lawrence before the Emperor Decius* – to the spatial and volumetric language of Piero della Francesca.

THE SISTINE CHAPEL

We now descend to the Sistine Chapel, finished in 1481, possibly by Baccio Pontelli under the direction of Giovannino de' Dolci, for Sixtus IV (1471–84). In October 1481 at all events, the pictorial decoration of the Chapel was entrusted to Domenico Ghirlandaio, Pietro Perugino, and Cosimo Rosselli. It was dedicated to the Madonna on 15 August 1483

(Redig De Campos). As Steinmann has pointed out, the building, apart from having a religious and artistic function, also served as part of the defence works of the Vatican palace, as attested by the Guelph crenellations and corbels.

Basically it consists of a basement, a mezzanine storey, an *aula* and, above the chapel itself, the quarters of the papal guards. The floor of the chapel is inlaid with polychrome stone in geometrical patterns. The marble screen and choir are attributed to Mino da Fiesole, Andrea Bregno, and Giovanni Dalamata.

For almost four and a half years, from 10 May 1508 to 31 October 1512, at the behest of Pope Julius II Michelangelo worked on the ceiling of the chapel; the *Last Judgement*, on the altar wall, where there had previously been frescoes by Perugino, occupied him from 1536 to 1541, during the pontificate of Paul III. The skirting of the chapel is decorated with trompe-l'oeil drapes.

Before Michelangelo painted the frescoes, the ceiling had been colored sky blue and studded with gilded wooden stars, the work of Piermatteo d'Amelia. The twenty-eight portraits of popes between the windows were painted by Ghirlandaio, Cosimo Rosselli, Fra Diamante, and Botticelli.

On the right wall, starting from the *Last Judgement*, the sequence of frescoes shows: *Baptism of Christ* by Pinturicchio (Christ, St. John the Baptist, and the half nude on the right are by Perugino); *Cleansing of the Leper* and *Temptation of Christ* by Botticelli (the hospital of Santo Spirito in the background was built by Baccio Pontelli during the pontificate of Sixtus IV); *Calling of Peter and Andrew* by Ghirlandaio; *Sermon on the Mount* and *Healing of the Leper* by Rosselli and Piero di Cosimo; *Christ Giving the Keys to St. Peter*, one of Perugino's best works, and a masterpiece of Renaissance painting (the scientific, abstract qualities of Piero della Francesca are echoed not only in the superb series of portraits in the foreground – the fifth figure from the right is a self-portrait – but also in the almost calligraphic rendering of the figures dotted about the piazza, which is itself a worthy forerunner of the 18th-century townscape genre); and finally *The Last Supper* by Cosimo Rosselli.

On the left wall there appears: *Moses and his Wife Zipporah in Egypt and the Circumcision of their son* by Pinturicchio and Perugino; *The Burning Bush* and *Trials of Moses* by Botticelli; the *Passage of the Red Sea* by Cosimo Rosselli; *Moses on Sinai* and the *Worship of the Golden Calf* by Cosimo Rosselli; *Punishment of Korah, Dathan and Abiram* (the earth swallowing them up, at Moses's command, after their revolt against Aaron), by Botticelli. The architectural elements on the right are the work of assistants. Then finally *Moses Giving the Rod to Joshua*, and *Death of Moses* by Luca Signorelli and Bartolomeo della Gatta.

On the wall facing the *Last Judgement* the frescoes of the *Resurrection of Christ* and *St. Michael Protecting the Body of Moses* were originally by Ghirlandaio and Francesco Salviati but were entirely repainted by both Arrigo Fiammingo and Matteo da Lecce.

As Michelangelo himself has recorded, he began work on the Sistine Chapel ceiling on 10 May 1508, having received an advance of five hundred ducats. He first laid brush on the entrance wall, working towards the altar. He chose as assistants Giuliano Granacci, Giuliano Bugiardini, and Aristotile da Sangallo; according to Vasari and Condivi, they were soon dismissed as unsatisfactory, and Michelangelo decided to work entirely on his own. Biagetti and Camesasca, however, maintain that he continued to work with assistants until January 1511, and perhaps even after that.

According to De'Grassis, Julius II's master of ceremonies, the work was completed on 31 October 1512.

Interpretations of this stupendous work are both varied and complex. Henke, one of the most interesting and reliable of commentators, sees it as, a) the history of mankind before Revelation (visaged in the lunettes and ressaults); b) at the moment of consciousness (the sibyls and prophets and the *ignudi*); c) mankind's relationship with heaven (the Biblical scenes). For his source material, Michelangelo used, besides the Bible and Plato, the works of Sante Pagnini (a follower of Savonarola) and the *Decachordum* by Marco Vigerio. Not long after its completion, the work was restored by Carnevale. The most recent restoration to be carried out has stripped off the old varnish obscuring the frescoes.

This supreme figurative composition is held together and articulated by means of a grid of trompe-l'oeil architectonic elements which provide a setting for the painted 'sculptures' – which are yet typical of Michelangelo's 'true' sculpture, recalling the various designs for the Julian and Medici tombs. One only needs to compare the ceiling frescoes with those of the walls, which reflect the various schools of Humanist Renaissance art, to appreciate how completely Michelangelo had broken with the past, and indeed with his own times, to establish an artistic idiom that is at once taut and wonderfully rich, and to be seen again, more refined and intensified, in the *Last Judgement*, and again later still, with even greater intensity and mastery of drama, in the profoundly impressive Cappella Paolina frescoes (which were greatly to influence the Mannerists).

The various Biblical scenes depicted are: *Separation of Light from Darkness*; *Creation of the Sun, Moon and Planets*; *Creation of Trees and Plants*; *Separation of Land and Sea and Creation of Fishes and Birds*; *Creation of Adam*; *Creation of Eve*; *Fall of Man and Expulsion from Paradise*; *Noah's Sacrifice*; *The Flood* (assistants helped here); and *Drunkenness of Noah*. Interspersed between these scenes are medallions and *ignudi* (naked decorative figures). Between the ressaults are seven prophets (*Zechariah, Joel, Isaiah, Ezekiel, Daniel, Jeremiah*, and *Jonah*) and five sibyls (the Delphic, Eritrean, Cumean, Persian, and Libyan). In the corner ressaults are: *Judith and Holofernes, David and Goliath, The Brazen Serpent*, and *Punishment of Haman*. In the lunettes are family groups representing the forerunners of Christ. The compositional format is completed by putti as caryatids or supporting plaques.

In 1534 Michelangelo accepted the commission to paint the *Last Judgement*. There was an interruption with the death of Clement VII (1523–34) in September of the same year, but Clement's successor, Paul III (1534–49), continued with the project, and in April 1535 the scaffolding was put in place. The work was concluded in 1541, and the *Last Judgement* was officially unveiled on 31 October of that year.

This massive composition hinges on the vast figure of Christ in Judgement, with Mary at his side, amid a throng of saints and the blessed. Above, in a pair of lunettes, clusters of angels bear the instruments of the Passion; while at the bottom, on the left, are souls ascending to heaven, and on the right, the souls of the damned descending into hell. At the bottom is Satan-Charon, carrying the damned off to eternity.

Various critics have attempted to identify the saints, historical characters, etc. who are represented, but in some cases, it must be said, not very convincingly. The figure of St. Bartholomew has been seen as Pietro d'Arezzo, and the face on the skin he is holding in his hand as a self-portrait of Michelangelo. SS. Sebastian and Catherine are specifically recognizable by their appropriate attributes; while the figure of Minos encircled by a snake is said to be Biagio da Cesena, Paul III's master of ceremonies, who criticized the *Last Judgement* for having too many nudes; and finally the Satan-Charon figure, identified as the Bourbon Constable.

Justi describes the figure of Christ as being modelled on classical representations of Jupiter hurling his thunderbolts, or (and on this most critics concur) on classical portrayals of Apollo.

Pinacoteca Vaticana.
The *Virgin and Child with angels and SS. Dominic and Catherine of Alexandria.*
Beato Angelico.

Pinacoteca Vaticana.
The Agony in the Garden.
Giovanni di Paolo.

Pinacoteca Vaticana.
St. Benedict.
Perugino.

Other similarities have been noted: for example, between the souls ascending on the right and the cartoon of Cascina, with Signorelli's frescoes in the Cappella di San Brizio in Orvieto cathedral, and with certain elements in Bosch.

There was immediate criticism that the work contained an unseemly quantity of nudes. Thus, on 21 January 1564, the Congregation of the Council ordered the more 'flagrant' nudes to be draped – a task entrusted to Daniele da Volterra, who with three assistants duly bowdlerized Michelangelo's work with tempera draperies. When the floor level was raised, between 1572 and 1585, the lower twenty-seven and a half inches of the work were lost.

The *Last Judgement* breaks all the rules. The sheer conception of the work is a monumental achievement. A tremendous vertical dynamic is created by the way the figures grow in size as they rise higher, while the non-three-dimensional blue background – indeed *aere senza tempo tinto*, 'space with no taint of time' – forms as it were a spiritual stage for the eschatological drama. Structurally the composition is full of movement and contrasts of empty and crowded space; the figures seem to move upwards and

downwards, and rotate in turbulent whirlpools – all, however, within the overall vortex of movement created by the figure of Christ. The compositional knots of figures were later to be exploited by Mannerist painters such as Daniele da Volterra and Rosso.

THE SALA REGIA

We next proceed into the adjoining Sala Regia – the Royal Room, so named because royalty was received in audience here. It was built for Paul III by Antonio da Sangallo the Younger, and finished in 1573. The very beautiful stucco coffering of the ceiling is the work of Perin del Vaga after designs by Sangallo, while the wall stuccoes are by Daniele da Volterra. The scenes from the lives of popes and kings are by Giorgio Vasari, Lorenzo Sabbatini, Taddeo and Federico Zuccari, Francesco Salviati, Giuseppe Porta, Livio Agresti, Gerolamo Siciolante, Orazio Sammacchini, and Giovanni Maria Zoppelli, under the direction of Cardinal Marcantonio Mula. Salviati and Porta painted the *Reconciliation of Alexander III and Barbarossa*; Vasari and Sabbatini the *Battle of Lepanto*; Sammacchini the *Restitution of the Provinces to Agapetus*; Agresti *Pedro of Aragon's Offering to*

Eugenius III; Sermoneta the *Donation of Ravenna*; Taddeo Zuccari *Glory*, *Victory*, and the *Capture of Tunis*; and Federico Zuccari the *Blessing of Gregory VII* (Federico completed the *Capture of Tunis*).

THE CAPPELLA PAOLINA

Antonio da Sangallo the Younger built the chapel for Paul III. The frescoes are by Michelangelo, and date from the close of 1542, when this many-sided genius was almost seventy years of age. Partly because of recurrent illness, he did not finish them until 1550. In the *Conversion of St. Paul* there is a self-portrait. The other fresco depicts the *Crucifixion of St. Peter*.

THE PINACOTECA VATICANA

The origins of this collection go back to Pius VI (1775–99), but it has since been expanded with the addition of private donations, as well as works from the Lateran, the papal apartments in the Vatican, the palace of Castel Gandolfo, St. Peter's, and various other churches. After the Treaty of Tolentino (19 February 1797) several works were taken to France and added to the Musée Napoléon in Paris. These included masterpieces such as the *Apollo*, the *Discobolos*, and the *Belvedere Torso*, *The Laocoon*, Raphael's *Assumption* and *Transfiguration*, Caravaggio's *Entombment of Christ*, and Perugino's *Resurrection*. It was only with the appointment by Pius VII (1800–23) of Antonio Canova as Inspector of Fine Arts that they were recovered. Negotiations for the surrender of Napoleon's artistic booty began on Canova's arrival in Paris on 28 August 1815. Support was given by England, Austria, and Prussia. A first batch reached Rome on 4 January 1816, and between July and August, whatever else could be recovered.

Pius VII exhibited the paintings in the Borgia Rooms, but in 1882

they were moved to the Apartment of Gregory XIII, where they remained until Pius XI (1922–39) commissioned Luca Beltrami to erect a special new building for them in the northern section of the gardens, near the Atrio dei Quattro Cancelli. The idea of having a separate gallery for modern works came from Pius XII (1939–58); an advisory committee was formed, and works by various artists including Utrillo, Rodin, Fazzini, Greco, Sironi, Previati, Mancini, De Chirico, Carrà, Soffici, De Pisis, Morandi, Viani, Rossi, and Arturo Martini, were acquired.

The collection contains a panoramic selection of 20th-century Italian painting, and paintings of all schools from the 11th century on, as well as works by foreign artists. Room I contains a collection of 'primitive' panels, mostly Florentine, and a group of 16th-, 17th-, and 18th-century Greek, Cretan, and Russian icons.

Especially beautiful is the *Madonna and Child and Flagellants* by Vitale da Bologna; there is then a panel with *SS. James and Mary Magdalen* by Antonio Veneziano; a *Madonna and Child with Saints* by Niccolò di Pietro Gerini; a polyptych *Madonna and Child with Saints*, signed and dated 1371 by Giovanni Bonsi; a *St. Francis*

by Margaritone d'Arezzo; a remarkable *Last Judgement* dating from the 11th or 12th century, signed *Johannes et Nicolaus pictores*; a *Madonna and Child with Saints* by Giovanni del Biondo; a *S. Nicola*, an *Annunciation*, and a *Nativity*, all attributed to Mariotto di Nardo; and *Death of the Miser*, attributed to Bicci di Lorenzo.

Room II also houses panels of the 14th and 15th centuries, especially of the Sienese and Florentine schools. Among the artists represented are: Sano di Pietro, Taddeo di Bartolo, Giovanni di Paolo, Sassetta, and Vecchietta. Of note are the *History of St. Stephen*

by Ambrogio Lorenzetti; *Christ before Pilate* by Pietro Lorenzetti; and a number of 13th-century panels of the Rimini school by Spinello Aretino; and works by Allegretto Nuzi, Bernardo Daddi, and Lorenzo Monaco.

In the center of this room is the *Stefaneschi Triptych*, a large poplar-wood triptych, with predella, and painted on both sides. The central panel depicts Christ enthroned amid angels, with the donor, Jacopo Gaetano Stefaneschi; on the right panel is depicted the beheading of St. Paul, and on the left panel, the crucifixion of St. Peter. God appears in the central medallion, Moses in the right-hand one, and the sacrifice of Isaac is depicted in that on the left. In the predella there is the Virgin enthroned between two angels, with the Twelve Apostles. On the

back, in the central panel, is St. Peter with two angels, St. George, the donor holding a model of the triptych in his hands, St. Sylvester, and Celestine V; in the right-hand panel are SS. Andrew and John the Baptist, while on the left panel are SS. James and Paul; in the medallions in the cusps are heads of angels, and on the single predella panel in the center (though originally on the left) are two unidentifiable saints and St. Stephen.

The triptych was painted for the high altar of old St. Peter's. It was commissioned from Giotto by Gaetano Stefaneschi, Cardinal Deacon of San Giorgio al Velabro. It is dated between 1320–25.

Room III contains 15th-century panels of the Florentine and Marches schools. Especially noteworthy are the four small panels depicting the *Birth and Various Miracles of St. Nicholas of Bari* by Gentile da Fabriano. They were originally part of the predella of Gentile's polyptych of 1425, painted for the Florentine Quaratesi family, for the altar in the main chapel of San Niccolò oltr'Arno. This polyptych was split up in 1836, and the signature, said by Richa to have been *OPUS GENTILIS DE FABRIANO MCCCCXXV MENSE MAI*, has been lost. Other panels from the polyptych, those showing SS. Mary Magdalen, Nicholas, John the Baptist, and St. George are in the Uffizi, while a panel of the

Virgin and Child are at Hampton Court. Of the predella, a panel depicting the pilgrimage to the tomb of St. Nicholas is in the National Gallery, London.

Very beautiful too is Fra Filippo Lippi's triptych with the *Coronation of Mary with Saints*. According to Vasari and Borghini, this work was painted for the monastery of the Olivetani di Arezzo; in 1785 it entered a private collection; Gregory XVI (1831–46) then bought it and sent it to the Lateran, from where it finally came to the Pinacoteca Vaticana. Marchini identifies the kneeling donors as Carlo Marsuppini and his father Gregorio. Lippi himself is thought to have painted the central panel, while the wings may possibly be by the workshop.

A panel by Fra Angelico depicts the *Madonna and Child with Angels and SS. Dominic and Catherine of Alexandria*. Originally in the Bisenzio collection in Rome, it traveled to England (the Dudley collection) before eventually coming to the Vatican. It is datable to around 1434, about the same period as the *Reliquiari* of Santa Maria Novella, when Fra Angelico's work still retained the almost calligraphic 'preciosity' of late-Gothic art. The only critic not to accept this attribution is Pope-Hennessy, who proposes Zanobi Strozzi as the probable begetter.

By a follower of Fra Angelico are two small panels depicting scenes from the *Life of St. Nicholas*; these were initially part of a triptych (now in the Galleria Nazionale dell'Umbria) painted by Angelico in 1437 for the chapel of St. Nicholas in the church of San Domenico in Perugia. It was commissioned by Bishop Guidalotti. Finally it is worth mentioning Masolino da Panicale's *Crucifixion* and a *Virgin and St. Thomas* by Benozzo Gozzoli.

In Room IV are paintings by Marco Palmezzano; the fresco by Melozzo da Forlì, *Sixtus IV Appointing Platina Prefect of the*

Vatican Library, was originally in the Biblioteca Vaticana and transferred to canvas in the 19th century. Other fragments by Melozzo – *angels with musical instruments* and *heads of Apostles* – one from the apse of the church of the Santissimi Apostoli, destroyed in 1711.

Room V contains a *Pietà* by Lucas Cranach the Elder; a *Virgin and Child* by Bartolomeo Montagna; a *Virgin and Child with Saints and Dignitaries of the Sacra Rota* by Antoniazzo Romano; a *Virgin and Child* signed by Marco Basaiti; and the *Miracles of St. Vincent Ferrer* by Ercole de' Roberti, a small panel of a predella from the dismembered polyptych made for the Griffoni chapel in the church of San Petronio in Bologna. This work was attributed by Frizzoni, Gruyer, Berenson, and Jouffroy to Francesco del Cossa, and then correctly identified as being by Ercole de' Roberti, by Masini, Filippini, Longhi, Ortolani, Chastel, Nicolson, and others, from a mention to that effect by Vasari.

In Room VI is a remarkable group of 15th-century works from the Marches: a *Madonna and Child*, signed and dated 1482 by Carlo Crivelli (who also painted the *Pietà* panel formerly in the Campidoglio, which attracted the criticism of Longhi and Venturi.

There is a very fine polyptych of *Christ Rising from the Tomb, St. Anthony Abbot and other Saints*, signed and dated 1469 by Antonio Vivarini; a *Coronation of the Virgin and Saints* by Niccolò Alunno; the *History of St. Barbara* by Guidoccio Cozzarelli; and *Christ Carrying the Cross* by Marco Palmezzano.

In Room VII is a collection of works of the Umbrian school of the 15th and 16th centuries, by Spagna, Tiberio d'Assisi, Antonio da Viterbo, Bernardino di Mariotto, and Giovanni Santi. There is also a panel by Perugino of the *Madonna and Child with Saints*. Three other works by Perugino are the panels of *St. Benedict, St. Placidus*, and *St. Flavia*; there is also a *Resurrection* by him. This latter work was commissioned on 2 March 1499 for the family altar of Bernardino di Giovanni da Corneto, in the church of San Francesco al Prato in Perugia. Taken to Paris by the French in 1797, it came to the Vatican in 1816. Formerly attributed to Raphael, it dates from the first decade of the 16th century, according to Camesasca.

Room VIII boasts works by Raphael and his school. The ten tapestries – four with scenes from the *Life of St. Peter*, and six from the *Life of St. Paul* – were designed by Raphael and woven in Brussels by Pieter Van Aelst and Bernard Van Orley in 1515–16. The subjects depicted are: the *Miraculous Draught, St. Peter Receiving the Keys, Healing of the Cripple, Death of Ananias, Stoning of St. Stephen, Conversion of St. Paul, Blinding of Elymas* (this tapestry was damaged by the Landsknechte during the sack of Rome in 1527), the *Sacrifice at Lystra, St. Paul in Prison*, and *St. Paul Preaching in Athens*. Leo X (1513–21) had intended these tapestries as ceremonial decorations for the Sistine Chapel; and indeed when he celebrated Mass there on 26 December 1519 there were already, according to the contemporary account by

Marcantonio Michiel, seven tapestries on the walls. The remaining three (the *Death of Ananias, St. Paul in Prison*, and *St. Paul Preaching in Athens*) were probably delivered to the Vatican in 1521 (White, Shearman, Dussler).

Sanuto and Pastor mention that the tapestries were displayed in the Sistine Chapel some years later, at the funeral of the Bourbon Constable. Of the cartoons, three have been lost (the *Stoning of St. Stephen, Conversion of St. Paul*, and *St. Paul in Prison*), while the other seven are in the Victoria and Albert Museum in London. In designing the cartoons, Raphael had as assistants Giulio Romano, Gianfrancesco Penni, and Giovanni da Udine.

Regarding the subject matter of the tapestries, Dussler (working from Gaetano De Vio's *Tractatus de comparatione Auctoritatis Papae et Concilii*, published in 1511, and also from his part in the Lateran Council in May 1512), sees them as a reaffirmation of the role of the pope as the Vicar of Christ. Copies of the tapestries exist in the royal palace in Madrid, in the Palazzo Ducale in Mantua (made for Federigo Gonzaga), and in the Santa Casa di Loreto (formerly the property of Cardinal Sforza Pallavicino). A further copy in the Berlin Museum – made for François I – was destroyed in the last war.

This room also contains the *Three Theological Virtues between Pairs of Angels*, monochrome panels that were originally part of

the predella of the *Deposition of Christ*, now in the Galleria Borghese in Rome, signed and dated 1507, and commissioned from Raphael by Atalanta Baglioni in memory of his son Grifonetto, killed in 1500, during the Baglionis' struggle to win Perugia. Much to be admired too are the *Coronation of the Virgin, Madonna di Foligno*, and *The Transfiguration*. Although a gap of some ten years separates each painting, they give a good indication of Raphael's stylistic development from 1503 to the year of his death, 1520.

The *Coronation* was commissioned in 1502 by Alessandra di Simone degli Oddi for the family chapel in the church of San Francesco in Perugia, and duly delivered the following year (Wittkower dates it back to 1499–1500, maintaining that it was painted in Perugino's workshop). In 1797 it was included among the works sent as booty to Paris. It came to the Vatican in 1816. Parallels have been drawn with Perugino's *Ascension* in the Musée des Beaux Arts, Lyons.

The predella panels, transferred to canvas, depict the *Annunciation, Adoration of the Magi*, and the *Presentation in the Temple*. Preparatory studies exist in Oxford, London, Windsor, Lille, Paris, and Stockholm (Fischel). There is a copy of the *Coronation* in Bernazzone, near Perugia, of the *Annunciation* in the church of San Pietro, Perugia, and of the *Adoration of the Magi* in Copenhagen (Dussler).

The *Madonna di Foligno*, commissioned by Sigismondo dei Conti as an *ex voto* offering, originally stood on the high altar of Santa Maria in Ara Coeli in Rome, whence it was moved in 1565 to the convent church at Foligno. Carried off to Paris in 1797, it arrived in the Vatican in 1815. A copy was made for the church of Sant'Anna in Foligno. Dating from 1512, it reflects

Raphael's final abandonment of his great 15th-century Umbrian models, in which this theme was traditionally handled on two planes one above the other, in rigid compositional strictness. Now we have a homogeneous picture plane with no abrupt breaks, with a landscape fading off into cloud. The figures are given greater tactile value through brilliant graduations of light, inspired (as Cavalcaselle, Mendelssohn, Fischel, and Longhi already perceived) by certain works of the Ferrara school (e.g. Dosso Dossi) and the Venetian school as well.

The *Transfiguration* was commissioned in 1517 by Cardinal Giulio dei Medici for the cathedral of Narbonne, Raphael having beaten Sebastiano del Piombo for the honor (the latter painted a *Resurrection of Lazarus*). In 1523, however, the painting was placed in the church of San Pietro in Montorio in Rome. Taken to Paris as part of Napoleon's booty in 1797, it came to the Vatican finally in 1815. Both the design and most of the execution are Raphael's, as we know from Vasari and a letter from Sebastiano del Piombo dated 12 April 1520. Auxiliary work by Guilio Romano and Gianfrancesco Penni, dating from after the master's death, is confined to the lower part, as the critics have agreed. Dussler detected the hand of Penni in the head of Christ and some of the Apostles; Giulio Romano probably worked on the group on the right; while the

figure of the young possessed man and the upper section are thought to be entirely by Raphael.

The basis for these suppositions is the payments to Giulio Romano recorded in a letter from Baldassar Castiglione to the cardinal dated 7 May 1522, and a note from the clergy of Santa Maria Novella in Florence. However, as Vogel has pointed out, such payments would have gone to Giulio Romano in any case, as Raphael's heir. Recent restoration work has in fact revealed a masterpiece of the highest order, with no uncertain patches or other changes of style that could justify attribution of any part of it to the school. There can be no doubt that it is entirely by Raphael, as indeed Calvesi has recently acknowledged, and bears comparison with the contemporary *Assumption* by Titian in the church of the Frari in Venice.

In Room IX is a display of 16th-century works: a *Virgin and Child* by Gerolamo Del Pacchia; *Madonna Suckling Her Child* by Lorenzo di Credi; *Lament over the Body of Christ* by Giovanni Bellini; and Leonardo da Vinci's *St. Jerome*. This last is a panel painting, removed from its setting in the 19th century. According to D'Achiardi, it belonged to Angelica Kauffman before finally being discovered in a Roman junk shop by Cardinal Fesch. It was then bought by Pius VI in 1846 for two thousand five hundred francs.

All critics are agreed that it is an

original work, datable to the end of Leonardo's first stay in Florence, around 1481. However, Strzygowsky dates it from the first Milanese period, when Leonardo painted *The Last Supper* (in the refectory of Santa Maria delle Grazie). Ottino Della Chiesa regards it as an intensely analytical work, while Heydenreich stresses its dependence on the somewhat rough models of Pollaiolo. A bizarre monochrome work, highly expressionistic in tone, it is a marvelous example of Leonardo's experiemental and analytical brand of Humanism which put him in the vanguard of scientific thought of the time, during the very years that the great Umbrian and Florentine masters, with their mysticism, their cult of exquisitely refined decorative work, and their absorption in perspective, were employed on the Sistine Chapel frescoes.

This *St. Jerome* was intended as part of a huge composition, like the Uffizi *Adoration of the Magi*, with which it is linked chronologically. The new approach exemplified here implies a complete assimilation of the early Renaissance's poetic exaltation of perfect form into a sort of visual pantheism; there is no deviation from the process of enquiry into the causes and patterns of behaviour of living things. Painting, for Leonardo, had become a science. Yet it was no mere science of geometrical abstraction, as sometimes in Piero Della Francesca, because it remains first and foremost physical science, the science of the practical laboratory. And in a sense each painting becomes a figurative page of notes, as is the case of the Uffizi *Adoration* and this sublime *St. Jerome*. Plato and Aristotle have ceded first place to Archimedes.

Giovanni Bellini's panel painting of the *Lament over the Body of Christ* came to the Vatican from the Bolognese collection of Ulisse Aldrovandi, and is datable to

1471, the date of the altarpiece made for the church of San Francesco in Pesaro, from which it comes. Ascribed to Bellini by Frizzoni, it is one of this master's greatest works. The late-Gothic idiom is transcended in a profound mysticism, its wellspring being a more mature exploration of the deepest human feelings. The result is a more severe plasticity which comes from a complete understanding of the use of space through the balancing of figures and their daring disposition on different planes.

The panel with the *Coronation of the Virgin with SS. Paul, Peter,*

Jerome, and Francis also comes from this altarpiece now in the Museo Civico at Pesaro. On the right-hand pilaster are the figures of Blessed Michaelina, and SS. Bernadine, Louis and Andrew, and on the left-hand pilaster, SS. Catherine, Lawrence, Anthony of Padua, and John the Baptist; on the bases of the pilasters are St. George and the dragon, on the left, and St. Terence, on the right. The predella is divided into five sections with, from right to left, the *Stigmata of St. Francis*, *St. Jerome Repentant*, the *Nativity*, *Crucifixion of St. Peter*, and the *Conversion of St. Paul*. Pallucchini and Bottari

Pinacoteca Vaticana.
The Burial of St. Ephraem.
Emanuele Zanfurnari.

Pinacoteca Vaticana.
Rest on the Flight to Egypt.
Federico Barocci.

date the whole work to 1471, on the basis of comparison with a work by Marco Zoppo (dated 1471, formerly in the Berlin Museum) which derives from it.

Room X contains works of the central and northern Italian schools, especially the Florentine and the Venetian. They include a *St. Peter* and a *St. Paul* by Fra Bartolomeo; *Virgin and Child with Saints* by Gerolamo Genga; *Virgin and Child with St. Jerome* by Jacopo Boateri; *Virgin and Child with Saints* by Moretto; *Madonna Appearing to Augustus and the Sibyl*, dated 1544, by Benvenuto Tisi; *The Holy Family* by Bonifacio

Veronese; *St. George Killing the Dragon* by Paris Bordone; *The Circumcision* by Francesco Bissolo; *Madonna di Monteluce* by Giulio Romano and Gianfrancesco Penni; *St. Bernard Defeating the Devil* by Marcello Venusti (formerly in the church of San Bernardo alle Terme); and *The Madonna in Glory with Angels and SS. Catherine, Nicholas, Peter, Anthony of Padua, Francis, and Sebastian* by Titian.

This magnificent canvas, signed *TITIANUS FACIEBAT* in a central plaque, and painted around 1543 is remembered by Vasari as having been in the church of San Niccolò dei Frari in Venice. It was

brought to Rome in 1770. Here the classical, statuesquelike quality of other earlier works, for example *St. Mark Enthroned with Saints* in the sacristy of the Salute, the *Averoldi polyptych*, and the *Pesaro altarpiece*, is already beginning to dissolve in a wealth of color, enhanced by the emphasis placed on the figures and by the mobile graduations of light which led Titian in his old age, almost to the disintegration of line in favor of splendor and richness of color. This work belongs to a period of major change in the mid 16th century, but it also reflects the new artistic trends introduced to Venice by Giorgio Vasari, Giuseppe Salviati, and Giuseppe Porta.

Veronese's *Allegory* is to be related with the other two allegories, of Peace and Hope, in the Capitoline Museum, with which it was intended to be placed in a ceiling. Berenson at first attributed these three works to Giambattista Zelotti, but then changed to Veronese, dating them from the same period as the work carried out on the Sale del Consiglio dei Dieci in the Palazzo Ducale in Venice. According to Hadeln and Pallucchini, they can be dated to about 1556, that is contemporaneous with the ceiling of San Sebastiano and the Palazzo Trevisan on Murano.

Veronese's other canvas here, the *Vision of St. Helena*, was originally in the house of Pio di Carpi, whence it was acquired by Benedict XIV (1740–58). Chronologically it can be placed alongside the series of allegories painted for the Holy Roman Emperor Rudolph II in the late 1570s. However, it does not have the imposing, dynamic forcefulness of these works. The Vatican *St. Helena* is characterized by an architectural-like statuesqueness, the effect of which is softened by the color contrasts of the swelling draperies, a form of realism that Coletti has traced to the *Vision of St.*

Helena in the National Gallery, London; it is, however, a feature of much of Veronese's art.

In Room XI are paintings of various schools of the 16th century, among them a *Martyrdom of St. Stephen* by Giorgio Vasari; an *Annunciation*, signed and dated 1606, by the Cavalier d'Arpino; a number of works by Gerolamo Muziano; an *Assumption*, signed and dated 1515, by Cola dell'Amatrice; and *St. Francis Receiving the Stigmata, Head of the Virgin, The Annunciation, Rest on the Flight to Egypt*, and *Blessed Michaelina*, all by Federico Barocci. The *Rest on the Flight to*

Egypt was painted for Simonetto Anastagi by Barocci, as we know from a letter written by the artist to his sponsor, dated 2 October 1573. After Anastagi's death the picture was transferred to the sacristy of the church of the Gesuiti in Perugia. When the Jesuit Order was suppressed by Clement XIV in 1773 it was placed in the Quirinal palace, from whence it finally came to the Vatican.

Olsen has sought to trace the various versions of this particular painting. Besides the Vatican painting, we know one was painted for Count Antonio Bran-

caleoni, which is today in the church of Santo Stefano a Piobbico in Arezzo. The whereabouts of a third, mentioned by Bellori in 1672 as having been painted for Duke Guidubaldo della Rovere, and again recorded in 1824 as part of the Day collection in England, is now unknown.

The *Blessed Michaelina*, of which there is a copy in the sacristy of the cathedral in Urbino, was painted by Barocci in 1606 for Alessandro Barignani. Taken off to France in 1797 as part of the Napoleonic booty, it came to the Vatican in 1816.

In Room XII are some of the masterpieces of 17th-century Italian painting: *St. John the Baptist, St. Margaret of Cortona*, and *Mary Magdalene* by Guercino; the *Martyrdom of SS. Processus and Martinian* by Valentin; *The Holy Family* by Giuseppe Maria Crespi; and canvases by Poussin, Domenichino, Sacchi, and Caravaggio. The *Vision of St. Romuald*, by Andrea Sacchi, was painted in 1631 for the high altar of the church of San Romualdo in Vicolo del Piombo (destroyed in the last quarter of the 19th century during the building of Rome's Via Nazionale). The painting remained in this church until 1797, when the French took it to Paris. It next appears on the Pinacoteca Vaticana lists of 1841.

It is a work contemporary with the Palazzo Barberini fresco of *Wisdom*, and represents a deliberate rejection of the baroque style of Pietro da Cortona: the figures imbued with a classical grandeur that makes sense only in open pictorial space, defined by rigorously controlled composition, such as was quite alien to the dramatic, intense spontaneity of the baroque genius.

The *Crucifixion of St. Peter* was painted for the church of San Paolo alle Tre Fontane by Guido Reni, who had received the commission from Cardinal Pietro Aldobrandini (the cardinal having

Pinacoteca Vaticana.
St. Matthew.
Guido Reni.

Pinacoteca Vaticana.
Portrait of George IV, King of England.
Thomas Lawrence.

the tenure of the abbacy of the Tre Fontane). Hibbard dates it to 1604–05, on the basis of a part payment of fifty *scudi* which was made to the painter on 27 November 1604. Various copies of this famous work are known to exist, for instance in Genoa and Spain. The painting clearly reveals the influence of Caravaggio, a figure of ever increasing importance in the Roman artistic scene in the early 17th century. It was also inspired by the painting of the *Crucifixion of St. Peter* in the Cerasi chapel in Santa Maria del Popolo.

Guido Reni took from Caravaggio as much as was helpful in his own evolution as a painter, before adapting the idiom of Lombard realism: a crude bluntness, vivid reverberations of light and shade, the highlighting of anatomical details, the Cross planted obliquely. Yet in terms of compositional structure, he remained decidedly 16th-century, anchored in the peculiarly lyrical Bolognese academic tradition, hence the livid landscape in which the figures are disposed in vertically measured space, divided into mirror-like sections by the bisecting median of the Cross, upon which the naked figure of the martyr saint is stretched, remarkably at peace.

The Virgin and Child in Glory with SS. Thomas and Jerome was painted by Guido Reni for the Olivieri family altar in Pesaro cathedral, whence it came to the Pinacoteca Vaticana in the first half of the 19th century. It can be dated to around 1630, and is therefore slightly earlier than the *Pala della peste* (Plague altarpiece) in the Pinacoteca, Bologna, as noted by Giordani and more recently by Cavalli, who places this painting in the middle period of Reni's career.

St. Matthew and the Angel is one of Reni's most famous paintings and exists in numerous replicas and copies: the most beautiful of these and also the closest to the picture in the Vatican is the

version in Bob Jones University, Greenville.

The Communion of St. Jerome, signed and dated 1614, was painted by Domenichino for the Fathers of San Gerolamo della Carità; it came to the Vatican after the Treaty of Vienna, whereby works of art plundered by Napoleon in 1797 were restored to their owners. In this painting, Domenichino had as reference the painting of the same subject by Agostino Carracci, which is now in the Pinacoteca, Bologna. It is, however, quite distinct from the latter in its broader perspective and the generously conceived relationship between the figures and the picture space; whereas in Agostino's picture this is tightly packed, in Domenichino's picture the relationship is carefully calibrated, so that the figures are placed in a measured, almost metrical sequence, without the excited animation which characterizes the figures by Carracci.

The *Deposition of Christ in the Tomb* was commissioned from Caravaggio by Francesco Vittrici for the Vittrici chapel in the Roman church of Santa Maria in Vallicella. The commission took more than two and a half years to complete, from 9 January 1602 to 6 September 1604. This was much longer than Caravaggio normally

took to complete a picture, and Marini has reasonably suggested that this was because the artist was engaged in law suits with Baglione and with Pietro Fusaccia the waiter at the Osteria del Moro, and also because his attention was distracted by his trip to the Marches and by numerous other commissions which he received at that time. In 1797, the picture was carried off to Paris by the French, and came to the Vatican in 1815.

The most interesting of the many critical studies of the picture is that by Roberto Longhi who compares it with Simone Peterzano's *Deposition* in the church of San Fedele in Milan, and with the *Lament for the Dead Christ*, in the Cleveland Museum of Art: he reaffirms the essential unity of Caravaggio's compositions and thereby utterly refutes the hypothesis of Mary Cleophas being a later addition. Friedländer considered the cornerstone to be a reference to Christ's role as upholder of the world.

Several great painters made free versions of this picture, e.g. Valentin, Van Baburen, Fragonard, Géricault; several copies are also known: at San Marco in Milan; at the National Gallery of Canada in Ottawa; at the Prado in Madrid; at the Musée des Beaux Arts in Rouen; at the Brera in Milan; at the collegiate church of Offida, Ascoli Piceno; at the Fogg Art Museum, Cambridge, Mass.; in the Camuccini collection at Cantalupo Sabino, Rieti; in Santa Maria in Vallicella, Rome; and a series of engravings.

The work is a synthesis of Caravaggio's experiences during his residence in Rome, when he was able to know at first hand several major works of the Renaissance: thus Mary Cleophas is a quotation from Raphael and the body of the dead Christ recalls Michelangelo's *Pietà* for Jean Bilhères. In it, there are more of these echoes than in the other works of his Roman period, to-

gether with the viaticum of possibilities offered him by Lombard realism; but his vision is balanced and poetical without any tension or abrupt breaks; even where the presence of death is represented, it is without despair and with resignation, as if in a placid narration.

The Martyrdom of St. Erasmus, signed by Poussin, was painted for the basilica of St. Peter between February 1628 and October 1629. There is a replica of it in the National Gallery of Canada in Ottawa. Thuillier has pointed out that such a theme was foreign to French artists, though fairly common among Italian artists (Pordenone, Saraceni) and among Northern artists (Spranger, Troger), and was imposed on the artist as a part of the commission.

In Room XIII, there are paintings dating from the 17th and 18th centuries, representing various schools. A *Virgin and Child* by Sassoferrato, and another by Maratta; a *Holy Family* by Francesco Mancini; a *Judith* by Orazio Gentileschi; a *Vision of St. Bruno* and a *St. Jerome* by Pier Francesco Mola; two pictures by Gaetano Gandolfi; a *Holy Family* by Giambattista Castiglione; a *Virgin Appearing to St. John Nepomuk* by Pompeo Battoni; a *Martyrdom of the Maccabees* by Vincenzo Malò; a *St. Michael the Archangel*, at-

The Vatican Museum of Modern
Religious Art.
A Religious Panel.
Paul Gauguin.

The Vatican Museum of Modern
Religious Art.
The *Holy Robe.*
Fernand Léger.

tributed to Solimena, but now correctly reattributed by Bologna to the young Corrado Giaquinto at the time of his first visit to Napels; a *St. Francis Xavier* by Van Dyck which can be dated between 1622 and 1623, like the *St. Ignatius Loyola* rediscovered by Redig De Campos; a *Martyrdom of St. Lawrence*, formerly attributed to Ribera, but more probably a work from his studio; a *Virgin Appearing to St. Francis* by Pietro da Cortona, which can be dated around 1641 and is considered by Briganti to be an authographed replica of the altarpiece of the Montauto chapel in the church of the Annunziata at Arezzo. It came to the Vatican from the papal palace at Castel Gandolfo. Also by Pietro da Cortona are the pictures with *David Slaying Goliath* and *David and the Lion*, two authographed replicas of the scenes from the story of David which Berrettini frescoed on the ceiling of the Casino Sachetti in the Pigneto, which were recorded by Fabbrini as being in the Campidoglio in the 19th century; they were also linked by Briganti with two other canvasses with scenes from the story of David, in the Quirinal Palace, which he attributes to studio assistants.

In Room XIV are pictures of different schools and periods: an *Ecce Homo* and a *St. Ignatius* by Seghers; *Angels* by Baciccio; a 17th-century *Still Life*, and *Orpheus before Pluto and Proserpina* by Mathias Stomer; *The Astronomical Observations* by Donato Creti; the *Miracle of St. Toribio of Lima* by Sebastiano Conca, which was commissioned by Cardinal Ottoboni.

In Room XV, there is a series of portraits of different schools and periods: a *Pius VI* by Pompeo Battoni; two *Cardinals* by Scipione Pulzone; a *Clement IX*, signed and dated 1669 by Carlo Maratta; the *Doge Niccolò Marcello* by Titian: this picture came to the Vatican from the Aldobrandini collection

in Bologna when it was bought by Leo XII (1823–29). The sitter was identified by comparing the portrait with various medals and with the other portrait of this doge which was painted by Mazza at Bologna. It can be dated around 1542.

Room XVI is dedicated to 19th-century painting and sculpture: a bronze by Auguste Rodin; a *Crucifix* by Pericle Fazzini; works

by Ippolito Caffi, Antonio Mancini, Antonio Puccinelli, Gaetano Previati and Arturo Tosi.

Room XVII is dedicated to contemporary art, with works by Morandi, Soffici, Viani, de Chirico, Rosai, Utrillo, De Pisis, Carrà, Fazzini and others. Together with the works in Room XVI, these works are now included in the Vatican collection of modern religious art.

The Vatican collection of modern religious art has recently been arranged in the Borgia Rooms and it contains notable works, mostly religious in subject, and mostly of Italian and European schools be-

tween the 19th and 20th century. A sumptuous catalog was published in 1974 with a long introductory essay by Giorgio Mascherpa (G. Fallani, V. Maiani, G. Mascherpa: *The Vatican Collection of Modern Religious Art*, Milan 1974).

In this brief account, it is not possible to be strictly systematic, nevertheless, mention should be made of the following, among Italian works: a *Madonna*, *c.* 1860–65, by Carnovali; *The Mother*, 1907, by Boccioni; *The Mother*, 1928, by Balla; two drawings dated 1949 and five canvasses dated between 1938 and 1945, by Carrà; a mosaic, *c.* 1950, a canvas, 1964, and nine paintings on paper or card in oils, tempera or pastels, dating from 1927 to 1961, by Severini; five canvasses and panels, dated between 1944 and 1951, by Sironi; four canvasses, between 1932 and 1950, by de Chirico; a tempera painting on paper, an etching, two woodcuts and a lithograph, from 1936 to 1945, by Casorati; a fresco dated 1932 and an oil on board from 1946 by Ardengo Soffici; an oil on panel, 1923, two oils on canvas from 1932 and 1957, six drawings dated between 1959 and 1962, six etchings dated between 1924 and 1932, by Morandi; four oils on canvas dated from 1926 to 1951, and one oil on board from 1922 by De Pisis; twelve canvasses, panels, drawings, tapestries and mosaics, dating from 1937 to 1971, by Cagli; a charcoal drawing and a watercolor on board from 1957, a panel from 1965 and a canvas from 1973 by Guttuso; a canvas from 1958 by Capogrossi; a panel from 1958 by Omiccioli; a canvas from 1970 by Purificato; three canvasses, 1932, 1943, 1948, by Rosai; two *Crucifixions*, from 1973 and 1974, by Fausto Pirandello; the series of drawings in red ochre on paper of the *Via Crucis*, 1955, by Sassu; a canvas from 1970 and two mosaics from 1962 and 1969 by Cantatore; a series of fourteen

canvasses from 1901 by Previati.

Among the non-Italian paintings: a fine watercolor, *c.* 1818, by Goya; a carved and painted wood panel by Gauguin, *c.* 1892, at the time when the painter was in Tahiti; the tragicomic *Procession des Pénitents de Furnes* from 1913 by Ensor; a woodcut from 1902 by Munch; the series of lithographs, liturgical vestments and a crucifix, made in 1951 by Matisse for the chapel at Vence; the series of *Miserere* copperplate engravings by Rouault, between 1922 and 1927; gouaches from 1943 and 1956 and a lithograph from 1970 by Chagall; two dishes with mys-

The Vatican Museum of Modern
Religious Art.
A Church Interior.
Filippo De Pisis.
Bottom: *Deposition.*
Aligi Sassu.

tic fish by Picasso, from 1957; a watercolor still life from 1939 by Le Corbusier; a drawing from 1916 by Modigliani; four oils with views of churches, between 1908 and 1909 and between 1924 and 1925, by Utrillo; a canvas from 1944 by Orozco; two panels from 1963 and 1970 by Siqueiros; a study, dated 1961, for the portrait of Innocent X, after Velasquez, by Francis Bacon; a woodcut, c. 1905, by Kandinski; a watercolor from 1925 by Paul Klee; a cartoon by Odilon Redon; a canvas from 1960 and a watercolor by Salvador Dali; a lithograph by Braque; a drawing from 1946 and a water-color by Kokoschka.

Among the sculptures: three bronzes from 1880, 1890 and 1915 by Redon; the tragic, Mich-elangelesque bronze *Pietà* from 1946, and another bronze from 1950 and a wood carving, 1927, by Mestrovic; an icon-like representation of Pius XI, evoking the mysticism of statues of the Pharaohs, by Wildt; two pieces of pottery from 1949 and 1951, and seven bronzes from 1951 and 1956, by Fontana; the extraordinary series of six terracotta from the *Via Crucis* of 1926–27, a wood carving from 1925 and another terracotta of archaic flavor from 1934 by Arturo Martini; two watercolors from 1920 and 1923, a bronze from 1929 and a stone carving from 1971 by Marino Marini; a drawing with color wash from 1954 by Henry Moore; the furnishings for the Capella della Pace from 1951 and the bust of John XXIII from 1962 by Giacomo Manzú; nineteen bronzes and one silver piece, dating from between 1939 and 1972, by Messina; two bronzes from 1956 and 1963 and the series of fourteen bronzes for the *Via Crucis* by Fazzini; four drawings dating from between 1962 and 1968 and six bronzes from between 1961 and 1968 by Greco; seven bronzes from between 1946 and 1967 by Minguz-zi; a silver piece from 1942, a

bronze from 1967 and interlined cards from between 1954 and 1968 by Mirko; two bronzes from 1939 and 1950 and a marble sculpture from 1950 by Mastroianni.

SANT'ANNA DEI PALAFRENIERI

Let us close this itinerary by giving some account of one of the churches inside the Vatican walls, near the Sant'Anna entrance, which is an important example of architecture as it developed in Rome between the latter half of the 16th century and the late baroque period. The church of Sant'Anna dei Palafrenieri was built by the Confraternita dei Palafrenieri (the Confraternity of Grooms), who had been present in the Vatican since the 13th century and had been constituted a confraternity in 1378, being granted the privilege of being allowed to hold their meetings near the St. Anne altar, which had been erected in the basilica of St. Peter at the command of Pope Urban VI (1378–89).

Records show that the building of the church was begun on 29 June 1565 under the direction of Jacopo Barozzi da Vignola with the help of his son, Giacinto; the fabric of the building together with the façade had been completed as far as the cornice by 1576

when the work was interrupted. At the beginning of the 18th century, at the wish of Clement XI (1700–21), Alessandro Specchi was entrusted with the completion of the façade; by 1775, all the work was complete.

The interior is elliptical in plan and is decorated with 18th-century stuccos by Giambattista De Rossi and 18th-century frescoes with scenes from the *Life of St. Anne* by Ignaz Stern; the picture of *S. Carlo* (*Borromeo*) was painted in 1612 by Gerolamo Bertachiol.

On 16 April 1606, Caravaggio's painting of *St. Anne with the Virgin and Child Helping His Mother to Crush the Serpent* was placed in the church after having been exhibited on the St. Anne altar in St. Peter's on the 14th of the same month and immediately taken down again (Spezzaferro). The Confraternity had decided on 31 October 1605 to adorn the church with this picture; the work was finished before 12 March 1606. On 16 June, the picture was acquired by Cardinal Borghese for his collection, where it still remains (Rome, Galleria Borghese).

As Spezzaferro has convincingly demonstrated, the picture was rejected on account of the iconography chosen by Caravag-gio; traditionally St. Anne is

'Meeteer Theo' (Mother of God) by virtue of being mother of the Virgin, and therefore a participant in the Redemption from evil (the Serpent), obtained through Grace; whereas in this painting, she appears to the side, that is extraneous to the role traditionally attributed to her by orthodox iconography. At just this period, the friars of Santa Maria della Scala also rejected Caravaggio's painting of the *Death of the Virgin*.

SELECT BIBLIOGRAPHY

THE ROMAN PONTIFICATE
The ethos of a sacred city

Baldwin Smith, E. *Architectural Symbolism of Imperial Rome and the Middle Ages*, Princeton, 1956

Benedetti, S. *Architettura e riforma cattolica nella Roma del '500*, Rome, 1973

Bruschi, A. *Bramante architetto*, Bari, 1969

Castagnoli, F. *Topografia e urbanistica di Roma antica*, Bologna, 1969

Chevalier, J., Gheerbrant, A. *Dictionnaire des Symboles*, Paris, 1969

De Champeaux, G., Sterckz, S. *Le monde des Symboles*, Zodiaque, La Pierre-qui-vire, 1972

Delumeau, J. *Vie économique et sociale de Rome dans la seconde moitié du XVIe siècle*, Paris, 1957

Fagiolo dell'Arco, Marcello, *La Roma dei Longhi. Papi e architetti fra manierismo e barocco*, Rome, 1982

Fagiolo dell'Arco, Marcello and Maurizio, *Bernini. Una introduzione al "gran teatro" del Barocco*, Rome, 1966

Giovannoni, G. *Antonio da Sangallo il Giovane*, Rome, 1959

Hautecoeur, L. *Mystique et architecture*, Paris, 1954

Homo, L. *Rome médiévale*, Paris, 1934

Krautheimer, R. *Corpus Basilicarum christianarum*, Rome, 1937–77

L'Orange, H. P. *Domus Aurea, Der Sonnenpalast*, Oslo, 1942

Muller, W. *Die Heilige Stadt*, Stuttgart, 1961

Paronetto, V. *Agostino*, Milan, 1977

Pesce, D. *Città terrena e città celeste nel mondo antico*, Florence, 1957

Rykwert, J. *The Idea of a Town*, London, 1976

Schramm, P. *Kaiser, Könige und Päpste*, Stuttgart, 1968–70

Schramm, P. *Kaiser, Rom und Renovatio*, Leipzig, 1929

Valentini, R., Zuchetti, G. *Codice topografico della città di Roma*, Rome, 1940–53

Wassermann, J. *The Quirinal Palace in Rome*, in *Art Bulletin* 1963, pps 205–44

THE BASILICA AND THE BORGHI
From church to city

Adinolfi, P. *La Portica di S. Pietro, ossia Borgo nell'età di mezzo*, Rome, 1859

De Angelis, P. *L'arciospedale di S. Spirito in Saxia nel passato e nel presente*, Rome, 1952

Fontana, C. *Il Tempio Vaticano e sua origine . . .*, Rome, 1694

Francia, E. *1506–1606. Storia della costruzione del nuovo San Pietro*, Rome, 1977

Guarducci, M. *La tradizione di Pietro in Vaticano*, Vatican City, 1963

Magnuson, T. *Studies in Roman Quattrocento Architecture*, Stockholm, 1958

Marconi, P. *Giuseppe Valadier*, Rome, 1964

Orano, P. *L'Urbe Massima e l'architettura di A. Brasini*, Rome, 1916

Wittkower, R. *A counter-project to Bernini's "Piazza S. Pietro"*, in *Journal of Warburg Institute*, vol III, nos 1–2, 1939–40

THE VATICAN FRESCOES
A microcosm of the history of art

Baccheschi, E. *L'opera completa di Guido Reni*, Milan, 1971

Baldini, U. *L'opera completa dell'Angelico*, Milan, 1970

Béguin, S. *Le XVIe siècle florentin au Louvre*, Paris, 1982

Blunt, A. *The Paintings of Nicolas Poussin, A critical catalogue*, London, 1966

Borea, E. *Domenichino*, Milan, 1965

Costello, J. *Nicolas Poussin/The Martyrdom of Saint Erasmus/Le Martyre de saint Erasme*, Ottawa, 1975

Dacos, N. *La découverte de la Domus Aurea et la formation des grotesques à la Renaissance*, London, 1969

De Tolnay, C. *Michelangelo/Sculptor, Painter, Architect*, Princeton, 1975

Ettlinger, L. D. *The Sistine Chapel before Michelangelo*, Oxford, 1965

Freedbergh, S. J. *Painting of High Renaissance in Rome and Florence*, Cambridge (Mass.), 1961

Gere, J. A. *Taddeo Zuccaro/His development studied in his drawings*, London, 1969

Gould, C. *Raphael's Portrait of Pope Julius II/The Re-emergence of the Original*, London, 1970

Hartt, F. *Giulio Romano*, New Haven, 1958

Heimbürger Ravalli, M. *Alessandro Algardi scultore*, Rome, 1973

Marini, M. *Michelangelo da Caravaggio*, Rome, 1973–4

Nava Cellini, A. *La scultura del Seicento*, Turin, 1982

Shearman, J. *Mannerism*, London, 1967

Shearman, J. *Raphael's Cartoons in the collection of Her Majesty the Queen . . .*, London, 1972

Sutherland Harris, A. *Andrea Sacchi*, Oxford, 1977

THE LIFE OF THE PONTIFF
The Papal Tombs

Ettlinger, L. D. *Antonio e Piero del Pollaiolo*, New York, 1978

Dixon, A. M. *Arnolfo di Cambio, sculpture*, New York, 1980

Hartmann, J. B. *Bertel Thorwaldsen*, Rome, 1972

Minor, V. H. *The Roman Works of Filippo della Valle*, University of Kansas, 1976

Panofsky, E. *Tomb Sculpture, its changing aspects from Ancient Egypt to Bernini*, London, 1964

Sedlmayr, H. *Francesco Messina*, New York, 1978

Senie, H. F. *The Tomb of Leo XI by Alessandro Algardi*, in *Art Bulletin*, 1, 1978

Wittkower, R. *Art and Architecture in Italy, 1660–1750*, London, 1958

Zeitler, K. *Klassizismus und Utopia*, Stockholm, 1954

THE PALACES AND GARDENS
The Vatican as a secular palace

Battisti, E. *Rinascimento e Barocco*, Turin, 1960

Cassanelli L. et al, *Le mura di Roma, L'architettura militare nella storia urbana*, Rome 1974

Egger, H. *Der Uhrturm Paulus V*, In *Medeelingen van het Nederlandsch Historisch Institut te Rome*, 1929, pps 71–110

Ettlinger, L. D. *The Sistine Chapel before Michelangelo*, Oxford, 1965

Kaori Kitao, T. *Circle and Oval in the Square of St. Peter's*, New York, 1974

Letarouilly, P. *Le Vatican et la basilique de Saint-Pierre de Rome*, Paris, 1883

Magnuson, T. *Studies in Roman Quattrocento Architecture*, Stockholm, 1958

Rodocanachi, E. P. *Le Pontificat de Jules II*, Paris, 1928

Schöter, E. *Der Vatikan als Hügel Apollons und der Musen. Kunst und Panegyrik von Nikolaus V. bis Julius II*, in *Römisches Quartalschrift*, 1980

Smith, E. B. *Architectural Symbolism of Imperial Rome and the Middle Ages*, 1956

Thoenes, C. *Studien zur Geschichte des Peterplatzes*, in *Zeitschrift Für Kunstgeschichte* 1963, pps 97–145

Westfall, C. *In this most perfect Paradise. Alberti, Nicholas V, and the Invention of conscious urban planning in Rome (1447–55)*, The Pennsylvania State University Press, 1974

A STOREHOUSE OF THE ARTS
The Archives, Library and Museums

Ackermann, J. S. *The Cortile del Belvedere*, Vatican City, 1954

Bignami-Odier, J. *La Bibliothèque Vaticane de Sixte IV à Pio XI*, Vatican City, 1973

Calvesi, M. *De Arti in Vaticano*, Milan, 1980

Mancinelli, F. *La Torre dei Venti*, Vatican City, 1981

Moroni, G. *Dizionario di erudizione storico-ecclesiastica*, Venice, 1840

Scarpignato, M. *Correde de oreficerie da una tomba vulcente nel Museo Gregoriano-etrusco*, "Bollettino dei Monumenti, Musei e Gallerie Pontificie", Vatican City, 1981

INDEX

273

277

PICTURE SOURCES

a = above; b = below;
c = center; l = left; r = right;

Alinari 49
Archivio Fotografico Arnoldo Mondadori, Milan 8, 10, 31 a.l., 33 b.r., 35 a.l., a.r., c., 43 a., 61, 76, 77, 80, 83 b., 129 a., 148, 149, 150, 151, 152, 153, 174 a., 182, 183 l., 187, 190 a., 194, 205, 210 a., 210 c., 214 b., 216, 224/25, 226, 227 a., 228 a., 232, 234 a., 235 a., 237, 238 a., 242, 244/45, 249 a., 249 c., 250 l., 251, 256 b., 257, 258, 259, 260 l., 260 a.r., 261 l., 263, 264, 265, 266, 268 r., 269.

Biblioteca Vaticana 36 a., 42/3 b., 50, 51, 216.
British Museum (Freeman) 35 a.r., a.l., 35 c., 190 b.l., 205.
Civica Raccolta delle Stampe Achille Bertarelli, Milan (Giancarlo Costa) 47, 201 a., 210 b.
Maurizio Di Puolo, Rome 11.
Istituto Fotografico Scala, Florence 2, 7, 15, 17, 20/21, 25, 30 a., 34 b., 60, 74, 78, 79, 82, 83 a., 85, 86, 87, 88, 89, 90, 91, 92, 93, 94/5, 96/7, 98/9, 100/1, 102/3, 104/5, 106/7, 108/9, 110/11, 112/13, 114/15, 116/17, 118/19, 120/21, 122/23, 124/25, 126/27, 128, 129 c., 129 b.,

130/31, 132/33, 134/35, 136/37, 138/39, 140/41, 142/43, 144/45, 146/47, 154, 155, 156, 157, 158/59, 160, 161, 162, 163, 164, 165, 166, 167, 172, 174 b., 175, 177, 179, 180 l., 181 r., 198 a., 199, 204, 208, 214 a., 215, 218, 219, 222, 223, 227 b.l., b.r., 233, 234 b., 235 b., 236, 238 b., 239, 240, 241, 243, 244 l., 245 r., 246, 249 b., 250 r., 252, 256 a., 260 r.b., 261 r., 262, 267, 268 l., 270, 271.
Kodansha 212, 224/5, 226.
Toni Nicolini, Milan 12, 28, 38, 39, 44, 45, 48, 52, 53, 56, 57, 59, 62, 63, 64/5, 66, 67, 68, 69, 71, 72,

73, 81, 168/69, 170, 173, 178, 180/81, 183 r., 184, 185, 188, 190 b.r., 191, 195, 196, 197, 198 b., 201 b., 202, 203, 206, 207, 208/9, 209, 211, 217, 220, 221, 228/29 b., 229 a., 230, 231, 253, 254, 255.
Takashi Okamura 70.
S.P.A.D.E.M 270 r., 271 a.
Enrico Valeriani, one of the authors, supplied the photographic material on pages 30 b., 31 a.r., 31 b., 32, 33, 34 a., 35 b., 36, 37, 40, 41, 42, 42/3, 46, 49, 50, 51, 54, 55, 248.